THE MODERN NOVEL
Volume 2

Modern Languages and Literature

Literature Editor
J. M. COHEN

The Modern Novel

PAUL WEST
*Visiting Professor of English, Pennsylvania
State University*

Volume 2:
The United States and Other Countries

HUTCHINSON UNIVERSITY LIBRARY
LONDON

HUTCHINSON & CO. (*Publishers*) LTD
178–202 Great Portland Street, London, W.1

London Melbourne Sydney
Auckland Bombay Toronto
Johannesburg New York

First published 1963
This edition 1965

This book has been set in Times New Roman,
printed in Great Britain on Antique Wove paper
by The Anchor Press, Ltd., and bound by Wm.
Brendon & Son Ltd., both of Tiptree, Essex.

Contents

PART FOUR: OTHER COUNTRIES

PART THREE

The United States

I

A mystique of documentary

I

ONE difference between the America of Henry James's time and that of today has been well expressed by John Bayley in his intriguing study *The Characters of Love* (1961):

> What strikes us most about James's feeling sketch of the emptiness of the American scene is that it is no longer true—a mass of institutions, atmospheres and social complexities have sprung up to fill the gap—but that the American novelist still feels bound to behave as if it were true. Faulkner, Hemingway, Fitzgerald, O'Hara, Carson McCullers etc., all import the needful requirement which will fill their literary consciousness; they have no confidence in Nature manifesting itself in their surroundings.

Against this thickness of social texture (amply illustrated by the novels of O'Hara, Cozzens and Marquand as well as Faulkner) the American novelist is always tempted to work his sense of myth. And his sense of myth is really his subjectivity. I have already suggested that, of three principal views of man, the abstract and the private entail each other and are closer to each other than either is to the social. Man in the abstract is just as isolated as man in private. He is Man separated from Nature and, like man in private, thrown back on his own resources. Naturally enough, then, modern American novels continually transform the enterprising hero into Man *versus* Nature, and back again, as well as pretending that society is Nature. Not only that: the myth-making of the modern American novelist is usually accompanied by dense social documentation (whereas, say, most German

219

myth-novelists go in for bare outlines). It is as if their predilection for myth makes them doubly anxious to avoid 'unreal' abstractions. On the other hand, however, their facility in myth-making enables them to make the recital (and the over-recital) of social data seem a catechism of the cosmos itself. In America massive technological feats have followed epic pioneering feats in the subjugation of Nature. Heroism and pride in sheer invention have become indistinguishable from each other; I cannot pretend to divide them. What can be done, however, is to indicate the American novel's extremes and to consider how their simultaneous presence gives the modern American novel its unique quality.

The extremes I propose are bare myth and voluminous documentary as exemplified in the novels of Hemingway and O'Hara respectively. Most other novelists come somewhere in between. An early fusion of the extremes is Charles H. Sheldon's *In His Steps* (1876), a sermon in serial. A devout young preacher persuades certain members of his congregation into promising that, for one year, each will conduct himself like Jesus. The first to attempt this ambitious emulation is the editor of the local newspaper; before long he is refusing to print prize-fighting items, tobacco advertisements or to publish on Sundays. Bankruptcy is averted by another member of the congregation—an heiress. And so on: the book becomes tedious with gravid, pat sincerity. But its forced juxtaposition of sacred and secular and its pious game of repercussions have secured it a total sale of about twenty-three million copies. Ironically, pre-empting Sheldon's share of this world's goods, faulty copyright lost the author his chance of royalties. His type of mixture, however, still appeals even though *In His Steps* is no longer pirated.

Hemingway (1898–1961) the romantic creates his own code—metaphysical and religious; O'Hara (1905–), the equally romantic reporter, photographs and analyses codes which already exist and then, like Hemingway, leaves us to guess his opinion.

II

Hemingway's novels might almost have been written to prove that a novelist can be realistic without creating the 'Indiana novels' derided by Ambrose Bierce. Yet Hemingway's is merely a token gesture, for he just transfers his Michigan forest-awe to the woods of Spain, his trout-fishing mystique to Spanish streams, his local idiom into pidgin Spanish or pregnant telegraphese, his cult of hunting to Africa and the bull-ring. He is, essentially, a son of one half of the native tradition which, with Charles Dudley Warner and Marion Crawford, splits into realistic documentary and romantic escapism. Warner, who collaborated with Mark Twain on *The Gilded Age* (1873), wrote a trilogy about money, which reads like Dos Passos out of Balzac. Crawford was both a realist and a romanticist: as well as such contemporary studies as *An American Politician* (1884) he wrote a host of other novels set as far away in time and place as fifteenth-century Venice. Hemingway has more in common with Crawford than with Warner, and more with Crawford the exoticist than Crawford the near-sociologist; but he introduces into romance other commodities just as traditional: the steady-eyed scepticism shown by W. D. Howells to such idealized institutions as marriage (compare, for example, *A Modern Instance*, 1881, with Hemingway's tart story 'A Canary for One'); Howells's fascination with Americans abroad—in Italy especially; Howells's concentration on dialogue rather than on explanations; the cult of the frontier almost worked to death in the later novels of Hamlin Garland; Stephen Crane's newspaperman's and correspondent's romanticized cynicism; Frank Norris's fatalism; the strong-man cult of Jack London; and the sense of pity which Dreiser introduced. Of the swarming, accelerating and pullulating industrial society devotedly chronicled by these writers, Hemingway has next to nothing. He prolongs, idiosyncratically, the romance tradition: a sympathetic imaginativeness remote from the everyday life of the nation, and set to rhythms created by Gertrude Stein.

Keeping the urban American scene out of his novels, he expresses himself through a colourful but thinly realized mythology of Europe. In this way his American exiles seem as much at odds with their environment as Hemingway with the world. Survival and dignity depend on a virile code of inverted sensitivity. Both the mythology and the code are autobiographical, resuming Hemingway's experiences of war and merging the privileges of his roles as ambulance-driver and war-correspondent: in the thick of it, yet not quite *of* it. Similarly, the Hemingway code prescribes that, being in the thick of it, men should nevertheless admit no more of the truth than they can stand. Without this code of self-denial and self-defence, man finds life meaningless.

Such extreme views are not promised in *The Torrents of Spring* (1926), his parody of Sherwood Anderson's *Dark Laughter*. The gibing literary prattle of that negligible work and the romantic evocation of Michigan woods in the short stories collected in *In Our Time* (1924) have virtually nothing in common with the world of *Fiesta* (1926).[1] Jake Barnes, sexually maimed in the war, and Lady Brett Ashley, his promiscuous *inamorata*, share a code with Brett's fiancé Mike and an American writer called Bill. Crudely stated, the code is 'making do' and 'not squealing'; from it Robert Cohn, maliciously apostrophized in the novel's first pages, is excluded. Alcohol is their emblem, bull-fighting their ritual (at which they 'assist') and articulateness their pet hate. Cohn, talkative, gauche, heart-on-sleeve, has an affair with Brett but behaves badly when she drops him. Not having studied defeat sufficiently, he epitomizes the antithesis of the regimen Hemingway pieces together out of Twain and Crane, the euphemisms of Englishmen, experience of hunting (*The Green Hills of Africa*, 1935), the theory of the bull-fight (*Death in the Afternoon*, 1933) and his own near-death from wounds. Hemingway's cult of action and violence resembles that of the early Malraux; and he stayed with it, never paring it down into any kind of apocalyptic aestheticism. Or so, at first thought, one might conclude. True, he advanced from utter pessimism to the noble stoicism depicted in *The Old Man and the Sea* (1952). But his cult of despair seemed at times as much an affair of literary formula as of judged experience. His simplifications (courage into virility, inarticulateness into mental blankness, love into forbearance, wisdom into glibness, heart-masking repartee into stylish juggling) gave him a chance to play with prose at the expense of psychology and milieu. He too often indulges in a kind of literary damascening while emotion is suspended or unnecessarily sustained. One can see the need for such manœuvres when he is dealing with the head-numb Harry of *To Have and to Have Not* (1937) and the aged-eagle Colonel in *Across the River and Into the Trees* (1950): these characters are

1. In America, *The Sun Also Rises*.

mere diagrams. After thirty pages we have the point; the theorem is seen to be proved, so Hemingway colours in the diagram as if to distract us, and himself, from wondering why the novel continues.

Not exploring, but recommending a 'seeming marble heart' like Childe Harold's, Hemingway did his best writing about fairly intelligent heroes whose minds he could not petrify entirely. Robert Jordan in *For Whom the Bell Tolls* (1940) and Lieutenant Henry in *A Farewell to Arms* (1929) are examples; so are the intellectuals and politicians of warring Spain. The main trouble with Hemingway is his conception of the alien princes who arrive to put things right—not the quiet or the ugly Americans, but the dedicated self-escaping ones who seek some kind of 'virile fraternity' in the face of death. All fail. Not because the price is too high; there is no price. It is simply a matter of snatching at justification and ecstasy *en passant*. And the reader may well feel that Hemingway's heroes either try too hard or not at all. His leaning to myth denatures his characters at the very moments when we ought to be shown how painful it is to blunt one's perceptions in order to survive. Too often Hemingway blunted his own too; and sometimes the performance looks more like idleness than anguished shorthand. In his short stories, however (*Men without Women*, 1927; *Winner Take Nothing*, 1933), his thin psychology—vast hints but no exposure or commentary—is just right. What in the novels seems a skimped tribute to human sensitivity becomes, in his stories, an ideal economy. The 'philosophy' compressed into the following exchange is one that can be practised as a short-story technique but not made the structure of a novel:

'I can't stand to think about him in the room and knowing he's going to get it. It's too damned awful.'

'Well,' said George, 'you better not think about it.' ('The Killers')

Unless we are shown how the character avoids thinking about it, all we are likely to get is an adventure story of brilliant surface texture. Which is, too often, what we do get from Hemingway. We are constantly reminded, when reading Hemingway, that the verbal wool of our century has been developed to give both rapid and slow thinkers something to say while they work out an idea ('In view of the fact that the nature of the case is such that . . .'). Both the inarticulate and the cautious resort to such gobblede-gook. And Hemingway too uses his own special version of it while he marks time or his characters daydream (since they are not allowed to 'think'). No wonder he has to be cautious or seems inarticulate. You never trust a talker, any more than, confronted with novels which preach despair, you take them entirely seriously. The question is whether Hemingway would have done better to make less of simple despair and more of society's complexity.

He confronts us with a naïve staginess which, if it is not in-tended to mean more than itself, is unworthy of the attention of the thoughtful reader. Only one side of a contrast is ever pre-sented at a time; and there are various hints that we should infer the rest of the truth behind what is given, and so, for ourselves, complicate the novels. In this way the characters are exempted from rhetoric, and Hemingway himself from the needless formu-lation of a despair which, for the most part, is left inchoate. The occasional passionate outbursts of his characters have a colossal effect of cloudburst. For those of us who elect to read his novels not as adventures purely, there is an immense brooding grimly withheld. When the cloudbursts come, they bring philosophizing which, through being explicit and sententious, sounds *blasé* and out of tune with its context of restraint:

> Poor little kid. I wished the hell I'd been choked like that. No I didn't. Still there would not be all this dying to go through. Now Catherine would die. That was what you did. You died. You did not know what it was about. You never had time to learn. They threw you in and told you the rules and the first time they caught you off base they killed you. Or they killed you gratuitously like Aymo. Or they gave you the syphilis like Rinaldi. But they killed you in the end. You could count on that. Stay around and they would kill you. (*A Farewell to Arms*)

Impassioned and laconic passages of this kind, like the tight-lipped suffering which is more usual with Hemingway, must not be imputed beyond the characters to the author. What the characters are made to say, as well as what Hemingway tells, constitutes one side of that perpetual and gathering irony which the story forces us to complete. In fact, the novels of Hemingway, usually regarded as the antithesis of gentility and subtlety, depict these qualities in an ingenious way. If we are not prepared to surround the text with irony, we find not the numbed responsiveness of a sensitive character but the terse reportage of a simple-minded tough. We can please ourselves in deciding whether or not the hard-boiled slickness of such passages as the following is almost tragic in its implications:

> What a business. You go along your whole life and they seem as though they mean something and they end up not meaning anything. There was never any of what this is. You think that is one thing that you never will have. And then, one lousy show like this, co-ordinating two chicken-crut guerilla bands to help you blow a bridge under impossible conditions, to abort a counter-offensive that will probably already be started, you run into a girl like this Maria. Sure. That is what you would do.
> You ran into her rather late, that was all.
>
> (*For Whom the Bell Tolls*)

The real irony of this low-gear realization is what we ourselves devise; not that a Maria should arrive at this time, but that a man, a former lecturer at Montana University, should so fumblingly spell out his predicament; that an intelligent response is precluded by the facts; that you have to anaesthetize your mind if you want to go on living. The mentality of the dumb-ox type has fascinated Hemingway no less than the ineffectuality of philosophizing has haunted him. The unfortunate thing is that his heroes' glib acceptance of horror, and Hemingway's own blatant mannerisms, happen also to be features of slick thriller fiction. And Hemingway's own attitude vindicates his literary practice: if you cannot read between his lines, then you are not likely to have enough subtlety to resent the straitened reality which characterizes the novels on their primary level of adventure story.

This does not apply to *The Old Man and the Sea*, for in that short novel the moral is the whole. It is a tract about the value in suffering, the fulness in destitution. Here, once again, is a favourite theme of the American novelist: man alone against, or contrasted with, the cosmos. In a large sense, Santiago is a representative of suffering humanity which finds no purpose in its pain, no prize for it efforts, and experiences (like Santiago) destruction of the thing long sought-for. The good is not in the fish's skeleton, but in the man; Hemingway's little novel celebrates man's power to endure what appear the inexorable ways of an impersonal Nature. But notice the qualities which enable Santiago to gain from his loss. He is humble: 'He was too simple to wonder when he had attained humility. But he knew he had attained it.' He has too an immense compassion for all creatures —for the marlin itself, for the exhausted bird that perches on his line well out to sea, for the flying fish, for even the rich who have radios to talk to them on their luxury yachts.

The old man has too some inexhaustible sources of spiritual power: he dreams of the powerful young lions he saw on the white sands of the African coast; he recalls a long bout of wrist-wrestling which he won; he sees the great Di Maggio as a symbol of power and resolution. The facts are plain to Santiago; he addresses the small bird that perches on his line: 'Take a good rest, small bird. . . . Then go in and take your chance like any man or bird or fish.' But there is something to be added to that picture of the world as a violent lottery. It is this. 'Man,' says Santiago to himself, 'is not made for defeat. . . . A man can be destroyed but not defeated.' It is the theme of the old heroic poems: whatever happens to the body, the spirit need not yield. And so, during his battle with the ravening sharks, he fights and fights; he is stripped of everything—his harpoon, his knife, his oar, his tiller— until he is as helpless as the dead marlin. He spits blood once; then he puts what is left of the tiller back in its slot and steers for home. Yet all the time he is thankful: for an intact boat, for the wind, for his bed waiting. The sea, like Huck Finn's river, is now an enemy, now a friend. When he gets into port, he does something that recalls his exclamation on seeing the first of the sharks. ' "Ay", he said aloud. There is no translation for this word and perhaps it is just a noise such as a man might make, involuntarily, feeling the nail go through his hands and into the wood.' It is a crucifixion image—put in to give the action the widest possible significance. And that image is evoked at the end when, having unstepped the mast, he carries it up the hill and has to stop five times on the way. But he is carrying the mast *away* from his own ordeal; and after a sleep, he is soon asking for the baseball news and planning to make a new killing lance. He has to; the marlin is worth nothing in money. But in spiritual restoration its value is incalculable.

This, I think, is the most moving and most heartening of Hemingway's books. It is also a typical American parable-novel. The old man, we might say, has pioneered his way into a new country of the spirit, with the help of his faith and sheer resourcefulness. We are back where we began, with the story of the meaningful ordeal: Odysseus and Santiago go together.

III

In 1893 Marion Crawford told an interviewer that America offered novelists the richest subject-matter in the world. It is beside the point that Crawford was the arch-Romantic; he also wrote novels about the social scene of his own time, including *An American Politician* (1884), unsparing in its exposure of corruption. It was natural enough that, in the last forty years of the nineteenth century, American writers—whether escapist or realists —should feel that the only way of coming to terms with and understanding the new, industrial society was to amass data. 'No ideas but in things.' W. D. Howells (1837–1920), preferring the realism of Daudet to that of Zola, was preferring the honest catalogue to the garish revelation. *The Rise of Silas Lapham* (1885) shows Howells at his best: Lapham the self-made man is contrasted with Corey the genteel. This is the epic of social rise seen under the aspect of old Boston refinement; Howells documents both manners and the psychology of the *parvenu* family. This is his reality: not rebellious, not laboured, but an honest attempt to distinguish between different kinds of people and their differing assumptions about life. He takes pleasure in human diversity and material acquisitions, eventually raising the novel to a severely moral plane by confronting Lapham with a choice between ruin and deceit. Lapham plays fair and goes bankrupt. And his choice sends us forward to another of Howells's novels, this one more openly didactic, *A Hazard of New Fortunes* (1890). The title explains itself and in turn sends us forward to Hamlin Garland's aim to write the epic of the ordinary man. Garland side-tracked himself, however, into limiting his theme to the Western farmer he knew so well and could present with a coarse awkwardness that convinced better than (as he said) the more sophisticated methods of Howells and James, Lowell and Holmes, and 'the other fossil representatives of classicism'.

One of the most solid achievements of the time is Frank Norris's unfinished trilogy, *The Wheat*, which in the two volumes that exist gives a chastening account of wheat-farming in a California torn by the struggle between the railroad and the farmers (*The Octopus*, 1901) and the Chicago wheat-market (*The Pit*, 1903). Unfortunately Norris's rant not only makes parts of these novels unreadable but also fattens out the exaggerations already present in the plot in the shape of a wandering, mystical shepherd. Just as doctrinaire as Norris, Jack London provides both socialism and evidence in *The Iron Heel* (1907). Both Norris and London view their characters as creatures of circumstance; determinism precludes satire because satire presupposes man as a free agent. So their novels lack Howells's lambent ironies and present history as a judgment to be shaken off only by Nietzschean efforts.

Another, much subtler, version of this determinism is that of Theodore Dreiser (1871–1945), who saw men trapped in their temperaments: we are all 'chemisms', and no amount of knowledge can alter that fact. As soon as we are born, the universe has won; therefore Dreiser wastes no time in apportioning blame. *Sister Carrie* (first published in England in 1901, in America not until 1908) presents Carrie as a pawn who, in her turn, triggers off events because of the effect she has on certain other temperaments. The truly strong persons (*The Financier*, 1912, and *The Titan*, 1914) are masters of themselves, but these are rare. Dreiser has no conception of the agonies of choice: to him, man is not condemned to be free, but condemned to wrestle with inconquerable powers which manipulate him through chemistry. So when Dreiser piles up the detail (and he really knows the surface texture of his America) he is demonstrating the complexity of a life that demands clear-cut answers to moral questions: is Carrie to blame? To what extent is Clyde Griffiths in *An American Tragedy* (1925) guilty of partly accidental murder? How, in fiction or in life, 'can' the heroine of *Jennie Gerhardt* (1911) perform, as she does, decent actions? Such questions ask too much: life did not come into being to supply clear answers. To be clear and unequivocal we must necessarily distort; to be utterly honest we must affirm everyone's right to a degree of innocence. Dreiser simply (sometimes crudely) reports on the milieu: pityingly, untidily; and he shows how man's intelligence is always forced to simplify in order to judge. Meanwhile, as his novels powerfully exemplify, the world of objects gets fuller, both a solace to the ineffective mind and a challenge to man's incapacities.

It is not surprising, then, that the dense documentary method typified in John O'Hara's novels should seem one way of illustrating man's powerlessness. True, as O'Hara exhaustively proves, men excel at manipulating physical objects. They mine, smelt, refine, design, sell, re-sell, create markets, fortunes and a whole civilization of manufactures. But human nature gets its own back. Man, able to apply determinisms of his own contriving, is himself subject to one determinism he cannot beat. The craving for love and power (*Ten North Frederick*, 1955), physical compulsion (*A Rage to Live*, 1949), innocence pickled in alcohol (*Butterfield 8*, 1935) and innate egregiousness (*Pal Joey*, 1940)—to take a few examples—make Dreiser's point all over again. And Julian English in *Appointment in Samarra* (1934) cannot really help himself once he throws the highball in Harry Reilly's face. Some unwritten, indetectable law of conglomerate psychology whirls him on towards his own destruction. He cannot know all the repercussions his action will have; how it will chime in with other actions and create a momentum he not only cannot control but cannot even discern. No amount of fieldwork, exploration or knowledge can save a man from a capricious destiny: capricious because unpredicted.

O'Hara's massive albums of facts, then, can fairly be interpreted as brave attempts at the impossible. We can never have enough information; and, in the circumstances, since there is never enough, how much we take depends on preference: if we like the illusion of being able to explain, we take the lot; if, on the other hand, we merely require such basic facts as make the fiction comprehensible, then we need no more than Hemingway gives. O'Hara adds things up; Hemingway explores the highest common factors. O'Hara's characters are trapped in confetti that does not quite explain them; Hemingway's stand out like monoliths from a landscape which seems no more than a setting for them. Neither method of presenting man is wholly satisfying, although each novelist is presenting the same kind of determinism.

Before going on to discuss methods more complex, we must explore a little further the O'Hara fact-fetishism. It is significant that many American novelists have done apprenticeship as picaros. O'Hara has spent time as an evaluating engineer, ship's steward, railway freight clerk, gas-meter reader, guard in an amusement park, labourer in a steel mill, soda-fountain clerk, press agent and newspaperman. It is as if encountering the world explained it. Thus Saul Bellow's Augie March roars through a succession of roles: newspaper boy, clerk in a toy department, flower-shop assistant, agent and companion to a paralysed estate agent, women's shoes salesman, model for riding gear, union organizer, trainer of eagles and so on. At the opposite pole to this cult of miscellaneous experience is the view that all reality and all explanations are within one's own mind. In the long run, myth sums things up and gives an illusion of control through understanding; and self-analysis explains just as well as exhaustive note-taking. So far, however, the only major American novelist to practise the personal-mythical method has been Faulkner, to whom I shall come presently.

O'Hara's novels teem with the resurrected data of lives lived: the expense of love, luck and hubris; parturition, weaning, the rebuffs of puberty, deprivation of all kinds, rift, scandal, salaries, lust, deceits grandiose and miniature, names and reputations towering, the cycle of economic and moral fall, the graph of social rise in an unsettled society, success bringing constriction, failure and *Schadenfreude*, and senility dogging the very heels of supremacy. Yet there is so little illumination of the protagonists' spiritual lives. O'Hara's gods are mundane. His giants are giants of data, and it is as such, not as persons, that they are distinguishable from the data stacked around them. On the other hand, the dwarfs in the major novels—the near-nonentities offered as diversion—are more like believable people, precisely because they remain comparatively undocumented. His Lilliputians drag at our emotions; his Gullivers do not—especially in *From the Terrace* (1959).

This is the story of Alfred Eaton, born 1897, unloved second son of a Pennsylvania steelmaster and a powerless, cool mother. The father, after the elder son dies from spinal meningitis, is unable to transfer his devotion and dreams to Alfred, who matures early through self-reliance and yet is always seeking a father-substitute. The novel's 897 pages massively record the context and detail of Alfred's rise from wealth to imminent millionairedom: after Princeton, the Navy; then into civil aviation and so to Wall Street where he is groomed for power. He distinguishes himself as Assistant Secretary to the Navy, learns the higher calculus of human wickedness and, after a 'massive haemorrhage', resigns. The rest is milk, rest, taking probanthine, the Legion of Merit, convalescence (and obsolescence) on the terrace of a rented house in California. Once out of things, he finds return difficult: his phone is silent for days on end. In fact he is to remain a spectator, well-to-do, gifted, experienced, but irrevocably shelved. Success and power, like his father, have made and abandoned him. At the end of the novel his second wife has a still-born son, and they are left with waning passion and a pathetic craving for 'something to do'.

Alfred Eaton is no Jay Gatsby, starting from scratch; he begins in a privileged enclave of the open society. Why does he fail? Or at least why does he find himself excluded from power? He makes enemies through chance and disdain, but omits to choose and adapt his friends according to the power-politics of high finance. He is essentially lonely. His towering sexuality and his passion for a guiding love are his only means of bridging the gulf: they are the godhead invading his life. Yet their invasions are catalogued in much the same way as the landscape, the syllabus (inserted with a Defoe-like flourish) of the Princeton entrance examination, the desiccated puerility of Long Island society and the exploits of casual acquaintances. Does O'Hara imply that Alfred demeans the one power capable of regenerating him? Partly, yes. Neither twister nor idealist, Alfred is (as his one remaining friend puts it at the end) 'a very attractive man with an unattractive outlook on people'. He has no spiritual centre, which is perhaps why O'Hara presents him inconsistently, promising a monolith but offering fragments only.

Yet one's discontent is the measure of a grand ambition all but realized. The O'Hara of *From the Terrace* is trying too hard, attempting excessive objectivity. Only rarely (like H. G. Wells in another novel about a wrecked career, *The New Machiavelli*) is he fully behind even the emotional passages. But for comprehensive and sometimes ferocious intelligence, sifting without interpreting the substance of human downfall, *From the Terrace* is unforgettable. It has power, grandeur, accuracy and the ghastly pressure of this industrial century. Possibly, even, its very lack of integration is meant to force upon us more depressingly than usual the O'Hara theme: man at odds with himself for ineluctable reasons. Only several readings would find the strategy behind this overwhelming saga of human miscarriage.

On second reading, O'Hara's major novels appear to be perfectly phased and built: accurate and worthy pyramids to the memory of considerable men. Yet their considerableness is that of size, not of spirit. There is a plethora of fact, a dearth of simple soul-searching and self-defining. If we use the word 'remorse', we may have difficulty in applying the word's literal sense: self-biting. Where is the self? Does it consist in the documentation? It seems nowhere; and this fact, in one way, is O'Hara's main asset as a tragedian. For in tragedy there is no hope; no reckless aspiration in face of the hostile sky. The essential facts are there; so is the emotional outburst; but what is presented in such a play as Sophocles's *Antigone* is the impact, not the imagined alternative. No one except Creon in an off-moment expects things to improve. The same, *mutatis mutandis*, is true of O'Hara's novels: what they miss in sheer evidence of men's hoping they gain in tragic matter-of-factness. The main characters have no faces: they do not appear to us; neither do the protagonists of Greek tragedy.

The disturbing truth seems to be that we are accustomed to seeing too much of a character's inner life. Proust and Joyce have created in us an excessive appetite for soul-searching. And O'Hara, at the expense of seeming a Tolstoy of the zombies, has restored to the epic novel *some* of the balanced techniques of the nineteenth century. So that within an O'Hara context, a bout of introspection achieves an effect of outburst impossible in, say, a volume of Proust's vast exploration. The novelist who taps the stream of consciousness or the sea of the unconscious has to attempt the reverse trick. He has to be content with a sudden act, something pungent in the way of detail, a sudden absence of meditation altogether. Both effects are within the scope and, indeed, the practice of O'Hara. The main trouble is that he contrives a stream of mere consequences just as cloying as Proust's *roman-fleuve*, and yet punctuates it with spells of non-pungent introspection. The consequent effect is of the same process in two differing materials or of different processes *in pari materia*. In other words, one kind of viscosity will not serve to accentuate another. The only contrast consists in the motive, not in the method.

But it is only fair to illustrate here O'Hara's mastery of the euphuistic, rambling presentation of life's flux. This is Alfred Eaton:

Today was not Tuesday, it was Wednesday, because on Wednesday you saw *him* and on Tuesday you did *that*. And a little girl grew and a little boy grew, and a woman got older and a man aged, and a tooth came out and a muscle ached and a man did not get his money and a waiter fell dead, and thunder slapped and a bell rang and paper crinkled and an elevated train abraded the track and a flying machine fanned the air, and a letter came and a sweetness was tasted and a taxi was found and a piss was postponed and a door would not close and a party hung up and a lion escaped and a woman's oil brought joy and the approximations of peace and the approximations of happiness.

Such item-by-item recapitulation of life's miscellaneous phenomena has something in common with the undifferentiating perception of a child. It conveys, in fact, the sudden, perhaps aghast, abdication of the adult, organizing mind. There are many familiar and notorious passages in Hemingway's prose that attempt a similar significance. The technique is rather like that of the collage, in which, say, haphazard scraps cut from newspapers are included in a design otherwise fairly orthodox. These cuttings are presented in their own right as objects and specimens: it is as if art cannot cope, cannot make artificial: the writer or the painter comes forward, negative in capability, explaining or implying that in this instance he chooses to go no farther. He will not adapt the object in question to his style's convention. He elects for rawness, 'real life', aiming perhaps at something like Aristotle's τὸ ὅμοιον, 'likeness to life', allied with τὸ πιθανόν, 'convincingness'. Such a specimen is, in the literal sense, obscene, for it affronts the gracious world of considered and organic style. It barks out from its context and shocks. But, in O'Hara's novels, and in *From the Terrace* especially, it does not quite disrupt things enough: the method's very unselectivity hinders its success in the familiar O'Hara context of amassed data.

There is a further significance of this deliberate lapse into cumulatively meaningless catalogues. Not only discrimination is put into abeyance; so also is the moral sense—the whole moral identity of the character concerned. Everything in the long, free-wheeling list is as good as everything else; every action is in the same ethical category; every motive is null. O'Hara's aim in this respect is clear: when a character has had enough, when society's machine has flung him to the periphery, he lets go and defaults for a while. An introspective anarchy ensues. And it is here that O'Hara's ambitions as a novelist of modern American manners appear most forcefully. In these ambitions, traditional for the novelist, he proves himself superior to such epic-tasters as Norman Mailer, James Jones and James Gould Cozzens. His is a laudable aim: to strip the facile labels off things, to remove the surfaces, to expose the naked self which disguises and ramifies itself through so many habitual subterfuges. But this is not to say that he ever fully succeeds. He never does. And one of the principal reasons for the failure is the fact that his free-wheeling monologues seem to parody the structure of the whole novel—whichever one is in question.

It might be said that, in some respects, he intends these interior monologues as crystallizations of the epic's progress. If they actually were such, they would be very welcome indeed. We sympathize with the writer who, attempting a vast panorama of men, manners and history, now and then gets the urge to say it all out in one word, to encompass all in one vision. Joyce's *Ulysses* is an expansion of such an urge. So too are the poems of the Imagists, although (of course) expansion constitutes an admission of failure. Our difficulty with O'Hara's manner of self-interrupting honesty is really with his monotony of technique. If only he would fight more scattering, he could become the Tolstoy of present-day America. He is close to Faulkner in many ways. They both aim at depth and attain density; they both document so fully as to invert the narrative. Faulkner supplies more emotion and massed ambience than we generally expect characters to have; O'Hara tells us more about the configurations of a man's life than we can assimilate. Both surfeit us, both interpret emphasis as an increase of weight. No doubt, of course, that O'Hara in particular intends to show his characters as much weighed down by time's sheer multitudinous endlessness as by success's responsibility and simply by having too much to do, too many things to think about.

Epic is essentially a religious mode of literature, entailing inclusion of a whole cosmology. O'Hara too has to include it. Yet we ourselves should be able to see it as included merely, not as all-devouring: such an illusion is essential in any form of art. The convincingness is incredibly well achieved; but that illusion of the author's supremacy over all his material is missing. O'Hara seems to be too close to his theme; his obsession seems unadaptable to deliberate art. All he has to do is to redispose his emphases; but at present, wary of becoming subjective with his massive theme, he overconcentrates on externals. Consequently his presented moments of inwardness are powerless to diversify the sheer bulk of his novels. Such a theme as his comes alive only through a proportionate amount of a character's ordinarily unobservable reactions. That was Tolstoy's trick. But whether or not it can become O'Hara's depends upon his ability to transfer his own spirituality into his novels without overdoing it. Dynamos have to produce power, not use it. One has the impression that O'Hara has failed to turn the vital switch. It should be easy; for he has accomplished with such majestic thoroughness tasks which other novelists merely set aside. When those dummies really quiver, when those giants engulf the data in self-colloquy, O'Hara's art will be fruitful indeed. The unexamined life is not worth having, or, for that matter, worth writing about. Significantly, the narrator of *Ourselves to Know* (1960) shows a compulsive interest in Robert Millhouser's motives for committing a *crime passionel*. The psychology rather than the physical environment is what counts in this novel. Why Millhouser went to Europe with a homosexual and eventually married a teen-age nymphomaniac cannot be explained in terms of social data. For once O'Hara strikes just deep enough. Fatality for once seems vested in the man himself. This is the kind of probing O'Hara does best in the *novella*; there is room for just the amount of psychology he usually puts into a novel, but not for his usual amount of surface data. So, as in *Sermons and Soda Water* (1960), the psychology wins out and so does the reader's sympathy. O'Hara seems already to have taught himself that the facts of life are ruinously elusive and also that one's own fictional mannerisms can obscure them entirely. Life is not *quite* the shuttle from lust to boredom, from boredom back to bed. O'Hara's complicated simplifications can be maddening—even when, as in *The Big Laugh* (1962), an upright wife, for once in an O'Hara novel, abandons a reformed rake of a spouse. All the same, as Lionel Trilling has said: 'More than anyone now writing, O'Hara understands the complex, contradictory, asymmetrical society in which we live.'

Edith Wharton (1862–1937) adds the necessary footnote to O'Hara: the novelist, she said, must 'bear in mind at each step that his business is not to ask what the situation would be likely to make of his characters, but what his characters, being what they are, would make of the situation'. It is an honourable view, substituting for the determinism of Norris and his contemporaries the emphasis Dreiser placed on people 'being what they are'. It is not a pendulum swing back to free will, but the kind of modified will to be found in *Huckleberry Finn*, *The Red Badge of Courage* and *Daisy Miller*. Evoking as it may the myth of the conquering pioneer, it amounts really to an acknowledgment of cosmic forces compelling men to face their environment with a handicap.

To Edith Wharton the handicap was the vulgarity of the majority: society is always changing, always erasing old codes of behaviour. *Ethan Frome* (1911) gives the extreme version of man's helplessness, even in the comparatively impregnable life of a New England farm; and her New York novels paint the same condition in harsher contrasts. Society imperceptibly at first, then brutally in the open, defeats those who refuse to move with it: Lily in *The House of Mirth* (1905) is too honest and has too much integrity; Ralph Marvell in *The Custom of the Country* (1913) has too much taste to fight the groundswell he is intelligent enough to observe. Vance Weston in *Hudson River Bracketed* (1928) moves from Euphoria, Illinois, to a house on the Hudson, and thence to the maelstrom of New York, which he cannot survive. He seems to belong nowhere. Logically enough, Edith Wharton portrayed the world as a destructive element. Less minutely analytical than Henry James, less sustained in observation, she wrote her novels as if in disdainful proof of something she had known for a long time. Sometimes, as with Ralph Marvell, and even more with Undine Spragg, the mid-Westerner in *The Custom of the Country* (1913), she seems uninterested in her characters: either because she sees them as beaten before they start or because they embody what she detests. Either way her novels suffer. The myth (the general outline re-personified) inhibits her documentary intentions; and her novels themselves die victims to the pressures she tries to display. Even her war novels, *The Marne* (1918) and *A Son at the Front* (1923), took war too seriously to hit the fashion; once again, society—American post-war society— proved impervious to standards she treasured even though she also regarded them sceptically.

Edith Wharton's passionate beliefs were only as passionate as her very fine intelligence permitted. She hovered between un-critical conviction and a proud isolation, with her strong humanitarian streak and her care for the decencies always hindering her respect for logic. She fought, as did Henry Adams, a sense of her own obsolescence and embodied the virtues and graces that Adams cherished in the heroines of his novels *Democracy* (1880) and *Esther* (1884). But her bewilderment emerges casually, whereas *The Education of Henry Adams* (1918) foreshadows the panorama (of social change and ideological upheaval) to come from John Dos Passos. Adams, having admitted to himself all he felt, could work it up into a vision; Edith Wharton was too impatient with a changing world to manufacture something worth while from it. What appalled her, as it appalled Gertrude Stein, was the rapidity and grossness of change: she wanted to experience change in a settled context, not one change hot on the heels of the last. And she, like the other expatriate writers, developed a kind of literary schizophrenia: not divided, so much as shattered, mind, the fastidious aristocrat merging into the secessive artist, the uprooted American seeking a *planche de salut* from which to justify a guilty conscience and meditate reconciliations in the abstract. Of course, the longer the Henry Jameses, the Hemingways, the Whartons and the Steins stayed in Europe, the more abstract their notion of America became. Their novels epitomize the idealized realism and the glamourized myth we have come to expect from people who are uncertain where they belong. James's casuistical analyses of manners and motives, Hemingway's defeated exiles, Edith Wharton's resentful elegiacs and Gertrude Stein's francophilia add up to a refusal to take the world on its own terms, the antithesis to which is O'Hara's eagerness to specify what it is and even to make it seem more so. George Santayana's novel *The Last Puritan* (1936) is a more accurate reproof to American gentility (at home and abroad) than anything O'Hara has written.

I do not mean to suggest that the stay-at-home realists, of whom O'Hara is the extremest example, experienced no conflicts. What we find in the novels of Sherwood Anderson, Sinclair Lewis, John Dos Passos, James T. Farrell, as well as those of Steinbeck, Faulkner and Wolfe, is the mind which reassures itself by accumulation while pursuing a purpose either reformist or satirical. Whereas, in the work of the expatriates (among whom we must include Fitzgerald for *Tender is the Night*), there is a compensatory near-idealism of remote America, the muck-rakers and debunkers piled up facts not without a certain pride that these were American facts and no other kind: repugnant but their own. So it is not surprising to find Sinclair Lewis (1885–1951), the creator of the novel as expert reportage, hammering the 'booboisie' in *Main Street* (1920), the Babbitts of Zenith in *Babbitt* (1922), the pretentious venal nation as a whole in *Arrowsmith* (1925), religiosity in *Elmer Gantry* (1927) and the plodding car manufacturer turned tourist (*Dodsworth*, 1929), half in love with his targets. Towards the end of his life he told a European audience (not entirely playfully) that he wrote *Babbitt* 'not out of hatred but out of love'. Always in Lewis, anathemata slide into anthems.

The reason is partly the need to belong. Mencken and Ring Lardner could exploit to the full the contemptuous role; they were not writing novels; and it is hard to write many novels without wishing to celebrate life's fulness. To pore over characters, to describe landscapes exactly, to dwell in and on the life of a generation, is to go through the motions of a kinship. And Lewis, assaulting the Gopher Prairies, the George Folansbee Babbitts, proving with mordant elation how crass, crude and narrow most of his contemporaries are, cannot resist either the creative artist's feeling for his characters or the feeling that, out of sheer creative exuberance, he might have gone too far in denigration. So he restores Carol Kennicott to the hebetating husband she has left. Just so, out of some infiltrating fidelity to the only context he himself has, he goes back on his own scorn. We have to choose. If we enjoy Lewis the slightly Dickensian anatomist of manners, we have to allow his allegiances; if we value him most as a satirist, we have to wish he were less wrapped up in his work.

The novels of Sherwood Anderson (1876–1941) are those of an expatriate who stayed at home. They are repopulated versions of the Anderson story rendered as homage to the Midwest. His semi-autobiographical *Windy McPherson's Son* (1916), although too thin in texture to be as atmospherically bemusing as his later work, typifies the Anderson method. Fundamentally Anderson had no abiding centre but himself: a late starter, he walked out on his job and family, and understandably discovered his main subject-matter in that act. He muddles wistfully. He looks in on dreams being dreamed, fills in from his own reveries. He studies loneliness and distinguishes it from self-sufficiency; gregariousness from companionship. *Winesburg, Ohio* (1919), a collection of studies in human bafflement, is somehow too desultory to be the enthralling spectrum of scenes-from-provincial-life it would have been. The participant-narrator, George Willard, seems dazed; but, of course, he is growing up and cannot, as an older character might have done, identify himself with all ages. But the groping and fumbling of young love is exquisitely set against the brooding, the remorse and the crippled dreams of the small town. What one misses in Anderson is the pressure of the century: it is as if he has chosen to transfer *mal du siècle* into a town where the century counts for very little. The self-tormenting seekers for

liberty are too confused, too tepid, to have conceived of liberty
in the first place. Anderson himself, perhaps exaggerating the
severity of the step which took him from respectability into
writing, worked out his guilt in the form of similar small-scale
rebellion. Juxtaposed with Faulkner or Hemingway, he is deficient in heroic pretensions, and is perhaps all the more persuasive for that. We are only just learning how to read him; and
what we have learned of the Willy Lomans should send us back
to Anderson with renewed perception and a clearer idea than he
himself had of the mild refusals which are the unheroic hero's
heroisms. Anderson made his protest by accumulating instances
of thwarted lives. Only the innocent keep on aspiring when they
are getting nowhere; only the innocent resort to violence. Anderson's very mildness is a welcome change from the American cult
of violence, and makes the same points with captivating stoicism.

F. Scott Fitzgerald (1896–1940) takes up aspiration where
Anderson leaves off. Jay Gatsby and Dick Diver both aim high
and come toppling down; they aim higher than any Anderson
character and topple harder. (Fitzgerald, in fact, is to Anderson
as Wells is to Gissing.) *The Great Gatsby* (1925) is a fable about
the pursuit of perfection: the rich cannot find perfection because
money contaminates it (*vide* Huck Finn) and the poor cannot find
it because poverty makes people lower their sights. Fitzgerald
knew. Above all, as the fate of Gatsby and Dick Diver demonstrates, men are born to spoil the precious gift which their life is:
the way up is always the way down. And while they are worrying
how to make the most of the one life they have, they are wasting
it.

Nick Carraway is a young Midwesterner who sells bonds in
New York. He lives at West Egg on Long Island. His neighbour
there is Jay Gatsby whose fabulous at-homes are financed by
bootlegging and various other nefarious arts. Gatsby has come
from very little. As an army lieutenant, Gatsby had fallen in love
with Nick's cousin, Daisy, who later married a wealthy boor
called Tom Buchanan. Through Nick, Gatsby meets Daisy again
and makes her his mistress. Her husband turns to Myrtle Wilson,
the wife of a garage-owner; but Myrtle is killed on the highway by
Daisy, who drives on. Gatsby tries to protect Daisy. Then Tom
Buchanan tells Myrtle's husband that it was Gatsby who killed

her. Wilson therefore shoots Gatsby and then himself. It is a dream—a bad one; the Jazz Age raised to its highest power.

Gatsby wants to impress Daisy, or the ghost of what Daisy once was. He knows he is living, is buying, a lie; but there is an insane nobility about him. He riots in his ready-made waste-land; his happiness is precarious, but he rarely speaks in his own person in the novel, and who are we to know? Gatsby is America: between power and idyll, between Mammon and the Territory, he epitomizes the spirit which feels it can make the world to its own order. As the novel tells us: 'Jay Gatsby of West Egg, Long Island, sprang from his Platonic conception of himself.' And his story is an American fable: this is how the open society will let you up; giddily, hastily, intoxicatingly, ecstatically up; and then sordidly down. As Lionel Trilling says: 'To the world it is anomalous in America, just as in the novel it is anomalous in Gatsby, that so much raw power should be haunted by envisioned romance. Yet in that anomaly lies, for good or bad, much of the truth of our national life, as, at the present moment, we think about it.'

Gatsby's dream of luxury and civilized conviviality and lost love regained, as well as of remaining undiscovered for what he really is, seems just as futile as Daisy Miller's innocence and Huck Finn's escapism. Fitzgerald gives us a superb picture of the social manners of the time; he also tells us a fairy-story. The godmother has done her work; the means are to hand; and Gatsby, like some demented impresario, sets about building a world out of his own personality. It is megalomania: he seems a god—he never seems quite real. But there he is, the endless provider, feeding the thousands merely to draw a girl back into his power. He has created his own élite; and he is rich, rich in people and rich in money. He seems to have proved himself: the self-imposed test was success. He passed with flying colours. But the Buchanans are rich too; they are together at the end when Gatsby is dead. He has aspired and failed; like the old story of the young prince deprived of his kingdom *The Great Gatsby* shows the prince trying to move back in. Gatsby moves in and vanishes through the door on the other side. The corrupt and entrenched have worsted the trusting and the aspiring. After Gatsby has been killed, his father arrives from Minnesota and talks to Carraway:

After changing my clothes I went next door and found Mr Gatz walking up and down excitedly in the hall .... 'Jimmy sent me this picture.' He took out his wallet with trembling fingers. 'Look here.' It was a photograph of the house, cracked in the corner and dirty with many hands. He pointed out every detail to me eagerly. 'Look there!' and then sought admiration from my eyes.

The pathos is clear: Mr Gatz, rather shabby and very proud of his son, who is both prince and prodigal, is the ashes of the American dream. He has even brought along one of the books Gatsby had as a boy: *Hopalong Cassidy*. And at the end of the novel, as if to ram home the painful point, Gatsby's effort is related to that of the early settler who, three hundred years earlier, 'must have held his breath in the presence of this continent . . . face to face for the last time in history with something commensurate to his capacity for wonder'. Nothing could be more poignant in the context than that.

Tender is the Night (1934) is more ambitious. There are more people and more twists; Fitzgerald probes deeply into Dick Diver and Nicole; the ending is not the accidentally melodramatic bang of the previous novel, but a dying fall. Dick, too wealthy and too devoted to other people, loses his identity; his wife and associates prey upon him and he ends up preying on himself. This is the novel Gatsby himself might have written once his soaring confidence had yielded to self-pity. It is a pappier novel, not quite controlled, with much dark stuff flooding into it, and too autobiographical to have the almost impersonal authority of *Gatsby*. But it is neither as bad as the thirties critics said nor as good as some present-day critics pretend. It is Fitzgerald without the gloss of the early novels *This Side of Paradise* (1920) and *The Beautiful and the Damned* (1922): it goes beyond the meretricious and mannered, even beyond the crisp economy of *Gatsby*, and, after establishing Dick's 'trick of the heart', sprawls into the muddy waters of his crack-up and Nicole's reversion to family type. The novel must be read as the Fitzgerald dossier cast as an anticipatory obituary. Along with the personal emptiness revealed in Stahr, the Hollywood tycoon in the unfinished *The Last Tycoon* (1941), and in the papers collected posthumously in *The Crack-*

Up (1945), we must place the near-hysterical cleverness of Fitzgerald's stories about threatened or missed marriages. He always made a great deal out of nervous collapse, neurasthenia and scenes—partly because they offered a springboard for technical contrivances, partly because his own life was full of them. One story, 'The Curious Case of Benjamin Button' (1922), tells how a man grows steadily younger: an ironic inversion of Fitzgerald's vernal mania.

But if youth fades, heritage does not. Fitzgerald was always proud of the cachet an Irish name gave him (or seemed to give). He badly needed a gorgeous ethos and just as badly feared having to admit, *from his own experience*, that life is a drab affair. In some ways a true child of the nineties, in others pure Hollywood, he was also a master of sharp prose and, in *Gatsby*, of the classical manner we find only in *Manon Lescaut, Adolphe* and *Les Liaisons dangereuses*. Eventually the facts of life pierced him: there is no glamour-worship among the dry sentimental analysis of *The Last Tycoon*. Sexual love in *Gatsby* has an air of childlike prank; in *Tender* Dick and Nicole suddenly retire from a gathering in order to make love—but rather like two close friends with the same passion for ice-cream: they will share an ice together, so to speak; and, finally, Stahr, getting romantic, hears the girl who reminds him of his dead wife utter a lewd, provocative word. Not that things get shabbier; they just come to earth—for most of us the natural element, but for Fitzgerald the region of defeat. It was, sadly and significantly, the impossible at which his dreams aimed and the improbable on which they broke. Where Anderson aims low, Fitzgerald describes a parabola and re-describes it until the rapidly moving wand prevents it from fading.

Unfortunately the Budd Schulbergs and the Sheilah Grahams have added their wads of melodrama and self-concerned revelation to the generous efforts of Edmund Wilson and Alfred Kazin. We are in some danger now of losing the intelligent Fitzgerald for the corruptible dreams of the defeated one. It was the intelligent one who wrote that 'the form of so many modern novels is less a progression than a series of impressions . . . like the slowly turned pages of an album', who described *Gatsby* as a *tour de force* and *Tender* as 'a confession of faith' by Dick Diver 'the spoiled priest', and explained to Maxwell Perkins that 'A short

story can be written on a bottle, but for a novel you need the
mental speed that enables you to keep the whole pattern in your
head and ruthlessly sacrifice the side-shows as Ernest did in *A
Farewell to Arms*.' He told a friend that his own novels were
either selective (*This Side of Paradise*, *Gatsby*) or blown up (*The
Beautiful and the Damned*, *Tender*), based on 'the views of [the]
Theodore Driesers [*sic*] and the Joseph Conrads—that life is too
strong and remorseless for the sons of men'. He was thinking
mainly, but not entirely, of Zelda; and we have to remember that
he had an almost liturgical sense of life's precariousness. There is,
in almost all his novels and stories, a constant suggestion of his
being a stranger on earth, an ethereal misfit popped on to the
clay while God busied Himself with something better. And
then, without warning, off, like Peter Pan. Fitzgerald lost his
Catholicism at Princeton but never lost the sense of awe; 'He was
not even a Catholic,' he wrote of the hero in *This Side of Paradise*,
'yet that was the only ghost of a code that he had.'

Fitzgerald has his successors. Paul Darcy Boles, for instance, in
Granville Hicks's symposium *The Living Novel* (1957), recalls an
early meeting with an editor: 'I looked good in a white summer
suit, and the girl has always been beautiful.' But he and the editor
disagreed; Boles terminated the interview, picked up his manuscript and walked out: 'I felt wonderful, going down in the
elevator with the girl, and stepping out on Wabash into the close,
quick, adventurous night.' Those sentences spell out an intoxicating sense of possibility, of young life unspoiled. They also
present an urban version of the pastoral hinterland cherished by
Huck Finn; and this pastoral appears too in Boles's account of
his growth as a novelist: 'I was also like the pioneer scout free in
the limitless forests and grasses of early America, with the same
voraciousness, casual waste, and minute-by-minute exaltation at
the unrolling of experience. . . .'

IV

No American novelist can escape a dilemma which might be
formulated as follows: until the Frontier reached the West coast,
there was always the physical presence of unexplored, untamed

land to substantiate the magical idea of the place where, because
nothing was fixed, any ideal was realizable. All manner of dreams,
aspirations, escapes and reversions clustered round the notion of
such a place. Raw fact could still be seen as pastoral; the west-
wards-moving frontier, rapidly chased by urban and industrial
civilization, typified the American principle and could be treasured
as a literary concept. But, with America opened up, made uni-
form, raw fact became a spoiled ideal; what once was fluid set.
'The only regions left', as Wright Morris says in the above-
mentioned symposium, 'are those the artists must imagine. They
lie beyond the usual forms of salvage. No matter where we go, in
America today, we shall find what we just left.' What the imagination could conjure up out of the unknown land has now given
way to imagination in its own right. So many possibilities have
been excluded for ever; many other possibilities have become
permanent facts. And the partly religious, partly adolescent zeal
of Huck Finn has to yield to an ineluctable net of railways, urban
developments, money-making projects and stereotyping media.
Possibility has become fact; and imagination has to cease speculating about things it cannot change.

Except in one respect. It can still mythologize: not vaguely,
coining 'dark fields of the republic' or the 'fresh, green breast
of the new world' (nostalgia even in *Gatsby*), but precisely and
tenaciously. The world has to be coped with as it is, either through
enumeration (impossible) or conceptual effort. Thomas Wolfe
(1900–1938), lately commended by William Faulkner for attempting the impossible, was on the right—the only—lines. Wolfe, in
fact, recognized what was impossible; he chose to transform,
to create a rhetoric of national metaphor. It is the O'Haras who
fail, seeking to master through completeness rather than through
essence. To some extent, Wolfe is O'Hara's antithesis: he adduced
rather than added. He dared to discover in the America about
him what he found in himself; he defined myth as 'distorted fact'
and thought of himself as a slave to 'the dark, ruined Helen of
[his] blood'. Unresolved contradictions did not frighten him over-
much, however; and so, romantic as he was, he still aimed at
some objective version of what America was. The largely unwritten *Hound of Darkness* was to have been 'a great tone-
symphony of night—railway yards, engines, freights, deserts, a

clopping hoof, etc.—seen *not by a definite personality*, but haunted throughout by a *consciousness* of personality'. Perhaps it was because this work was not to be his usual style of confessional that it remained a fragment.

Wolfe is good because he responds intensely. He towers, shovels, self-pities, loathes, plunges and tramps—a gargantuan Huck. The hero of *The Web and the Rock* (1939) 'has the face of a demented angel . . . and there is a madness and darkness and evil in his brain. He is more cruel than death, and more lovely than a flower. His heart was made for love, and it is full of hate and darkness.' Wolfe writes the epic of raw nerves as they are played on by phenomena, and he can only think of concluding when the nerves do not respond. So he never concludes. Looking for his notorious 'father'-figure, he finds Mrs Bernstein, who is brilliant and mature, Maxwell Perkins, who is both long-suffering and unyielding, and the notion of the Great American Novel—a kind of cosmic insurance policy for something invaluable. He fails to realize that he is writing mythological autobiography and not a catalogue; he does not know he is epitomizing. Writing selectively, able to transform the scene about him, he yet refuses to excise a single word.[1] In other words, he is too self-centred to know the difference between the cataloguer and the expressionist. Writing metaphors, he wants his metaphors to be as big as the world they suggest. In pursuit of 'the image of a strength and wisdom external to his [man's] need and superior to his hunger', he forgets that the image is imaginative. He wants to be Panto-crator the Second. 'I have at last discovered my own America,' he exclaims, responding lyrically and then interpreting until he seems almost to have uttered the ineffable.

It is odd to find him, on the one hand, transcribing Asheville almost undisguised in *Look Homeward, Angel* (1929) and, on the other, first planning *Of Time and the River* (1935) as 'Antaeus' based on Heracles, Poseidon, Gaea, Helen, Demeter, Kronos, Rhea and other figures. His response to the world of the senses is

---

1. Cf. Maxim Lieber in the *Times Literary Supplement* (16 June 1961) who recalls, in a letter, trying to persuade Wolfe to lose 5,000 words by eliminating the literal reproduction of one character's stammer. Wolfe 'turned livid with fury, ranted, stormed, and literally foamed'; justifying his refusal, he said: 'he did stammer . . . he was my brother'. Art as artifice eluded him.

balanced by his passion (especially in his last years) for high-sounding abstractions; and that balance is perhaps explained by his early studies in Hegelian dialectic under Horace Williams ('Hegel in the Cotton Belt'). Wolfe the romantic self-emptier constantly betrays Wolfe the reporter of the American scene, and *vice versa*. His concern with the middle-class, its poverty, its prejudices and its liberalism, its real-estate pipe-dreams and its influence on his parents, has to survive as best it can his enthusiasm for Joyce's *Ulysses*. *Look Homeward, Angel* is of all his novels the most purely Wolfe's own; and its account of Eugene Gant's childhood, early youth and adolescence shows how Wolfe could, at his best, combine lyrical deluge with an almost metaphysical sense of order, even though that sense had to be expressed in imaginary conversation with a ghost.

His short novels, *A Portrait of Bascom Hawke* and *The Web of Earth*, reflect the same sense; so much so, in fact, that *Of Time and the River* might have been a more coherent work if Maxwell Perkins had not dissuaded Wolfe from tackling his new vision of America in any way but that of a young man's apprenticeship. As it is, the novel follows Eugene Gant to Harvard, New York, Europe and into two love affairs. But it lacks the momentum of its predecessor; it impels us towards no Lawrence-like moment of revelation and resolution; it sprawls, it yawns, it pumps itself up, bursts, then sprawls again. It is a glutinous self-indulgence of a book, too much so to maintain a vision of a vast country or even of a vast soul. The digressions are the best bits; they at least hang together. So do the excluded portions published together as *From Death to Morning* (1935)—not, in Bernard De Voto's phrase, 'placental matter', but pieces neither malleable nor vague enough to be fitted in. *The Web of Earth*, a reminiscence by Eliza Gant, will stand comparison with the best shorter works of Faulkner; and 'Only the Dead Know Brooklyn' shows that Wolfe could occasionally mythologize the American scene with scarcely a word wasted. From time to time Wolfe the rhetorical mammoth ran out of breath, and 'the Lost, the Never-Found, the Ever-Here America' suddenly crystallized into a profound vignette free of mystagogic cobwebs.

After Wolfe's death in 1938, Edward Aswell of Harpers produced three books from the manuscripts that remained. *The*

Web and the Rock (1939) does the usual prolix romp around childhood, college, New York, Europe and love; it almost comes off, especially in the early sections which Wolfe himself had been able to pare and tighten. Aswell's next compilation, *You Can't Go Home Again* (1940), is more of an untidy conspectus than it is a novel. George Webber of the preceding book reappears but merely as a mirror for such entertaining characters as Lloyd McHarg (Sinclair Lewis), Mr Katamoto, Judge Bland, Mr Green who jumps from twelve storeys up (once), and for such incidental sections as the account of Nazi-dom, the publication of George's novel and the moral inanition of Lybia Hill (Asheville once again). Much the least lyrical of Wolfe's 'works', it feels harder and creates clear characters in meticulously realized settings. For once, the apocalyptic is short in supply, and the drama free of Wolfe's self-dramatizations. Aswell's third excavation produced *The Hills Beyond* (1943), a collection of fragments and episodes the best of which are the two stories 'The Lost Boy' (noteworthy for a compact presentation of Wolfe's attitude to time) and 'Chickamauga'. Part of the title piece was originally conceived of as 'The Doaksology', a label which aptly suggests a tenacious realism sustained throughout. It shows the Wolfe who said he moved from lyricism to 'concern with the designs and purposes of life'; and it also illustrates how he could use words for purposes other than incantation.

Wolfe had an acute ear for the idiosyncrasies of speech; to him oddities in talk amounted to an attempt to personalize the void and its silence. The way a person spoke was to Wolfe a sample of privately arrived-at lyricism, and it had to be revered as an effort to bridge the gulf between lonelinesses. He always wanted to understand his fellows, and one can respect the notion even though he felt equal to understanding men in their thousands. Only a very lonely man dares to indulge so grandiose a dream without assuming that most people are alike. Wolfe pined for massive sodality; for the thoughtless togetherness of childhood when all children are made free of the 'great forgotten language, the lost lane-end into heaven'. Wordsworth coincides with Sterne in Wolfe: the young heroes trail their clouds of glory into the irremediable isolation of adulthood. W. O. Gant (with Walter Shandy) represents the last stage of the enveloped, stifled heart. And Wolfe, who tots up the past rather than re-living or refurbishing it, proves his point by saying, in fact: 'You can't go home again.' In the story already mentioned, 'The Lost Boy', Wolfe writes: 'And out of the enchanted wood, that thicket of man's memory, Eugene knew that the dark eye and the quiet face of his friend and brother—poor child, life's stranger, and life's exile, lost like all of us, a cipher in blind mazes, long ago—the lost boy was gone forever, and would not return.' Wolfe goes seeking a vanished spell: it is in the air but can no longer possess him. In other words, it is America's childhood that he seeks, and his efforts are as futile as those of English novelists who seek the Arthurian, the magical, in the modern industrial world. The only way of re-establishing contact with an early atmosphere is through myth and the imposition of it on alien elements. Wolfe wants the pastoral version of the condition he describes as 'so lost, so naked and so lonely in America'; it is a primitive innocence—*euetheiâ*, felt in its most acid version at night when the trains trundle by and time itself seems to whistle past. His only compensation is to show, in his writing, how he understood his characters, those thinly disguised creatures of his own actuality.

With his sympathy went infatuation with vigour. For a time he thought the Nazis the ideal of vigour, but he got over that when he saw what the ideal entailed in Germany and upon Europe. Wolfe's trouble was that when he found the personal, private way impossible, he averted his gaze to the social and general, and thus prepared to deal in cult, fable and myth. His time in Brooklyn during the depression taught him about penury and drove him to quasi-Marxism, to what Pamela Hansford Johnson in *Thomas Wolfe* (1947) calls 'a young man's socialism, based on the generous rage, the infuriated baffled pity'. *You Can't Go Home Again* contrasts the wealthy with the needy, the charitable with the statistical view, and condemns the acquisitive society's early phase. Sinclair Lewis's influence is obvious, but Wolfe gives it a peculiar twist. He rages against the ugly just as much as against the unjust, and one cannot help noticing how he always harks back to a condition of complete simplicity: a mythical condition available only to the Huck Finns and to them only intermittently.

In a word, his social conscience is anarchic. His hope for

America is a pious wish based on fine, private emotion; not on facts. Like another Southerner, William Faulkner, he believed—in spite of his manicheanism and his loneliness—that man's inhumanity to man was not the only truth. He spoke of 'the final deposit, a burning memory, a certain evidence of the fortitude of man, his ability to suffer and somehow to survive'. Faulkner's version is similar: man not only can endure; he may even prevail over his own collective sin and folly. The main question is: what is man? Both bestial and divine. The question and the answer are Malraux's too, as well as Faulkner's. But naturally such a view, vague and hopeful, cannot be communicated in terms of social data: all the relevant facts cannot be added up and presented for scrutiny. Instead, Wolfe creates his own distorted, teeming kind of *Bildungsroman*, Malraux evolves both a myth of committed fraternity and a mystique of art, and Faulkner invents Yoknapatawpha County—a phantasmagoria of the aspiring and the unhoping. In order to relate their convictions to fact, all three have to tamper with fact. Their basis is life's paradoxical nature. Their superstructure is a lyricism as private as the intuitions of a child. And the specifically American agony is that entailed in having to create a tradition of some kind; a tradition which Malraux takes to naturally but which Wolfe and Faulkner deny themselves. Wolfe put it clearly:

> . . . in the cultures of Europe and of the Orient the American artist can find no antecedent scheme, no structural plan, no body of tradition that can give his own work the validity and truth that it must have. It is not merely that he must make somehow a new tradition for himself, derived from his own life and from the enormous space and energy of American life . . . it is even more than this, that the labour of a complete and whole articulation, the discovery of an entire universe and of a complete language, is the task that lies before him.

Notice how, once again, the intoxication of possibility goes hand in hand with the fear of possibility, and how the emphasis on private vision is made without reference to a society already set in its ways, in its own kind of industrial landscape. A great deal of the *Angst* and violence in American writing comes from a recognition that the original experiment has gone too far to be revoked. What has taken place between the early establishment of a divine polity in a new land and the creation of a railway network (which fascinated and appalled Mark Twain) is wished away. *Euetheiâ* flourishes alongside the Stutz Bearcat and the Monroe Doctrine. Violence pioneers, even when it is the violence of gangsters: it is primal, evocative, and in the headlong, chafing prose of Wolfe and Faulkner we find an image of the main complaint: why have things come to this? It is an odd complaint which resents the advent of civilization (the fruit of pioneer courage) and yet extols the pioneer stage of American history.

For, as Marius Bewley has pointed out in *The Eccentric Design* (1952), the complaint comes from sensibility formed during the critical years of the Republic. In theory there should have been no Civil War, no slavery, no economic crashes, no self-consciously Cinderella region such as the South. Most of all we notice how the sense of an experiment gone wrong produces desperate efforts to reclaim; and how myth enables the thoughtful American to get a new hold on things. He has to choose between a factuality which includes evidence of good intentions and a dreamier view which, in Wolfelike paradoxes, posits the inevitable arrival of new virtue: the bad brings forth its opposite and their synthesis eventually (according to the Wolfe and Faulkner faith) confers a new chance. None of this appears in the O'Haras; but, strangely enough, in the sin-conscious Wolfes and Faulkners the corresponding hope of redemption is blatant. In the long run we find ourselves back at the personal inspiration 'derived', as Wolfe said, 'from his [the American artist's] own life'. Once again the private and the abstract—the Huck Finn dream and the puritan-democratic abstractions noted by Marius Bewley—go together, feed each other. What is in between is the wages of ambition, the peelings from the gilded age, the inspired founders' neglect of the nature of man, the impact of money upon an open society beginning to close up and rigidify. And where we find overt faith in the American experiment, we always find the novelist blurring his view. The faith entails romanticism; the romanticism forgets that it cannot go home again and is usually expressed in regional rather than national terms.

The cult of innocence has also given rise to a near-apotheosis of the unlettered and the backward. Both Faulkner and Steinbeck make a great deal out of naturals; and this habit reflects an American distrust of book-learning which shows in Mark Twain: 'as the most valuable capital, or culture,' Twain wrote to an un-identified correspondent, 'or education usable in the building of novels is personal experience, I ought to be well equipped for that trade. I surely have the equipment, a wide culture and all of it real, none of it artificial, for I don't know anything about books.' That folksy boast tells us much. Raw life gives its own degrees: to the American tradition of physical vigour, of initiative across the unmapped, books are a substitute reality, etc. One has heard the argument from philistines of all kinds. (It has turned up in the young English picaresque novelists too.) It assumes that there is more 'reality' in a man's saying 'Git arff mah laynd' than in, say, Hart Crane's

> Pennants, parabolas—
> clipper dreams indelible and ranging,
> baronial white on lucky blue!

Nonsense, of course. Crane's heady version of the Gatsby dream is just as real, just as integral, to the American experience, as any unlettered assertiveness. The point is that intellectual control failed America; the facts of life proved intractable; and the War, fought with bodies—just as the clearings were cleared by bodies—depressed the notion of 'reality' to the point at which the literate Twain had to pose as a yokel. The guilt of intelligence, the shame of being lettered, appear too in Wolfe's verbal orgy and are implied in almost every novel of violence. The republic was created by main force, not by eggheads; and raw experience still has tremendous appeal. After the impotence of ideas and mental exchange comes the impotence that violence is; and after the complexities which only the skilled mind can handle comes the essentially simplifying act of brute force. Innocence, animality and simple-mindedness go together; and together they exemplify the impotence that is one of the romantic agony's main assets. Perfectionism, the bane of America, causes intellectuals to feel useless and drives all sorts of men into outbursts of violence. Then follows the perfectionism of literary art and the limitedly perfect world of gadgets, stereotyped attitudes and mass-media cant. Both types of pseudo-perfection eventually produce rebellion and exasperation: Faulkner rants at the everyday world until it vanishes or he creates the strange peace of the moron; the other-directed man mutely lives out his anger in TV westerns, gangster-movies and, perhaps, novels of violence. Man, realizing the risks attending creation, knows he can also destroy or mutilate and so get his own back on the aberrational First Cause.

Rebellion is responsible for much of Faulkner (1897–1962). He takes the raw world and, through sheer technique, makes it into a rawness of his own. He creates two kinds of rebel—the one who fights for others and the one who fights for himself only. His procedure is to set the action in a world he has already transmogrified by style and technique—thus making his own exasperation plain. (He spoke many times of 'the impossible' and 'perfection', even appearing to identify the two, and praised Wolfe's heroic attempt to create the vision that life cannot automatically provide.) His own protest made, and volcanically evident in every sentence, he presents *non-literary* attempts to salvage some kind of perfection—whether an integrity or a decent standard, whether pride or purity. Byron Bunch, Lucas Beauchamp, Dilsey, Ike McCaslin, Uncle Gavin, Benbow, Ratliff and Hightower are examples. Quentin Compson in *The Sound and the Fury* (1929) dies to preserve the purity Caddy has already lost. Levine, the young flier in *A Fable* (1954), feels obliged to die in order to prove (to himself and others) that sacrifice is an act of life-affirming. Hightower inveighs futilely from his pulpit. They all suffer; they all serve; they serve the suffering. Jewel Bundren in *As I Lay Dying* sacrifices everything to get his mother's body home to Jefferson. Chick Mallison in *Intruder in the Dust* (1948) sacrifices all his prejudices and pride to save Lucas Beauchamp from being lynched. Joe Christmas, the tortured product of miscegenation in *Light in August* (1932), is hedged about with analogies from the Crucifixion; he is determined to suffer, to act in such a way that his own misfortune becomes a jussive example. He is a walking indictment. And, murdering Joanna Burden, turning against his foster-father McEachern, shoving the preacher from the pulpit and raving obscenely, and even dying, he makes his point. One woman calls him Satan; Percy Grimm finishes him off with a butcher's knife. Offering himself as a means of exorcism, he has to make his point through violence always—rather like Fosca in Simone de Beauvoir's *Tous les hommes sont mortels* who cuts his throat to prove he is immortal.

Behind all this there is Faulkner's belief in the possibility of regeneration, expressed in Gavin Stevens's appraisal of Lucas Beauchamp. The South, America, the world, can be made new; there are remedies still available to us:

> We—he and us—should confederate: swap him the rest of the economic and political and cultural privileges which are his right, for the reversion of his capacity to wait and endure and survive. Then we would prevail; together we would dominate the United States; we would present a front not only impregnable but not even to be threatened by a mass of people who no longer have anything in common save a frantic greed for money and a basic fear of a failure of national character which they hide from one another behind a loud lipservice to a flag.

So, history can be put right. Even the machinations of politicians can be stopped dead: the rebellious, saintly corporal in *A Fable* proves that an apparently impossible ideal can be achieved. He temporarily stops a war. But he is executed as a traitor, and we are left wondering with Faulkner whether an example is enough even when 'all of us, Germans and Colonials and Frenchmen and all the other foreigners in the mud here' are 'saying together: Enough. Let them that's already dead and maimed and missing be enough of this—a thing so easy and simple that even human man, as full of evil and sin and folly as he is, can understand and believe it this time.' This is the personal vision, not only transcending any notion of a divine polity but raising to its highest power the sentiment, 'Make it new'.

Yet Faulkner, just as trapped in the paradoxes of life as Wolfe, is just as often to be found brooding on mere survival, which is to be won only through a disciplined indifference. He makes failure so heroic as to suggest that nothing else can be managed. He is torn between a seductive dream of regeneration and a strong possibility of endurance: between the self-sacrificers and

the exasperated, wilful destroyers. Jason Compson, seeing himself
as the saviour of his family, destroys it; Darl, under a compulsion
to hurt, goes laughing into the Jackson asylum; Joe Christmas
has a Cain-like aspect. Temple Drake in *Sanctuary* (1931) turns
instinctively to evil; Harry Wilbourne in *The Wild Palms* (1939)
accidentally destroys Charlotte Rittenmayer, but the terrible
logic of inadvertence is of his own making. He has eloped with a
married woman, has made her pregnant, has used his medical
knowledge to destroy the embryo. He has tampered, and he
almost demands disaster, believing as he does in 'the passionate
idea of two . . . damned and doomed and isolated for ever against
the world and God'. Yet, in the prison cell with a cyanide pellet
in his hand, he chooses life; or rather, having to choose between
'grief and nothing', he takes grief. He is innocently of the company that includes the gangster Pop-eye who corrupts Temple
Drake, the footballer in *The Hamlet*, Bayard Sartoris, Pete,
Gowan Stevens and Percy Grimm. Those who do evil in Faulkner
tend to do it in a daze; they are enslaved. So are those who do
good, for they often do it bemusedly—like the convict in 'The
Old Man' sections of *The Wild Palms*.

Faulkner creates a world of mystery; no explanation covers it.
But from time to time revelations are made and epiphanies happen. Consequently his frequent patches of Christian symbolism
are more than facile. We notice the presence of Holy Week in
The Sound and the Fury and the heroic, last-ditch self-sacrifice
of Nancy Mannigoe in *Requiem for a Nun* (1952): Nancy, taking
the baby's murder upon herself, seeks to redeem those who
survive. She, in all her illiterate naivety and outcast's rebellious-
ness, knows more of the natural law of love than either Temple
or her husband. As Gavin Stevens says, she will die for the unwritten principle that children 'as long as they are little children,
shall be intact, unanguished, untorn, unterrified'. Gavin Stevens
voices it; Nancy knows it, and she has not learned it from any
book. Here at its most severe and most dignified is the principle
voiced by Gail Hightower: 'How false the most profound book
turns out to be when applied to life.'

We notice again the American belief in truth as revealed direct
to the heart. Literature can help a few, but not many; and
Faulkner illustrates that fact, scenically and ritually exposing the

ways in which evil can be countered and power guided. Young
Isaac McCaslin, taking part in the hunt for Old Ben, the supreme
bear, engages in a rite which confers a blessing. He divines an
ethic, a sense of aboriginal purity, which prompt him to repudiate
the corrupt history of his family and, through *ascêsis* in the
dwindling forest, to live out his life in moral freedom. But he is a
solitary, a voice in that wilderness, and of limited experience.
The equally self-regarding but more beleaguered corporal in
A Fable attempts not merely self-purification but the redemption
of others. Yet even he is not a complex enough human, just as
Isaac McCaslin occurs in too simple a setting. Faulkner's fat
rhetoric urges us towards an inward operation of the spirit and
envisions a 'new age' similar to Ignazio Silone's Abruzzese dream:
spirit not law. The paradox is that Faulkner seems to identify
being human with a refusal to be involved, and self-thwarting
with impurity. Before a man can be valuably involved with
others, he has to be himself—have a clear sense of himself. But
identity is a process, not a fixity, and the result is that, as Gide
complained of Henry James's characters, men 'never seem to
exist except in relation to each other'. That is the price of the
religion of fraternity; that or solipsism. Faulkner's corporal
believes in the need for a symbolic death: 'It's not I but you',
the general tells him, 'who are afraid of man; not I but you who
believe that nothing but a death can save him.' This is the other-
worldly confronting humanism with, in both senses, a vengeance.

One's final response to Faulkner's vast, idiosyncratic achievement is to his double obsession. Blame cannot easily be calculated:
the human condition acting upon, running riot within, the
peculiarities of American history, and the history of the South
in particular, urges the individual in inscrutable ways. Temperament, accident and revelation complicate each individual life
beyond the point where absolute guilt can be established. On the
other hand, Faulkner is anxious to stress responsibility within
limits, to affirm that nothing is done that does not begin, somewhere, somehow, with an individual's decision. And about the
area of responsibility that can be measured he is desperately clear.
Gavin Stevens, often garrulously tedious, but as expert in the
natural as in the written law, points the attributions of blame,
explains the baffling act and vindicates the efficacy of reasoning—

even when reasoning merely clarifies the nature and supremacy of passion. In the presence of all this, Faulkner celebrates the life he finds, revels in character-creation (Mink Snopes, for example) and composes long tributes to the land in the tradition of Augustus Baldwin Longstreet's *Georgia Scenes*. He is copious, verbose, dynamically emotional, obsessed, never quite in control and sometimes too ambitious. His finest achievements—the brilliant crop of seven novels published between 1929 and 1936 and the 'Snopes' trilogy—display the least self-consciousness, whether that which produced the Dixie gongorism of such early works as *Soldier's Pay* (1926) and *Mosquitoes* (1927) or that which we associate with his recourse to overt allegory. Since *Absalom, Absalom!* (1936) he has not bothered much with unity of structure, preferring to collect previously published pieces into a tolerable congruity (*The Unvanquished*, 1938; *Go Down, Moses*, 1942) or to write novels episodically (the Snopes trilogy).

In a prefatory note to *The Mansion* (1959), the final novel in the Snopes trilogy which began with *The Hamlet* (1940) and continued in *The Town* (1957), he said that *The Mansion* was 'the final chapter of, and the summation of, a work conceived and begun in 1924'—which seemed to imply that he had finished with Yoknapatawpha too. It is instructive to set the Snopes novels alongside his post-war homilies (*Intruder in the Dust, Requiem for a Nun, A Fable*) and to note how, through the rise of Flem from Frenchman's Bend to Jefferson, the presidency of the Sartoris bank and occupancy of the De Spain mansion, and through Mink's thirty-eight years in gaol, we had been kept waiting for a revelation both complete in itself and crucial in the Yoknapatawpha situation. Mink, whom Faulkner suddenly decides to present with considerable sympathy, is eventually let out among 1946's trucks and skyscrapers. He buys a gun in Memphis; then, calm as a sleepwalker, heads for Jefferson and the brother who has failed him. All Yoknapatawpha's hatred is embodied in this vengeful, resurrected man, formerly the most brutal although not the most vicious of the clan. Flem, whited sepulchre that he is, clings to his poses and the mythology he has made himself into. With his death, something is exorcized from Faulkner's county: Flem, the arch-Snopes, the ace parasite and master-hypocrite, the man who led an infestation that ousted the old order, is made to dwindle in comparison with Mink. For Mink is a man of the earth, albeit a murderer three times over. Faulkner's nostalgia suddenly transforms him into a redeemed prince:

> equal to any, good as any, brave as any, being inextricable from, anonymous with all of them: the beautiful, the splendid, the proud and the brave, right on up to the very top itself among the shining phantoms and dreams which are the milestones of the long human recording—Helen and the bishops, the kings and the unhomed angels, the scornful and graceless seraphim.

No moralizing here. Notice that he is 'inextricable', a guiltless energumen whom Faulkner hymns (not, I think, ironically) almost as if anything, anyone will do as an emblem of wonder. The conscienceless Faulkner of this is far from the committed Faulkner of *A Fable*. If the world cannot be put to rights, then, he seems to say, let us relish the world for what it is. And this world of Yoknapatawpha County ravishes him, the pathetic, sinning Mink notwithstanding. In the long run, pageantry and colour prevail over virtue. And if Faulkner has to choose between Mink all at sea in the materialistic mid-century and the right-minded who would condemn Mink on moral grounds, he chooses Mink. The American romance wins out because the thought of paradise regained always enthralls the adult and sometimes (see *The Reivers*, 1962) entertains the young.

In the novels of John Steinbeck (1902–) and John Dos Passos (1896–) we find rebellion, certainly, but of a much more political complexion than that of Faulkner. Steinbeck's 'land-mysticism' conflicts with his politics in much the same way as Faulkner's mystagogy conflicts with his moral earnestness. Steinbeck's early novel *To A God Unknown* (1933) sends its hero, Joseph Wayne, from Vermont to California in search of land. 'I've a hunger for land,' he tells his father; but Joseph is so portentous and vague a figure that it is hard to conceive of him as a person rather than an animated principle. He belongs to the world of *euetheiâ*, and his innocent ignorance, although fitting the heavenly pastures he has in mind, tells us little. Before he has had a chance to meet adult complications or return to the family home he is dead. The traditional pattern is not completed until Jim Casy in *The Grapes of Wrath* (1939), having abandoned his vocation of preacher and gone off to ponder, returns to counsel Tom Joad and to die for a newly found cause. Industrialized society can never quite forget the pasture, and—in American fiction particularly—the disillusioned or baffled hero withdraws in order to straighten himself out; he withdraws to the pastoral or its equivalent: the state of Nature. Adam unparadised, as R. W. B. Lewis points out in *The American Adam*, is always wanting to go home again.

Steinbeck's other novels show the American withdrawal to be as creative as fugitive. In *East of Eden* (1952) Adam Trask leaves Connecticut for California, and the Joad family in *The Grapes of Wrath* move from Oklahoma for the West coast: in both cases, with a better, fuller life in view. Whatever the motive of the man who withdraws, whatever his degree of success, he always goes in the shadow of Thoreau, leaving Concord for Walden (and returning), Huck Finn lighting out and Natty Bumppo quitting Templeton for the woods, Herman Melville seeking out the pure Taipi valley and James Michener doting on South Sea islands. Saul Bellow's multi-millionaire in *Henderson The Rain King* (1958) seeks and finds profound, revitalizing experience in Africa. Hemingway's green hills and Henry Miller's Big Sur extend the list. To them all, the untainted is always mythical, and their experience of it readily mythologized. In fact Steinbeck, in *Of Mice and Men* (1937), mythologized so daringly as to create something verging on maudlin melodrama, clogged with importunate symbolism and heavy allegory, and yet in its hermetic way both moving and purging. Lennie, the pathetic man-child, is the fruit of a paradise lost: he is both godlike and ignorant. And the mercy-shooting which ends the novel signals, quite naturally and with as little staginess as possible, the advent of fallen man. Steinbeck's heroes do not embody wisdom; they are foragers and searchers who have to submit their inexperience to the characteristic Steinbeck witch-doctor—the lapsed preacher, doctor or armchair sage. The heroes inhabit a paradise Steinbeck presents in terms of California, while the sages inhabit a world in which man is a wolf to his fellow and accentuates man's isolation from man.

Unfortunately Steinbeck fails to make his themes interpenetrate.

His innocents are too little contaminated; his sages too complacent. Perhaps this is because innocence prompts him to be
poetic and worldly wisdom tempts him into an almost beery
euphoria. Preoccupied with the possibility of regeneration, he
chooses the Salinas Valley and, in the prefatory matter to *East of
Eden*, speaks happily (shades of Tocqueville and Gatsby) in the
persona of the first man setting eyes on fertile land. He presents a
common human impulse which, in fact, and in the world of fact,
will eventually have to pursue the unspoiled out into the Pacific
once California is tainted. The trouble is that, in his poetic
fervour, he turns commonplace wishful thinking into actuality; he transforms metaphor into pseudo-fact. And the result is
the cheery sentimentalities of *Sweet Thursday* (1954)—cute and
refreshing reading, but too remote from the world of most wage-
earners. The vision is eccentric: it disdains what comes between
the two brackets of first innocence and affably welcomed failure.
East of Eden, for example, seems to set out to portray an ancient
pattern in which the pre-human suddenly arrives at the human:
at the overweening pride, idle or frenetic concupiscence, hopeful
and sinful muddling, hypocritical confidence and cosmic cheek in
which we all share. Particularly, the novel seems to promise an
analysis not only of terrestrial lapse but of the exclusively American territorial romance and its disregard for the cumulative
results of rash ambition. One expects something of those untapped
American themes that Emerson listed: 'Our log-rolling, our
stumps and their politics, our fisheries, our Negroes and Indians,
our boasts and our repudiations, the wrath of rogues and the
pusillanimity of honest men, the northern trade, the southern
planting, the western clearing. . . .' But no: *East of Eden* remains
a framework erratically and unilluminatingly filled by the story
of Adam Trask who, coming to manhood in the East a century
ago, marries a slut, takes her off to California where she deserts
him and sets up a brothel. Adam's twin sons, Cal and Aron,
evoke Cain and Abel but Steinbeck expects the outlines, the
mere presence, of the old metaphor to intensify such an irre-
levance as Cathy Trask's perverted eccentricities. In its own
right—without biblical signals and portentous labels—the Trask
story is of interest; but Steinbeck insists on involving it with an
allegorical pattern with which it not only does not coincide but

to which it seems tangential. Faulkner's Temple Drake is a more persuasive portrait of evil than Cathy Trask: Temple is not announced as operating under specific anagogic auspices—which gives us all the more reason for supplying them ourselves. It is hard to resist the feeling that Steinbeck hoped to gain a cut-price profundity from his scriptural allusions.

Steinbeck has never, with Wolfe and Faulkner, asked the vital questions about human nature. He always succumbs to his vision of what man should be. He likes to rhapsodize, so much so that he usually shunts off original sin (or whatever one calls that condition) into the merely mechanical shortcomings of systems. Misfortune rather than tragedy supervenes when the landowners combine against the Joad family. Jim Casy works himself into a rhetorical pantheism ('We was one big thing. An' that one thing was holy') and Tom Joad himself tells his mother 'I'll be ever'-where—wherever you look'. Steinbeck trying to repair rents in the pastures of heaven is suspiciously like Croce trying to explain a war as a temporary short-circuit of the Immanent Spirit. Time and again he fails to keep his eye on the distinct individual, on the individual act: it is the oversoul that attracts him and stimulates him into fluent prose. He has no sooner spotted human corruptness than he begins to explain it away as an organizational mishap. Too fond of life-affirming to admit the full measure of human depravity (just like Faulkner at the end of *The Mansion*), he works from mellowness to whimsy: *Tortilla Flat* (1935) and *Cannery Row* (1945) prepare us for the moonshine can of *Sweet Thursday*. He hovers uneasily between fatalism and apathy: somehow things come about, he says; look what the oversoul gives us, and be glad. This is why *In Dubious Battle* (1936) fails although nobly meant; it lacks a Dostoevskian probing into the secret springs of action; it has the shallowness of Chaucer without that poet's sense of 'aventure or cas' as it affects intimate motives. Where Dreiser speaks, a little pompously, of 'chemisms', Steinbeck speaks with resolute lyricism of 'bust . . . holiness'. Whether he is considering social injustice or military mania he keeps stopping short. In *The Moon is Down* (1942) he studies heroism under Nazi occupation, but simplifies until it seems that personal attitudes have nothing to do with the evil in the world. It is as if *As You Like It* has been crossed with John Buchan. Only the

Nazi commander is a mixed personality; all the others are simplified, homogeneous humours.

Steinbeck's allegiances have always been ambivalent. *In Dubious Battle* speaks up for Communist labour organizers but *Tortilla Flat* for an amiably anarchic spectatorship; *The Grapes of Wrath*'s suffering, migrant Okies contrast with the celebration in *The Red Pony* (1937) of a boy and horse in the wilderness. Outcasts have always beguiled him, and he has rarely been able to distinguish clearly between criticism and rejection, between injustice and society itself. In *The Winter of Our Discontent* (1961) he rebukes a money-worshipping society in which the decencies—honesty and pride—have succumbed to materialism. Ethan Allen Hawley, lapsed son of whaling captain forbears, works as a clerk in the grocery store he once owned. Although he has come down in the world, so far he has stoically survived. But, lacking both car and TV, and having to reckon with status-conscious wife and teen-age children, he begins to weaken. Before long he has betrayed his boss (an illegal immigrant) who, unsuspectingly, gives him the store. By the end of the book, Ethan Hawley has done a Flem Snopes; he owns New Bayton, but has lost his soul, and the son who condescendingly offered to buy him a car has won a national TV contest by cheating.

Such is the rather laborious parable of moral turpitude with which Steinbeck followed *Sweet Thursday*. Hawley the status-seeker is the escapist inverted; his trouble is that he wants to escape the one good thing he has—his conscience. It is all over-simplified: Decency *versus* Prosperity is a false opposition and Hawley *versus* his former principles belongs to fable rather than to the novel. An old question recurs: is Steinbeck against society altogether or just its evils? Of the psychology that creates evil or permits its creation, he shows too little. 'You can't see units, Joseph,' Joseph Wayne's sister-in-law admonishes him in *To a God Unknown*, 'only the whole.' The cap fits. One can understand why Steinbeck attacks conformists: 'I can understand', we hear in *East of Eden*, 'why a system built on a pattern must try to destroy the free mind, for this is the one thing which can by inspection destroy such a system.' What one would like to see is that conviction illustrated in depth. He is acutely aware of man's essential egregiousness: 'Every man', he told *Newsweek* (26 June

1961), 'is moral. It's only his neighbours who aren't.' Perhaps he has finally decided that, in a world of conformists, the overall pattern is less interesting than the component units. But not all units are psychological eunuchs, nor is the pattern as clear as he would have us think—whether we are escaping from it or trying to surrender altogether. That, perhaps, is the 'meaning' of his priapic allegory *The Wayward Bus* (1947). We are all stranded but obliged to travel.

The usual tripartite simplification—whimsicalist, plebeian and radical—conflicts with his own plaintive self-explanation: 'I just like to have fun with whatever equipment I have'—a lewd-sounding gaucherie to silence the critics for ever. But one critic, F. W. Watt,[1] has done Steinbeck some justice in contrasting the Olympian with the sentimentalist. It is a duality which has led Steinbeck into various sectors of the bizarre no-man's-land between naturalism and metaphysics: into fable, historical romance, myth, ironic realism, the mock-heroic, the folk-epic and farce (see *The Short Reign of Pippin IV*, 1957). These are the ingenuities of Steinbeck's reluctance to dispense with analytical intellect and its power to elucidate individual psychology. His ways are metaphorical, not ratiocinative, which is not to say that he does not wax philosophical or that he is always wrapping things up. Indeed, his very versatility has bewildered the label-minded: Antonia Seixas (Mrs Edward Ricketts) contends that he has been 'wrongly classified and thus misunderstood, misunderstood and thus wrongly classified, in an automatically circular process'.[2] Steinbeck's sensibility is Californian, but he mythologizes the Salinas Valley, the Monterey area and the 'sea of Cortez' into what F. W. Watt calls 'a vast, fascinating, paradoxical universe . . . a sprawling continent of discordant extremes'. Yet the Olympian has to reassure himself, and there is more than a tint of *chosisme* in Steinbeck's emphasis on *is* rather than *why*. It is an emphasis which suggests escapism and also ties in with his medievalism, his obsession with the group and his oddly ambivalent attitude to machinery. In one sense, his stock-in-trade is relativism; always a little bit muddled (he does not simplify

1. *Steinbeck* (1962).
2. Tedlock, E. W., and C. V. Wicker, *Steinbeck and His Critics: A Record of Twenty-Five Years* (1956), p. 276.

as much as Hemingway and does not use language to mask incoherence, as does Faulkner), he steadies himself by minute
scrutiny of the physical world: no morals drawn, no reasons
asked, no preconceptions and no catechisms. It is a very American
spiritual turbulence which he records: the turbulence of a society
that lauds kindness and generosity yet admires the consequences
of bustling, ruthless success. As Gide observed of *In Dubious
Battle*, 'the most noble and generous characters find themselves
corrupted'.

We are only just beginning to recognize Steinbeck's mastery
of medley, of *melo*drama, of the heterogeneous and the untidy.
This, surely, is why he himself found *Of Mice and Men* 'thin'
and 'brittle'—just not complicated enough—and why he rewrote
The Grapes of Wrath because a first attempt came out satirical
and 'In satire you have to restrict the picture'. The final product,
almost certainly his masterpiece, loads a simple story with overwhelming reverberations and large meaning. So far, most critics
have missed his large effects and over-studied his mannerisms;
but it is surely insufficient to find him, as R. W. B. Lewis does,
only 'a suggestive . . . representative, and a completely honourable
failure'.[1]

Of the national pattern, John Dos Passos's version is even
more arresting, more persuasive. Dos Passos complicates everything:

> Wars and panics on the stock exchange,
> machine gunfire and arson,
> bankruptcies, warloans,
> starvation, lice, cholera and typhus:
> good growing weather for the House of Morgan.

In *U.S.A.* (1930–6) it was big business which complicated and
corrupted; in his first novel, *One Man's Initiation—1917* (1920),
it was the incomprehensible world of large-scale war; in the less
pallid *Three Soldiers* (1921) it was the failure of war-born ideals—
'work and comradeship'; in *Manhattan Transfer* (1925) the city,
the urban machine; and in *Mid-Century* (1961) it is big labour

1. 'The Fitful Daemon' in *The Young Rebel in American Literature*, ed.
Carl Bode (1960), pp. 121–41.

unions. Against these destructive agencies and their even more destructive interaction, Dos Passos pitted his own idea of escape: aestheticism, embodied in John Andrews, the young composer in *Three Soldiers* who enlists but ends up 'Under the Wheels', and Jimmy Herf of *Manhattan Transfer* who has aesthetic leanings and eventually walks away from his marriage and the city. In Steinbeck one always feels that the facts are being partially ignored; in Dos Passos that they are presented in too much detail —as if to show man hemmed in with undue complexity, with numerousness and variety. Where Steinbeck chooses the disguised aesthetic protest, Dos Passos advances from that to an immersed dissent. Steinbeck's social protest conflicts with his near-mysticism; Dos Passos, from *Manhattan Transfer* to *Mid-Century*, protests from more than one point of view, and the result is less like propaganda than like a tragedy under the microscope. Dos Passos's indignation increases as he gradually proves that the unaided, unscheming individual has little chance against any collectivity.

Manhattan Transfer is crowded, ingenious, diligent and occasionally inspired. The *U.S.A.* trilogy—*42nd Parallel* (1930), *1919* (1932) and *The Big Money* (1936)—is less coherent: the scene is not just a city but America; the aspiration is Thomas-Wolfeian; the technique is still that of dogged enumeration—of the vicissitudes of swindlers and drinkers, of thwarted wives and poseurs of taste, but enlivened (or impeded, according to one's point of view) by notorious devices, the Newsreels and Biographies—the dry sediment of progress or at least of the succession of headline on headline, of obituary on obituary. The other device, the Camera Eye, written in idiosyncratic poetic prose, recalls the early Dos Passos, the man of sensibility and taste. These devices come off; and yet they also fall off as the vast pageant unrolls. They become tropes in their own right: a relief from the unyielding hard world of labour and capital, ambition and acquiescence. *U.S.A.* is a capricious work, as irritating for its repetitions and lacunae as exhilarating for its suggestion of urban, industrial bustle and economic tumult. It is easy, though, to see why Sartre has extolled Dos Passos as 'the greatest writer of our time': for social realism, for his unique sense of malleable man among the shifting patterns of unchanging motifs. At the same time, one cannot help feeling that he prefers the impersonality of catalogues to the self-revealing undertaken out of self-defence in *The Adventures of a Young Man* (1939), part of the *District of Columbia* trilogy. Not surprisingly he tends to regard his own convictions as factual and (like Tocqueville) to base other convictions upon them. The facts of society—New Deals vitiated by bureaucracy and duplicity—are such as to provoke either complete cynicism or unsatisfactory partisanship. Between being partisan and being cynical, he becomes a pessimist, as if to say that, in the long run, no appraisal of the facts can hearten. So his opinions are often to be found juxtaposed with facts they do not quite fit; and such lack of care for synthesis cripples *District of Columbia*. Too often in Dos Passos, the movie techniques betray a mind made up and lapsing into stylistic exercises or a mind so convinced of the corruptness of all ideologies as to try them on like a woman sampling dresses. Something revulsed in him—whichever side he takes—resorts too gratefully to the random kaleidoscope of social change. He has all the answers and yet, as Arthur Mizener has said, hates 'our failure . . . humanity's failure, to be what it professes—and what it ought to be'. Such a position cannot really produce anything but a bemused 'that's that'. For Dos Passos, no matter how much things change, they remain the same and continue to depress.

The panorama of *Mid-Century* is organized along the same lines as *U.S.A.* The theme is disillusion: 'So long as a man got his handout, who cared?' After the iniquities of capital comes the pendulum-swing of malign labour organizations (compare with the Steinbeck of *In Dubious Battle*). Three lives predominate, as they were supposed to in *Three Soldiers* in which two petered out. Blackie Bowman, dying in a Veterans' hospital, meditates on the ruin of labour; interspersed with his meditations is the story of Terry Bryant, a rubber worker who falls foul of a corrupt union, becomes a taxi-driver and eventually finds himself (in both senses) siding with the bosses. Jasper Milliron, the subject of the third narrative strand, declines and falls while trying to modernize a baking-powder company. On this tripod Dos Passos balances the good advice and accurate foreboding of a Polonius. He is up-to-date, of course: Eleanor Roosevelt, Dave Beck, James Dean the actor, James Hoffa and Sam Goldwyn appear, and the account of present-day 'sluggings, shootings, embezzlement, thievery, gangups between employers and business agents, the shakedown, the syndicate, oppression, sabotage, terror' is painfully authentic. The montage is laboured, but at least there is neither saccharine patriotism nor overt ideology. What comes through is man's overriding need to create institutions, and their habit of coming to possess their creators, whether capitalists or labour-organizers. It is the small man who suffers. None of this is news; but then, the truth is never much of a novelty, even when its trappings are.

It is to the truth of American society that James T. Farrell (1904–) addresses himself: to the factual truth of what American society is like and to the subtler, imaginative truth which he describes as 'the patterns of American destinies'. Writing of Chicago and the Catholic Irish poor of his boyhood, Farrell readily guides facts into mythology: the face of a society corrupt at its roots develops into a mask emblematic of 'American destinies'; but there is no labouring after general significances. What does put one off is Farrell's fondness for emphasis by increase of weight; determined to be photographically accurate yet also to be thorough (to awaken the reader to 'patterns'), he cannot resist evidence. Everything becomes relevant. Everything points a tiny bit beyond itself; and every bit of transcendence adds reverberation. It is as if he is determined to mythologize without appearing to; by indirection to suggest intention and by volume to transfigure the everyday.

His effort is, however, sometimes misplaced, like O'Hara's. The *Lonigan* trilogy (1932–5) and the Bernard Clare, Danny O'Neill cycles take literary naturalism as far as it will go when combined with an almost painful moral seriousness going beyond political credo or merely economic man. With what has been called his 'buffalolike stubbornness' he makes Studs Lonigan, who fails to fulfil himself, either in modern society or privately, provide a sullen, massive postscript to the aspirations of Gatsby. Danny O'Neill prevails but Farrell remains hostile to America because it enforces, even upon the successful, a corrupt kind of triumph. Like Steinbeck and Faulkner he respects the rebel, prefers the jaundiced failure to the contaminated success, and, in tabulating the ills of a society, turns against the social contract itself. Radical sympathies and a vague pessimism combine in Farrell to transform the act of cataloguing into an ecological sneer and also make him confuse the endlessness of ecological truth (for we can never possess all the facts) with the self-sufficiency of anagogic examples. He documents resentfully and his mythology emerges more from his resentment than from the recorded facts. This confusion gives his best single novels (*Young Lonigan*, 1932; *The Face of Time*, 1953) a personal flavour lacking in the work of O'Hara. At the same time, his show of conscience weakens his evidence in the way that the evidence of all eclectics is weak. The man emerges and wins our sympathy—so much so that his ecological data seems to get in his way while dictating his predominant attitudes.

In one sense, Farrell is a Willa Cather bowed under a rucksack of evidence. Willa Cather (1873–1947) disdained democracy, industrialism and materialism for the same reasons as Farrell exhaustively and hostilely records them. His scorn is just as anachronistic as hers was; but also just as much on moral grounds. Her *O Pioneers!* (1913) typifies her novels about foreign-born farmers taming the West: a reverential pact with earth and Nature's simplicities is the image she opposes to an increasingly technological society. Her artists too (*Youth and the Bright Medusa*, 1920) detach themselves from the hubbub which she unsuccessfully tried to depict in *One of Ours* (1922) and *The Professor's House* (1925). The first, awarded a Pulitzer prize, tells how a young Nebraskan finds escape from his dreary marriage in war; he eventually dies in the Argonne. In the second novel, Professor St Peter finds himself unable to relish the affluence a successful career brings him; he gives up, a stranger in his own house, more in tune with Tom Outland, one of his students who explores cliff-dwellings in New Mexico, than with Mrs St Peter's eager donning of the badges of wealth. Outland, one is not surprised to learn, gets killed in the war. Willa Cather had as acute a sense of apathy as of the modern world's harsh way with dissenters. Clinging as she did to the gracious, the sophisticated and the traditional, she was never able to communicate tragedy—even that of war.

She has something in common with E. M. Forster: a well-bred reticence which, although respecting the springs of human vitality, lacks animal vigour, the urge to shout or thunder. Not desiccated, she makes her characters appear so; not quite in touch with chaos, she creates a wistful, aloof substitute world which needs to be contrasted with chaos and turbulence if it is not to seem sheer fantasy. Her classicism is not that of life tamed but of life avoided. She is at her liveliest in *Death Comes for the Archbishop* (1927), in which she combines the story of two French priests in New Mexico with Indian mythologies, and *Shadows on the Rock* (1931) which portrays the life of an Ursuline convent and the missionaries of early Canada. In these novels she manages to have vitality without vulgarity, spiritual uplift without vociferation; and she achieves something aloof without becoming precious.

She is with Farrell in remarking the absence of a decent matrix. Farrell records and deplores; she takes notice and disdains, confining herself to the ordeal of the sensitive in a world geared to the standards of clamant or complacent majorities. She has a great deal to say to us in an age in which the habit of concentration is dying a victim to intrusive TV commercials. Oddly enough, many of the angry denunciations of Admass made by the young novelists in Granville Hicks's *The Living Novel* recall Willa Cather: they find, as she did, that the life of standards is always on the defensive, can never take the offensive and tends to feed on itself. There are few realizable idylls left; even the promised idyll of prosperity is beginning to pall. Society is still wrong but the let's-do-something attitude of an Upton Sinclair (1878–) has lost its appeal. Dos Passos and Steinbeck worry away about the corruptness of modern America in things big and little. But the visions of reform implied in Sinclair's onslaughts have given way to caustic anatomies. No one now sets about the meat-packing industry as Sinclair did in *The Jungle* (1906), or the Colorado coal-mines (*King Coal*, 1917), or the Bostonian mentality which executed Sacco and Vanzetti (*Boston*, 1928), or pleads for co-operatives (*Co-op*, 1936) or knocks the trusts (*The Metropolis*, 1908, and *The Money-Changers*, 1908). Sinclair's *Roman Holiday* (1931) is more in tune with modern persuasions and apathies: an American, believing himself in Rome at the end of the republic, discovers little bits of home—Reds, class bigots, financial vanities and social turbulence. Sinclair could allow himself the notion of reform-to-come, whereas neither Steinbeck nor Dos Passos hopes for much at all, and the novelists in Granville Hicks's symposium look anxiously, desperately, for fit audience though few: 'Not irreverence', says Mark Harris, 'but craftsmanship, dismays the editors of the mass media' and the would-be contributor to *Reader's Digest* who had sexual intercourse with a bear in an iron lung for the F.B.I., and found God.

Fundamentally, the effort to create myth is an effort to perfect actuality: to blur it, redispose it, transfigure it and intensify it until it becomes both a source of pleasure and an index to human experience in general. Myth is a product of our dissatisfaction; actuality is there to start with. Not that deliberate creations turn out exactly as we intend them to; they often (as Leslie Fiedler points out in his voluminous study *Love and Death in the American Novel*, 1960) reveal suppressed nightmares of misogyny, incest, homosexuality, miscegenation, massacre, Gothic lugubriousness and wished-for insanity. The American hero is haunted by long-legged women who would drive him even beyond success, by wood-trolls and furious Puritan clergymen. He feels confined by being 'civilized': his daily behaviour has become stereotyped, unbestial; but primitive urges and lurid fantasies keep welling up from his unconscious. Man is much more than society admits.

Fiedler goes along with Henry James's lament about the dearth of interesting manners; but the nature of American Gothic is surely to be explained more as a consequence of man's recognizing his uncivilized self than of the texture of American society's being too thin. In any case, American manners have for a long time been just as profuse and substantial as those of Europe. People cannot help indulging in behaviour, and Henry James was merely saying that American manners differed from English ones. It is a matter of definition and of American closeness to pioneer experience from which, say, a Jane Austen, a Trollope and Proust are remote. If Edith Wharton and Sinclair Lewis are not writing about manners—manners as positive and staining as gravy—it is hard to see what their subject-matter is. Where they fall short is in omitting the monsters which breed when reason sleeps: they do not fit Fiedler's argument (or rather his assumption) any more than do the later Faulkner or the latest Steinbeck.

A simple point emerges. The American novelist can afford to let his mind play on the theme of a vast continent conquered; he knows what he is talking about, and his contrasts between Man and Nature are relevant to his portrayal of Society. The English novelist, on the other hand, is only qualified to compare Man with Society, and his sense of Nature is not metaphysical but empirical: stockades and clearings are centuries away from him and even his image of rural rhythm is the long-standing one of several hundred years. We might epitomize the difference by contrasting Mark Twain's ritualistic, empirical sense of Nature with the abstract view of Nature held by Hardy. In each instance, the cosmos imposes on man; but Twain deals in textures, Hardy in forces. Twain sees a nation emerging; Hardy finds one ready-made. It is American history which relates the American novelist, through his unconscious, to the simple behaviour-patterns and complex fears of pioneering into the unknown. The vast continent still awes, as the work of Steinbeck, Wolfe and Kerouac shows. There is much more in America than *mores*; in England, there is not much else. And the American novel documents, sometimes unwittingly, the nightmare of starting from scratch—of forcing to yield the Nature which produced Man himself.

V

Henry Miller (1891–), variously dubbed Patagonian, porno-grapher, saint, Caliban, Buddha of the Beatniks, one-man band, amateur writer *cum* professional mendicant, poor man's Whitman and Swiftian bladderflapper, illustrates what happens when a writer becomes voracious for the cosmos and ceases to value the mind's ability to systematize:

I believe that it is now possible for me to have my being anywhere on earth. I regard the entire world as my home.

His end is in his beginnings:

I began in absolute chaos and darkness, in a bog or swamp of ideas and emotions and experience. Even now I do not consider myself a writer. I am a man telling the story of his life, a process which appears more and more inexhaustible as I go on. Like the world-evolution, it is endless. It is a turning inside out, a voyaging through X dimensions. . . .

He sees himself, the writer, as 'An explorer, calling to life the slumbering entities of his dream'. He ridicules industrial civilization, trafficks in hypothetical simplicities such as a brave new world based on novel-worship and 'the man who has no feeling of class, caste, colour or country, the man who has no need of possessions, no use for money, no archaic prejudices about the sanctity of the home, or of marriage with its accompanying treadmill of divorce'. In a word, *euetheiâ* all over again.

This archetypal dream would be very boring if Miller did not turn his exemplifications, *pro* and *con*, into circus. 'Paff, paff!' go the lovers at their climaxes. *Tropic of Cancer* (1931) includes, as well as Tania, lush in garters, the prostitutes scratching themselves 'like chimpanzees', and Fillmore the homesick Puritan, a monstrously funny account of his experiences while working for Indians. Conrad Moricand, the sponging and malevolent ingrate guest in *Big Sur and the Oranges of Hieronymous Bosch* (1958), might have come out of Marlowe. Always, among the prophetic panting and the freewheeling mystagogy, sex has served as punctuation; but in grotesque, disdained form. This—especially in the two *Tropic* novels and *The Rosy Crucifixion* (1949)—has been Miller's saving. Reluctant to cherish, he has been free for farce—for its hardboiled percussion. Slop and rant ('all snow and lice, with the great band of Orion slung round the ocean's crotch') do not drown (quite) his carol of creation ('that same prehistoric look. The look of always'). And his boudoir boors, his coxcomb copulants, are the antithesis to the tenderness with which he writes about his children. The unspoiled enthralls him; the concocted (*The Air-Conditioned Nightmare*, 1954–7) sickens him. 'My aim in writing', he has said, 'is to establish a greater *reality*. I am at bottom a metaphysical writer, and my use of drama and incident is only a device to posit something more profound. Above all, I am for imagination, fantasy, for a liberty as yet undreamed of.' His works are an open letter about himself as the picaresque *voyeur* with the horse-laugh, a personage as unquenchably garrulous (but not as witty) as the doctor in Djuna Barnes's *Nightwood* (1936).

Perhaps he is not a novelist at all, or not even a writer. But his lack of art typifies the unorganized side of the American mind, the side which retreats from a world of chromium into an anachronistic reverie in which everything is still possible. His nostalgia for Paris notwithstanding, he captures all the reasons for all the Big Surs and all the pathos of a society reduced to an Automotive Passacaglia. To read him in conjunction with James Michener (1907–) is to realize why Michener's picaresque novel *The Fires of Spring* (1949), set in America, seems a less adequate account of Americans than *Return to Paradise* (1951) and *Sayonara* (1954), set in Asia. Adam unparadised resists the colours of his urban setting: he moves about, becomes increasingly restless. But, 'back' in paradise, he quickly learns to camouflage himself and, in so doing, symbolically sheds his civilized trappings. Michener's quaint 1,018-page ethnographical chronicle, *Hawaii* (1960), states and re-states the old formula. Once again the dry, tough guys yearn for softness: 'as the inspection team piled into the PBY for take-off and the return to Hawaii, no one spoke of the long-haired girls of Bora Bora, or their flashing teeth, or of the games they knew how to play. . . .' (Henry Miller's prose is insanely articulate, compared with that.) A general confesses his amazement at what a man of forty-nine can do; the aged or heartsick modern praetors devour the golden girls; the simplistic solemnities pile up ('she felt confused by the great passion that can exist between men and women'). Yet, for once, the *Kitsch* is embedded in a history so vast, so meticulously and grandly presented, that one's irritation is lost. The earliest Hawaiians, wandering the islands, live or die at the whim of a priest; to build a temple they bury a slave alive beneath each corner-column; later, to safeguard and advance themselves, they bury expatriate whites, and others, alive in their golden, chaotic families. One such, Hoxworth Hale, descendant of Rafer Hoxworth who in 1833 married Noelani Kanakoa, tells the people's story from scratch. And through him Michener makes a very fine attempt at putting the primitive mind into modern English. The account of the primogenitors' odysseys and eventual grapplings with Christian ethics is particularly well done. *Hawaii* is no masterwork, but, as vicarious confession and atavism, it extends and explains the work of Miller, Hemingway and, not least, Willa Cather.

Another novelist who turned against society and its shams is Nathanael West (1903–1940). In the early thirties manager of a

residential hotel in Sutton Place, New York City, and sub-
sequently a writer of film scripts in Hollywood, he knew all about
pretence, urban rootlessness and slick ballyhoo. Most of all, he
recoiled from the physical processes of the human body, and his
Swiftian scabrousness consorts oddly with Henry Miller's
rollicking prurience. Neither of them is as ingenious as Aldous
Huxley in communicating the body's baseness and limitations.

In *The Dream Life of Balso Snell* (1931) he sets out to shock.
Balso Snell, situated in the rectum of the Trojan Horse ('O Anus
Mirabilis!'), has a love affair with a beautiful hunchback who has,
she says, been seduced by one Beagle Darwin and bears his child
in her hump. Another character, Maloney the Areopagite,
occupies himself with self-crucifixion by thumb-tacks and a biography of Saint Puce, a flea who lived in Christ's armpit. For all
its scurrilous, resolute surrealism (one form of emotional
violence), it is a powerful novel. All vengeful blasphemy and
aggressive panache, it expresses loathing of the human condition.
West is sadistic and irresponsible; he finds only in the grotesque
a satisfactory image of his young experience. A schoolboy murders
an idiot and, symbolically, West murders himself. Few novels
have come so close to the ferocity of Dostoevsky without quite
shedding the sniggers of the schoolboy urinal.

West's next novel, *Miss Lonelyhearts* (1933), displays less
mania. The hero conducts a 'Can I Help You?' newspaper
column, suffers personally through an excess of empathy and also
from a gloating editor called Shrike. His problems are summar-
ized in a letter that Shrike writes to Christ:

> I read your column and like it very much. There you once
> wrote: 'When the salt has lost its savour, who shall savour it
> again?' Is the answer: 'None but the Saviour'?
> Thanking you very much for a quick reply, I remain yours
> truly,
>
>   A Regular Subscriber

Lonelyhearts, trapped in the urban web, tries love, drink and art
as means of possible escape. He retires into the country; but
rural peace, even with a doting girl for company, fails. Returning
to the Bronx, he sees a man entering a cinema to watch *Blonde*

Beauty, and a woman with a goitre extricating a love-magazine from a dustbin. Finally, embracing the crippled husband of a woman he has had an affair with, he miscalculates again: the cripple, thinking he is being attacked, shoots Miss Lonelyhearts. It is an involuntary, jittery cartoon of a novel, sometimes meretriciously slick in style and always baffled before the incompatability of dream and daily living. It epitomizes one type of religious neurosis but suggests no remedy, no explanation. West vents his disgust and compassion, and these are intense; but the novel is too jumpy and gaudy to hold one's interest sustainedly and formally.

A Cool Million (1934) shows the decent man, typified by Lemuel Pitkin, trying to make an honest fortune in the Land of Opportunity, but only managing to lose his teeth, an eye, a leg and his life: he ends up as a martyr of the fascist National Revolutionary Party. This could have been a savage *Gatsby*-reduced-to-absurdity; but West's prose is not subtle or sharp enough for satire. The result is burlesque: Pitkin is given a job with a famous comic team because he is well qualified, already having a wooden leg, a wig, a glass eye and false teeth. On stage, the comedians hammer him with rolled newspapers until his artificial bits fall off or out. Finally they poleaxe him with a vast mallet labelled 'The Works'. The audience rejoices as he disintegrates. This is the cruel percussive world of Jarry's *Ubu Roi*, Heinrich Mann's *Blue Angel* and Camus's *Le Malentendu.* Despairing of a world in which there is little tenderness, West theatrically, impatiently simplifies: farce is his natural mode of expression, being at once a supreme form of irresponsibility and a version of pessimism. *The Day of the Locust* (1939), a study of nondescripts on the fringe of the Hollywood studios, is a more conventional novel. The grotesques are still there, but are natural for Hollywood. There is one scene of mob violence, a brilliant metaphor of West's favourite theme. Violent religious mania demands miracles, even the facetious ones of Hollywood. So too did West. A brittle and impetuous writer, he expressed all the forms of private, religious and political despair without ever suggesting what could make life worth while.

West set the style for hyperbolical anatomies of civilized regimen which play exaggerative societies—Hollywood, advertising,

the military and commuterdom—at their own game. Compared with Anita Loos's Hollywood lampoon *No Mother to
Guide Her* (exhumed from *Cosmopolitan* magazine and first
published in book form in 1961) *The Day of the Locust* is caustic
and deft—a strong enough piece of writing to create a school,
but not as thoroughly a novel of social and private photography
as Fitzgerald's *The Last Tycoon*. Budd Schulberg's *What Makes
Sammy Run?* (1941), told in the first person by a scriptwriter,
explores the growing unscrupulousness of Sammy Glick, a poor
Jewish boy who 'rises' from nonentity on a New York paper to
becoming a Hollywood producer. Illusory and self-corrupting
self-promotion is shown to be the vilest of the devil's snares. The
lavish paradise of alcohol and co-operative authorship which
beguiled Fitzgerald into self-ruination (see *The Disenchanted*,
although this was based on the lives of fifteen or so scriptwriters)
is a parody of democracy's twin ideals of freedom and community. The open society has draughty stairs up which crazy per-
forming bears cavort to the delight of enthroned groundlings and
the disgust of the intelligentsia.[1] The decline and fall of practically
everybody is implicit in Mary McCarthy's mordant exposure of
utopias in *The Oasis* (1949) and of academic duplicity in *The
Groves of Academe* (1952). Howard Nemerov's *The Melodrama-
tists* (1949) and *Federigo, or the Power of Love* (1954) thrust
carefully aimed barbs into the smooth upholstery of the copy-
writer's world, depicting rather than explaining. His *The Home-
coming Game* (1958) is much less tart and much less exuberant;
a professor of English falls foul of the college football racket and
finds himself being blackmailed. The reproof creates no caricature,
whereas Kenneth Patchen's *Memoirs of a Shy Pornographer*
(1945), Jerome Weidman's spoof about the Bureau of Psychological Combat, *Too Early To Tell* (1946), and Herman Wouk's
Aurora Dawn (1947), in which not all the parody of big business
extravaganza seems intentional, give a foretaste of obloquacious
satire-fantasies to follow: from the 'coal-fiber-lined mink-dyed
natural stone-marten bed-jacket' and 'Potenca-Borg two hundred

---

1. Cf. Schulberg's comment: 'I believe Hollywood is rather an ideal
microcosm in which to study it [the theme of success]; and for this reason I
hope to write more novels about the dream factories and their heterogeneous
personnel.'

liter after-drive piston silver-coloured sports racer' of John Hersey's *The Child Buyer* (1960), with its 189 I.Q., $12.593 brainchild bought by the United Lymphomilloid Corporation, to Max Shulman's *Rally Round the Flag, Boys!* (1958), a riot about Connecticut 'exurbia' where $25,000 a year is the breadline, where Oscar Hoffe, TV executive, watches a screen with his dictaphone by him, and commuter husbands frenetically pursue therapeutic hobbies in elaborate workshops while their non-commuting wives confer about garbage-disposal—at least until the military arrive to build a disrupting rocket base.

Vladimir V. Nabokov (1899–) left Russia after the revolution, graduated from Cambridge in 1922, then spent some time in Berlin before leaving for the United States in 1940. He must now be considered an American novelist and, indeed, one of the most distinguished social anatomists and prose stylists of the present day. He usually takes a simple episode and works it up into parable. In *Luzhin's Defence* (Russian, 1930) he traces the disintegration of a young chess master; and the story of *Camera Oscura* (Russian, 1933)[1] goes like this (the summary and the English are his own):

> Once upon a time there lived in Berlin, Germany, a man called Albinus. He was rich, respectable, happy; one day he abandoned his wife for the sake of a youthful mistress; he loved; was not loved; and his life ended in disaster.

Poor Albinus, turning from insipid wife to voluptuous, scheming Margot, the cinema usherette, is one more scalp to the female juggernaut: a victim to the impossible male passion for ideal experience of the other sex. And one thinks of Nathanael West's Lemuel Pitkin; Albinus too loses all: mistress, wife, daughter, wealth, even his sight (in a car-crash). Finally, aware that he has been duped, he tries to shoot Margot but is shot by her instead. Nabokov presents this version of the absurd with unsentimental economy; his prose is spare, visual and swift, and his satirical intelligence always in evidence, adjusting the puppets into an ever

---

1. English translations: *Camera Oscura* (1936) and *Laughter in the Dark* (1938, 1961).

more ridiculous light but also underlining the *lacrimae rerum* of his theme. An ironic compassion characterizes his most macabre fictions—even the esoteric spoof *Pale Fire* (1962), in which a fantastic exegesis of a 999-line verse elegy enacts the absurdity of our civil sanities.

Despair (1934; English, 1937) is a masterpiece of cumulative tension and reads like a trial run for *Invitation to a Beheading* (1938), originally written in Russian under the pseudonym 'Sirin', the last of the seven pre-*Lolita* novels. Cincinnatus C., the hero, has been sentenced to death for 'gnostical turpitude'; he passes his last days reflecting on the invulnerability of the soul. In a foreword Nabokov disputes the 'kafkaesque' qualities which European critics attributed to the novel when it first appeared. He had not, he says, read Kafka when he wrote it. But certainly the wild hallucinatory atmosphere, the beleaguered and uncomprehending hero, the gallows Grand Guignol and bland exposure of man's perversity, all suggest Kafka. Other aspects of the novel, however, do not. Nabokov the tragi-comedian creates an almost joyous nightmare from the theme of anarchic self-respect. The festive accompanies the grisly, the surrealist the documentary, and the state's indictment is balanced by self-condemnation. There are, perhaps, too many antinomies for the novel not to bewilder. The prose glitters beguilingly, an antic veil that should have been torn here and there. All the characters, the hero included, languish and diminish in its mnemonic possession.

Nabokov treats his characters off-handedly—not as 'people'—and tends to detach their psychological processes from the social context. A novelist of essences and fundamentals rather than of social buzz, he envelops his personages in his own ceaseless, bizarre and highly ingenious musings. The expert on diurnal lepidoptera prompts the novelist to fit every character with spectacular, minutely patterned wings. In *The Real Life of Sebastian Knight* (1941), which Nabokov wrote in English, he is acutely self-conscious: afraid to look away and yet sensible of self-persecution. Sebastian Knight, a famous and somewhat precious writer, has died; and his half-brother sets out to discover the 'real life' which the official biography missed or omitted. The search whisks through Cambridge, Paris and a small German spa, and the suspense is brilliantly managed, working forwards into the next discovery and backwards into a definition of the solitary life as lived by Sebastian. The novel reads like an expatriate's self-catechism: Nabokov grows forward by journeying carefully back. *Lolita* (Paris, 1955; U.S.A., 1958), scandalizing though unscabrous, vividly describes the mutual seduction of a middle-aged man and a twelve-year-old girl. It has something in common with Edmund Wilson's *Memoirs of Hecate County* (1946), but has been more sensibly dealt with by the courts. After such of Nabokov's other work in English as the study *Nikolai Gogol* (1944), the rather outlandish novel *Bend Sinister* (1947) and the volume of childhood memoirs *Conclusive Evidence* (1951), all marginal to the American tradition, it seemed like a deliberate thumbing of the nose. After the unfashionable, the wilful *outré*: a cosmopolitan Dostoevsky-Voltaire turning sex and murder into a sardonic *détour de force*. F. W. Dupee explained in *The Columbia University Forum* (Winter 1959) how Lolita provided a twisted epitome of the American syndrome:

Here, in *Lolita*, are the common routines in plenty: the American small town, the house with the Van Gogh prints, the humdrum poetry of cars, schools, neighbours, the swimming lakes and country inns. . . . The melodrama turns this country of common routines into Lolitaland, a world of obscene innuendo, where the notices posted in motel bathrooms are cautionary come-ons, and the very highway signs are helpful-sinister.

As Dupee says: 'This raffish combination of the ordinary and the ghastly wasn't what influential people had in mind for the novel in 1954'; it rebuffed the 'ancestral Anglo-American pattern' and the taste which cherished William Dean Howells and 'his smiling horizons'. But *Lolita*, as well as capturing the surface of American life, struck through to the clammy suppressions studied by Leslie Fiedler: love and death.

The novel began, says Nabokov, with 'a newspaper story about an ape in the Jardin des Plantes who, after months of coaxing by a scientist, produced the first drawing ever charcoaled by an animal: the sketch showed the bars of the poor creature's cage'. This inspiration produced a thirty-page story with a French setting, a French Lolita and a central European Humbert Humbert. In 1949 Nabokov, travelling in the Far West in search of rare butterflies, began to work up the story into a novel. Paris provided the germ and America fed it. A lewd viper suddenly appeared in the nest of God's Own Country: to be reviled and extolled—and to bite. The same American background appears in *Pnin* (1957), in which a Gogolesque professor absurdly and thoughtfully gets nowhere. After the traipsings and perversions of *Lolita*, *Pnin* explores the static and the ordinary, embalmed in an acerb parody of slick-magazine prose. Nabokov's American stay has provided him with a manner remote from that of his 'Sirin' novels. Fixing on ballyhoo, he achieves the verbal panache that Nathanael West needed. He fits his baffled heroes into an air-conditioned, TV-sponsored nightmare and undertakes Dostoevskian probings into the American unconscious. His mythology anatomizes and his coruscating flow of words provides distorting mirrors in which we can watch the operation. Conrad never wrote in Polish; Nabokov, having written a good deal in Russian, German and French, writes a brilliant English. But, more important than this tremendous feat, there is his merciless image of American living, the kind of synthesis that only a highly trained outsider of mythologizing, morbid, satirical bent could manage.[1] In Nabokov folk-myth, folk-neurosis and intellectual independence fuse. His fables are as documentary as his photography of American life is homiletic. The *brouhaha* over *Lolita* proved the novel's very point. It is very much the novel of the Nabokov who, in one of his infrequent poems, noted that 'repaid' is 'diaper' reversed. Such cerebral ingenuities bring him close to Katherine Anne Porter who, after many enticing promises, has in *Ship of Fools* (1962) eventually kept faith by creating a meticulous allegory. What Glenway Wescott called her 'style of the mind' once again compels readers to choose, as Nabokov often makes them choose, between speculating on paradigm and delighting in precise observation. The choice is hard, peculiarly American, and in itself a commentary.

1. Cf. Robert Briffault (*Europa*, 1935) who, with similarly cosmopolitan sophistication, anatomizes pre-war Europe.

2

Time, South and Identity

I

EVEN to list (not to speak of reading through) such commentaries is enough to awaken one to a favourite American theme: time's erosion of man's accumulated achievements. It is a process of Nature, gradual and undifferentiating, impersonal and inescapable. Some things survive, others do not; and even massive, honest documentary novels get lost under the slow rain of accretion and obsolescence. The truly ambitious documentary novelist builds erosion itself into his works; he shows it as it affects generations and families, clans and parties. He makes it serve him but eventually succumbs to it. All that survives is the pattern of a century's repetitions: a pattern not so much archetypal as local. In short, a myth, by which I do not mean a legend but a communal frame of reference whose genesis the historical novel can keep on illustrating through hindsight and whose general usefulness continually prompts the writing of abstract, allegorical novels. The historical novel, *a posteriori*, shows us pattern forming; the mythological novel gives us a chance to test our own experiences against a baldly stated formula.

For example: Hervey Allen's novels of colonial America, Shirley Barker's study in *Rivers Parting* (1950) of early New Hampshire, and Henry Bellaman's account of how a small Midwestern town develops into a city (*Kings Row*, 1940; *Floods of Spring*, 1942; *Parris Mitchell of Kings Row*, 1948) provide the kind of empirical evidence which myth-minded novelists take as read. The Thomas Wolfes show myth burgeoning from the swarming phenomena of America; and those who in their respective ways follow Wolfe—Elliot Paul, Joseph Pennell, Edna

Ferber, Frederick Prokosch, Irwin Shaw, Wallace Stegner, Conrad Aiken (*Ushant*, 1952), Ayn Rand (*The Fountainhead*, 1943) —keep inferring pattern from events and then present that pattern in a non-documentary manner: they decorate it, philosophize about it, turn it into metaphor and allegory. But they do keep information coming, whereas other novelists turn pattern into fable, sometimes even turning the fable into private extravaganza.

Walter Clark, for instance, economically sketches the failure of an ideal in *The Ox-Box Incident* (1940)—an innocent person gets lynched—and in *The Track of the Cat* (1949) renders Lone Man *versus* panther as a heavily written parable. Thomas Wolfe haunts the same author's account, in *The City of Trembling Leaves* (1945), of a sensitive adolescence in Reno—just as he does James Agee's *The Morning Watch* (1951), which concentrates on one day in the life of an adolescent boy at an Anglo-Catholic school in the Tennessee hills. Isolation breeds extravagance, phantasmagoria and melodrama. The isolated individual fattens himself up to fill the void, and universal situations become pretexts for luxurious self-indulgence. Truman Capote, for example, says: 'The content of my work is "literary"; as opposed, that is, to writing inspired by political or religious convictions, of which I have, in the very orthodox sense, none.' Capote's *The Grass Harp* (1951), to cite only one instance, demonstrates not only the power of isolation to generate fantasy but also a principle not often heeded: an imaginative novelist need only attach himself to a familiar myth (or a familiar pattern); whatever he then says will be 'significant', will mean something, whereas the novelist (say Dos Passos or Dreiser) who keeps explaining his ideas, but not in the shadow of any mountain, may well seem to be saying nothing at all, or at least nothing universal. Tag along and even your irresponsibility makes sense; go it alone—ignoring the fund of myth—and your articulately made points are pointless because emotionally unpersuasive. Put, like Faulkner, a pregnant woman on a raft floating on a swollen river, and you have a potent image which dwarfs both the arguings of the sociologists and the erosions of time. Go further and set up the act of violence as a metaphor of liberty and autonomy, and you have the makings of the novel of destiny—the cosmic rather than the social novel:

the type of novel common in America and Europe but rare in England.

I mean that, in much the same mood as Malraux when he talks of art as an 'anti-destiny' and of 'carving a scar on the universe', the American novelist searches for master-images which sum up the fate and possibilities of a complex nation. It is not surprising that the south has become so heavily mythologized: the Civil War renewed the idea of possibility; a previously closed question was reopened, and the freedom to create was redeemed. But redeemed by violence in the belief that the immutable becomes so only through man's laziness and turpitude.

We have considered documentaries in most of which epic plainness and assiduous reporting have predominated over what I must label vaguely as poetic passion. Elliot Arnold may write vividly of the conquest of New Mexico in *The Time of the Gringo* (1953), but his epic does not strike into us deeply. Louis Auchinloss's historical panorama of the Millinder fortune in *The House of Five Talents* (1960) embeds us in extravagant minutiae; we are left to muse that people quarrel no differently over a hundred million dollars than over a hundred. Jessamyn West on Quakers in Indiana during the Civil War (*The Friendly Persuasion*, 1945), or on a rural section of 1916 California (*South of Angels*, 1960), convinces without piercing us. Even her most powerful novel, *The Witch Diggers* (1951), for all its Brueghel grotesques and bursting horror, does not quite force the poor Indiana farm to mean more than itself. Her accuracy restricts us. And another gifted novelist, Wright Morris, forges an unsuggestive massiveness from his native Nebraska plains.

The hard thing, the rare thing, is to combine passionate documentary (such as G. W. Brace's *Garretson Chronicle*) with an equally passionate demonstration of man's power to upset time's inexorable process. The chronicler's mind is dyed by what it works in: accretions, continuance, demise and replacement. It is against the nature of his work to pin all (as Erskine Caldwell does in *Trouble in July*, 1940) on one act of violence. Attrition, not explosion, attracts him. Dos Passos, Wolfe and J. P. Marquand are novelists who communicate the sense of procession and progression. Their sharpest pathos consists in the fact that, of a man's long, puzzled-through years, they make only a few hundred pages assimilable in a few hours. While they accumulate they telescope; the novel itself, while proving that time is long, mimes the brevity of an era's component lives. The only victory over time is through the imaginings of an articulate memory; our only impotence is that we are temporal in all save our imaginations, which we can preserve only in art.

It is, of course, deluded, but hearteningly so, to think that we defeat time by incessantly imposing our will upon circumstances —by precipitating change, revolution, novelty and crises. Such impositions of will necessarily exist within time, however much we magnify or minimize them. D. W. Brogan's quip that 'The French tend to think of the Russian Revolution as a step in the intellectual development of André Gide and of the Chinese Revolution as an incident in the literary career of André Malraux' reminds us that no amount of juggling with careers or events can humanize time. Our only cosmic power is that of creating life and causing death, accidentally or not. This explains Hemingway's preoccupation with hunting and with a whole etiquette of death-dealing.

Our power to stop a body from existing in time, at least from existing in the way it existed until we stopped its heart, develops into a Hemingway mystique, a Steinbeck main theme and, in the novels of James M. Cain, a meretricious obsession. As W. M. Frohock explains, in borrowing the term 'novel of destiny' from Jean Pouillon's *Temps et Roman*: 'The hero finds himself in a predicament such that the only possible exit is through inflicting physical harm on some other human . . . violence is man's fate. Thus the pattern of this kind of novel is in a sense tragic.'[1] When such a hero manages to fulfil himself only through self-destruction, the emotion of victory, as Frohock says, is left in the reader. The main point is that a man's intense humanity can drive him into delusion or inhumanity: say Robert Jordan's self-sacrifice or Harry Morgan's lucid killings at sea.

This is the literature of situations, not of the growth of personality, and for its sudden emergence in the thirties Frohock has suggested historical reasons which make commendable sense:

The depression [he says] had made us very conscious of the impermanence of our fortunes, good or bad. Violence had

1. *The Novel of Violence in America* (1957), pp. 6–7.

become the standard accompaniment of labor disputes. There was war in China, Ethiopia, and Spain, and we were facing—when we were not resolutely refusing to face—the prospect of war on a much larger scale. The thirties were the decade of Pretty Boy Floyd and John Dillinger, of Hitler, Mussolini, Franco, and Tojo. Violence was in the air, and Time's winged chariot was loud behind us.[1]

Without over-emphasizing such testimony—after all, human whims repeat themselves throughout history and often in defiance or disregard of National Predicaments—I want to consider the rebellion (including romanticized initiative) involved in three kinds of novel: first of all, the type of chronicle written by J. P. Marquand on the assumption that (in his own words) 'a slowly accumulated past lives in the blood—whether in the concrete image of the old house stored with visual memories, or in the conception of the house not built with hands, but made up of inherited passions and loyalties'. In this, Marquand presents his own version of Malraux's search for a continuing identity which time compels to keep on repeating and redemonstrating itself. In his novels the System (which you have to try to beat) is the resistant mass of the world, the universe and the cosmic powers. *Wickford Point* (1939), for example, is a comedy, a Yankee's Chekhov; but its serious point is that Wickford Point, 'where every small thing was of importance and where the mind wandered languidly to this and that with a strange midsummer's madness', is impregnated with 'an inexorable sort of gentleness, a vanity of effort, a sadness of pre-destined failure'. Accidia is not the South's monopoly; New England knows it too. And against such feelings—against the evidences of time's invincibility, as against the resistant mass of the financial and business worlds—a man has to fight to keep his human inheritance intact, including his tradition of being reconciled to ineluctable defeats.

Second and third, I want to consider the unique example which the South offers of a regional, semi-national identity maintained against time and man's aggression; and the experience of national identity, through the nation's uniforms, in the 1939–45 war. The theme of all three—the Marquand novel, the South and

1. Frohock, p. 13.

the war—is that of an identity made combative. To such a communal identity, the tentative individual can attach himself for purposes of self-definition. Svevo's distinction between the 'ancient hero . . . who confronted death' and 'the modern hero . . . who accepts life' is given a new twist: it is possible, by accepting death (which is really time's receipt for our bodies), to confront life fearlessly, even heroically. Death and time are as natural as love; violence does not efface either, any more than love's tenderness does. And the unheroic hero 'who accepts life' may not seem, on the surface, dynamic or spectacular, but he will most probably, in his respect for Tradition, Community or Cause, experience feelings of triumph: of metaphysical triumph, just like the twentieth-century painter who, as Malraux insists, finds himself echoing his predecessors not only because he has copied from them but also because the range of human longings is narrow and therefore rich with coincidences.

II

The novels of J. P. Marquand (1893–1961) show something of this triumph: obliquely, it is true, through dark glasses of Hawthorne and then of Howells, of sin both original and recent, both original and hackneyed. His stoicism makes no provision for ecstasy: we learn from Harry Pulham that love amounts not to 'passion or wish' but to 'days and years', and the novels' titles suggest more than a lip-serving response to time, e.g. *The Late George Apley* (1937), *So Little Time* (1943), *Repent in Haste* (1945), *Point of No Return* (1949). His characters' high moments are not moments in and out of time, not transcendences or escapes, but incidents in an unspectacular kind of fifth-column movement as old as time itself. Splitting himself into twin heroes (say Harry Pulham and Bill King in *H. M. Pulham, Esquire*, 1941), or melodramatizing his usual preoccupations in the *Moto* novels, Marquand never pushes retrospection into total recall (*something*, he admits, must always be lost) and never uses satire to demolish, only to rebuke. The effect of time, as Charles Grey concludes in *Point of No Return*, is to bewilder us with perpetual relativity:

They were caught in a current that jostled them and interfered with normal existence. All anyone could do was to try to adjust his life within the limits of a constantly changing frame. . . . Even the limits were constantly changing.

So his people keep on fidgeting. Cautiously stoical and stoically happy, they try to persuade themselves that present imperfections are mitigated by earlier instances of the contrary, by trophies of caste, class and clique. But they fail to convince themselves. Marquand demonstrates, in fact, the consolations of having in common with one's peers the craving to be convinced, the fortifying freemasonry of doomed aspirations.

His world is varied but of monotonous import: Boston, Hollywood, the South Pacific, Germany, Manhattan, suburban New York, Harvard, Washington. He himself is like Charles Grey's notion of the banker: regarding money 'in an impersonal way, as an astronomer might think of light-years in interstellar space'. Money can be made to work against and upon the physical world much as love against and upon people: avarice and romanticism are aspects of the same weakness, and his romances—*The Black Cargo* (1925), *Haven's End* (1937) and *Warning Hill* (1930) show him over-compensating for being too sensible. The very fact that *The Late George Apley* is explained as *A Novel in the Form of a Memoir* reveals a distrust of fiction, in which almost anything is possible. Apley, the New England Brahmin, understating and self-curbing, is an elegiac personification of a lost age; he goes into Memoir, and not Fiction, because (according to Marquand's little pretend-game) the memoir suggests lived experience and fiction fantasy.

Marquand found fiction too tempting. It invited him to consummate, in a fictive present, the promise of a golden past. In simulated memoir, however, and indeed in such historical studies as the Timothy Dexter books (1925 and 1960), Marquand disciplines himself out of velleity. His own town of Newburyport, Mass., home too of Timothy Dexter, the late eighteenth-century eccentric who began as a tanner and grew rich by exporting warming-pans to the West Indies and coal to Newcastle, who rode about in a basket strapped on a servant's back and gave a preview of his own funeral, is a chastening fact rather than a 'Clyde, Mass.' invented to chasten spry readers. For all his professed devotion to 'environment' rather than to 'the man', Marquand relishes Dexter the all-defying screwball. Although, as we read in *Timothy Dexter Revisited* (1960), 'death cuts down on continuity', a Timothy Dexter in his own zany way cuts down on death; Marquand, being antiquarian rather than historian, exultantly proves that. His flashbacks, perhaps the most brilliant part of his stereoscopic technique, are efforts at rehabilitation, and when the playwright hero of *Women and Thomas Harrow* (1958) tries to go home again, away from his carping third wife and even from the theatre-world which gave him success but could not save him from financial ruin, he dwells on his first wife who, by now, is just as talismanic as Jessica Lovell in *Point of No Return*. Thomas Harrow has been living lavishly and now, disliking the world he never made but certainly helped to modify, looks to some kind of intact goddess. It is the sense of failure which goads him to modify the immutable. Needing desperately to identify himself with the perdurable, he develops an almost medieval longing for the rose of love.

But love in Marquand is what makes marriage perilous: 'neither contracting party was in a normal state'; or so Jim Calder in *Wickford Point* believes. He goes on to assert that 'All the really good writers of my time had explored this field [love] at length and with conspicuous success, but had they gone any further than Tolstoy? Had they even said as much as Jane Austen, who said exactly nothing?' Tolstoy had drawn a bold line in *Happy Ever After*: ecstasy, being unstable, is a poor rival to middling contentment. Jane Austen's emphasis on charity's power to humanize reason takes us to the same position. To risk love is to risk disaster. Eventually Kay in *H. M. Pulham, Esquire* settles for the Tolstoyan kindness; Charles Grey, in *Point of No Return*, for garden and children. A lambent resignation takes the place of violent passion and, because it grows at time's speed, worsts time even more efficiently. Further, charity has nothing to do with possessiveness, whereas love and lust have. The truly charitable person is not expected to concentrate on one person. Charity is not apocalyptic; its movement is not, like that of love, exclusive. It is exoteric and it grows through being so. Love

isolates and confines; its messages are in code. But it is not impossible, even in Marquand, that love and all its fulfilments
should release the charity in people. Sometimes charity arrives
because of love, not instead of it.

In the long run, however, Marquand fails to satisfy because
he lacks depth. He skims and swoops but fails to suggest spiritual
desperation. His main feat is to have charted the world of wealth
as if it were a major religion, its adherents gaining the expanding
and stabilizing illusion of a great experience. They hold together,
spellbound by an ethos which makes them novitiates of love,
experts at making-do. They find they cannot buy off time or buy
back the life into a neglected tradition. So their only violence is
metaphysical, like fish bumping noses against the invisible wall of
the aquarium. Only a few of them esteem the glass as an invisible
but life-preserving window on death.

Where Marquand finds fiction too tempting, Erskine Caldwell
(1903–) succumbs to the picturesque-grotesque: he sets the
larger-than-life against time, keeps brutality and violence falter-
ing on the edge of comedy, and turns *fabliau* into *roman noir*.
His novels continually remind us of Freud's view that humour is
one form of aggression. Pa Stroup in *Georgia Boy* (1943) is an
underlord of misrule: he tolls a funeral peal at a wedding, buys a
paper-baler into which he throws his wife's hymnals and the
living-room wallpaper, and steals a heifer. He is like a redneck
Timothy Dexter, every bit as rebellious against both time and
mores. He embodies a careless detachment from others—the
kind of detachment Caldwell himself asks of his readers so that
wit can work through wormwood and humour through horror.
The difference between Caldwell writing about the folkways of
Maine (Bert Fellows retrieving his trousers in the story 'The
Corduroy Pants') and Caldwell writing about the folkways of
Georgia (Candy-Man Beechum the negro muleskinner in the
story of that name, inviting a gun-happy deputy, who has already
shot him, to finish him off) is this: pain, the pain of realization
according to conscience, forces Caldwell into caricature. He
fights back at the incredible and the discreditable by creating
enormities of his own; and these enormities—the belly-ballasted
Sheriff Jeff McCurtain in *Trouble in July* is one—readily develop
into macabre clowns. McCurtain, pretending he has been gaoled

by lynchers during the night, discovers at dawn that he locked himself in with, of all things, an attractive negress.

The folk patterns of 'comeuppance' and revenge, of heroic stolidity and vicious resolve, dominate Caldwell's novels. The mob in *Trouble in July* stones to death the white girl who accused a negro of rape; but only after it has lynched the negro. The compulsive violence of such a world is symbolic: a degenerate mode of self-emptying, as when the mob pours turpentine on the belly of an innocent negro girl. The same is true of the random, desperate lustfulness of Spence Douthit (*Tragic Ground*, 1944). It is unfair to complain that we cannot swallow so much farce and then switch, as Caldwell does, to violent catastrophe: death by axe, by bullet, by syphilis. We are jolted, it is true, but meaningfully, as by E. M. Forster. Life as the average reader knows it is not quite the hectic, degenerate farce of Caldwell; but then, the average reader is not a hillborn poor white slotted into an industrial slum. Caldwell selects his ethos, and then resorts to antic exaggeration in order to make the violence, when it comes, as monstrous and as jarring as possible. Without his exaggerations, all of them the stuff of folktale, *Märchen* and fable, the violence would *mean* nothing: it would just reveal life's absurd ironies rather than add to such revelation an intimation of violence's peculiar function in the South.

Caldwell does not, any more than Hemingway or Faulkner, write documentary novels. Even *Tobacco Road* (1932), for all its homilies, is an imaginative statement, a Gothic elaboration. And *A House in the Uplands* (1946), in which Caldwell eschews farce, is more of a melancholy fable about the decay of old decencies than it is a social document of the O'Hara type. True (like James Agee who reported on sharecroppers in *Let us Now Praise Famous Men*, 1941, and Carey McWilliams whose *Factories in the Field*, 1939, is a study of migratory workers in California) Caldwell has made a name as a reporter. But his novels offer metaphors of depravity: the dissolute preacher in *Journeyman* (1935), for instance, plays sexual and religiose havoc and then vanishes, during the night, like an incubus. It is simple-minded to look to Caldwell for comedy or documentary or mere grotesquerie. He is, in each sense of the word, *fearfully* involved with his material; and much of it is raw. To read him attentively is to begin to piece together for ourselves a whole mythology of the Old South, the new South, old gentility based on oppression, new oppression based on obsolete wrath, underprivileged whites doting on the physical prowess in which the negro surpasses them, gratuitous brutality regarded as a tradition and sexuality as religion. It is hard to see how Caldwell could have conveyed this without the Brueghel touch which saves him, on the one hand, from the sadness in sentimentality and, on the other, from the acute, guilty dispassionateness of the photographic reporter.

The most inscrutable version of the mythology of violence has come from Robert Penn Warren (1905–), one of the old Nashville Fugitive Poets, one of the old New Critics, and a university teacher. *Night Rider* (1938), *At Heaven's Gate* (1941), *All the King's Men* (1945) and *World Enough and Time* (1950) belong together. They argue the same principles in the same terms: agrarian *versus* urban, with Southerners on both sides, but with Warren's main sympathy going to Nature's gentlemen, the smallholders who have to fight both Nature and technocracy. The typical Warren hero gets caught between rednecks and eastern bankers, commits himself (sometimes recklessly) and gets destroyed in the process. For, as it happens, those who defend the old, rustic decencies usually have to resort to criminality. They subscribe, err and are punished, flee and fade into death or nonentity. A modern conflict has used them up It also (whatever side they are on) saps them sexually and morally; they act out their elected parts in a world that is meaningless or, at best, confusing. Everyone is busy selling someone else down the river: to cosmic treacheries add man's. (A familiar theme—the hanged innocent negro—turns up in *Night Rider*.) Father betrays son; son father; and it is not always clear why they do so. The enigmatic quality of life, which in Caldwell erupts in unnerving but explicable acts of violence (even though the stimulus is inherited prejudice), emerges in Warren as something much more idiosyncratic—a seeming *acte gratuit* such as Wilkie Barron's suicide in *World Enough and Time*.

Warren is always, to some extent, pretending that fiction is not a pretence: his characters baffle us just as our fellow-men sometimes do, and we have no sense of participating in a fictional world in which people are explained to us even if what they are is unbelievable. Warren's characters understand one another as little as those of Dickens: they fail to spot stratagem; they cannot justify stratagems which they have suffered from or which they themselves have devised. Their initiatives are dynamic rather than purposive; and, in the same way, the agrarian longing is lyrical rather than pragmatic. As W. M. Frohock observes, 'a young man assimilates his fortunes to those of the culture which produced him, and is destroyed by the same forces which are destroying the culture'.[1] The unprodigal son or tenacious prince takes his stand against Leviathan. We might as well guess at the psychology of the head-buried ostrich as search for the wisdom of the agrarian dream. We are as baffled as the narrator of *All the King's Men*; his bafflement no doubt intensifies the novel's realism but, passed on to us, it clouds our notion of Warren's point.

Like Marquand, although for different reasons, Warren mistrusts fiction: Marquand because it tempts him into a wishful dream, Warren because, concentrating on a defeated dream, and capable of sustaining that dream in subtly lavish prose, he can give a clearer idea of the thing defeated than of the moral dilemmas the conflict created. The dream is no longer an actuality whereas the dilemmas could be our own even now. In *World Enough and Time* Warren, in strangely Marquand-like way, sets a narrator-historian to the task of eliciting from documents the true story of Jeremiah Beaumont. (The actual Jeroboam Beauchamp left a confession behind him.) Warren the myth-dealer becomes Warren the interpreting archivist; for once trying to get to the bottom of a character and to get us there with him. For once, he is avoiding muddle: both the muddle which assists him to deal with a defunct dream as with a living force and that which obscures the characters' motives. The real temptation, we must conclude, is to mythologize the South, to idealize its former character, to make a mental climate live on even when its physical sources have disappeared. Many American novelists, anxious to provide a comprehensive image of human experience, construct dreams and particularly dreams based on American history. The sense of guilt eventually shows in the massive documentaries, the *Ourselves to Know* 'research' novel (of which Marquand's *Dexter* and Warren's *World Enough* are examples)

1 Op. cit., p. 103.

and the cult of sociology. In *All the King's Men* Jack Burden, having got his own story off his chest, elects to spend the rest of his time poring over the history of Cass Mastern. The myth gives resonance but, in the long run, it is history and biography which give the reader what he wants: the sense of lives being lived, near his own emotions, in minute particular. Without that sense, the novelist himself cannot operate convincingly; and, if he is trying to pit some enduring human pattern against disappearing time, he is all the more obliged to immerse the reader in minutiae. But before he can do that he has to immerse himself, even at the risk of disappearing. Otherwise he is bound to suspect fiction's usual formalities and therefore confront us with a bewildered narrator who, far from intensifying the illusion of reality, exposes art's limitations without making a virtue of their necessity.

Frank O'Connor has said that 'a novel is something that's built around the character of time, the nature of time, and the effects that time has on events and characters'.[1] Warren's novels are built around the idea of conservatism, a conservatism which defeats time's endless tomorrows and provides something to hold to in a manichean world. For Warren, no facile liberalism; but no blank uncaring universe, either: he sees everything in human terms, in terms of individuals' motives. And, in his idealism, the idea assumes flesh not to redeem but to be redeemed itself. At the end of *All the King's Men* we are told that 'The creation of evil is therefore the index of God's glory and His power': men are one another's pawns, not God's, and, such is the nature of things, are unlikely to treat one another decently. Jeremiah Beaumont says, 'I seek only to suffer,' and in this he attains the disinterestedness he thinks generally impossible. For that way lies knowledge, not grace. There is no escape, except the shameful fall from personal integrity and the noble refusal to take a logically just revenge. A dire causality moves through all things, and Warren's Miltonic-Aeschylean account of it simplifies into one principle: since we cannot evade the consequences of the past—since, in fact, we *are* its consequences—then we should hold to the human decencies explicit in our noblest traditions. In *The Cave* (1959) Warren starts with a young hill-

1. *Writers at Work*, ed. Malcolm Cowley (New York, 1958), p. 165.

billy trapped underground in Tennessee and vividly enacts ideas we first find in *Brother to Dragons* (1953), the verse play which expounds his view that Man, in fighting for identity against the cosmic process, only discovers how 'action is a constant withering Of possibility, and hence of life', as *Wilderness* (1961) severely and awkwardly proves. Warren's rewarding paradox—'by the act we live, and in action die'—brings him close to Faulkner, to Faulknerian Christianity even, and implies a major intellect too little acknowledged.

Naturally enough, such less obviously religious novelists as Allen Tate (*The Fathers*, 1938), Hamilton Basso (*The View from Pompey's Head*, 1954), William March (*The Bad Seed*, 1954), Hodding Carter (*Winds of Fear*, 1944; *Flood Crest*, 1947) and Eudora Welty (*Delta Wedding*, 1946) build, in various ways, their own versions of structures—traditions, idiosyncratic survivals, uniquely parochial horrors—which time has not ravaged. Tate, creating a brilliant panopticon-novel of furiously contending but hampered patriarchs, rebuts the New England which, in his essay in *I'll Take My Stand* (1930), he described as 'one of those abstract-minded, sharp-witted trading societies that must be parasites in two ways. . . . New England lived economically on the South, culturally on England.' In 1939, in a *Partisan Review* symposium, Tate went further, declaring that only the regional writer could demonstrate allegiance with both Europe and America. But his idealization of a Dixie squirearchy of planters and his apparent search for 'fathers' in his biographies of Stonewall Jackson and Jefferson Davis merely flexed his muscles for entry into a sterner fixity: the Catholic Church. More than New England is the enemy now.

Basso scrutinizes the rigidity of a small Southern town, implying in it the essence of a whole Southern ethos. Campbell takes a twisted girl and, in a numbingly matter-of-fact way, makes her depravity and eccentricity epitomize the dark side of Southern small-town life. Carter fills in the details of life in the Mississippi Delta more polemically than, but just as confidently as, Eudora Welty. Ties, heritage and family (as in the Virginia novels of Ellen Glasgow and the muted, upper-middle-class novels of Peter Taylor, whom Penn Warren has praised) develop into revered stabilizers guaranteed to keep any human in the correct living attitude. At such a level it is enough to tell the story, to ignore causality: even, at one extreme, a roll-call of ancestors will serve. But, at another level—at which we find Carson McCullers (1917–) and Lillian Smith (1897–) seeking both to exalt and terrify the reader—pride in the ineluctable Southern heritage and confidence in the South's uniqueness have fostered displays of style. This is the patina on the tradition, some of it natural, some of it elated daubing.

In many novels written by Southerners the ache to be special, the preoccupation with regional peculiarity, show themselves in a loving attention to freaks. This is violence done to the normal, the anagogue of the North's violation of the South. In Faulkner's novels it is the social hierarchy that is violated; in Tennessee Williams it is love, not to be purchased but not to be done without (*The Roman Spring of Mrs Stone*, 1950); and in the novels of Carson McCullers it is the comradeship of the innocent that is ravished. The typical McCullers novel is succinct, impersonal and heavily charged with symbolism. Her titles—*The Heart is a Lonely Hunter* (1940), *Reflections in a Golden Eye* (1941), *The Member of the Wedding* (1946), *The Ballad of the Sad Café* (1951) —epitomize both her staginess and her knack of complete self-control. There is black, perilous matter in these enamelled little fables. The sordid lasciviousness of the peacetime Southern Army post in *Reflections in a Golden Eye* is emblematic of the human condition in general and of man's essential loneliness in particular. The young heroine of *The Member of the Wedding*, clarifying her identity through successive self-naming (Frankie, F. Jasmine, Frances), finds, like the young heroine of Mrs McCullers's first novel, her isolation in sexuality more tolerable the more she realizes its wider significance. A child dying voicelessly of meningitis on 'a golden morning of the most butterflies' exemplifies a cosmic obscenity far worse than any human depravity. After all, humans' violations of others' privacies and intimacies often come with a genuine, aspiring love which, for inscrutable reasons, sometimes backfires. But when the universe violates us, it uses love without, however, evincing love.

Clock Without Hands (1961) is an untidy novel, full of false leads and false starts and as bewildering about motives as a novel by Penn Warren. But for its almost shivering presentation of

loneliness it is outstanding, and this time the loneliness of an
aged judge, two adolescent boys and a druggist, J. T. Malone,
who is dying of leukemia. But these characters find their links
with actuality inadequate; neither leukemia nor solo flying nor
colour prejudice nor negro paranoia convinces Malone or the
seventeen-year-old Jester or the judge or Sherman Pew, the
young blue-eyed negro orphan, that he really exists. So they
create fantasies: Malone believes he is not dying; the judge tries
to redeem $10,000,000 in Confederate bills; Jester broods on his
own father's unexplained suicide, and Pew dreams up a celebrated mother whom a white man raped. They all retreat, as
blind to life as to death. Malone turns anti-Jew because a Jewish
doctor diagnosed his leukemia. They are all stunned and des-
pondently evasive, and the novel itself is a gorgeous dream in
which the characters seem continually to be getting in the way
of some excruciating revelation. The prose rhythms keep on pre-
paring us for it, but there is always the same falling-away, back
into flux. The daydream permits of no exposition and Mrs
McCullers, extending faunish afternoons into glittering verbal
soirées, masters the ineffable only by ripping it out of context—
which is the only place where it meant anything at all. She is often
to be found impatient with her loving regard for the frustrated,
among whom she herself emerges the most elegant survivor.

It is not going too far to regard her characters as the most
substantial, most colourful tropes in a rhetoric that includes her
landscapes too. Her sophisticated pessimism has something of
William Saroyan's uneven, improvised quality but none of the
bonhomie he uses to mask his uncertainties. She is Flaubertian,
he too much what G. J. Nathan called him: the whirling dervish.
The McCullers exuberance is static; it seeps out and forms pools;
it rarely splashes. Her pace is similar to that of the Anderson of
Winesburg, Ohio, but even slower, suggesting heat, brooding,
corruption and a gently peeled malignity.

These ingredients can be found in a variety of novels by other
Southern authors. Flannery O'Connor, for instance, in The
Violent Bear It Away (1960), describes a battle for the soul of a
fourteen-year-old boy, but without nuance: the warped boy and
another child, this one an idiot, linger on in the mind. Their
futile dialogue, both apocalyptic and banal, suggests the presence

of devilish eavesdroppers. Less demonic, and rather like a less exotic *The Member of the Wedding*, Harper Lee's *To Kill a Mockingbird* (1960) has for narrator an eight-year-old girl: there is the usual crisis—a negro accused of raping a white girl, and Scout Finch, the narrator, tells how her lawyer father incurs the whole town's hostility by defending the negro. We are here, as in so many Southern novels, in the presence of ritual: brutal, atavistic ritual with the colour-blind being stalked by tradition-minded experts of hate. Seen through the eyes of a child or an adolescent, it all seems fiercer—a kind of witch-sabbath in Gogol-guignol. The tortured mind evokes physical punishments the South cannot forget; and William Styron's anguished girl in *Lie Down in Darkness* (1957) implies the guilt of a region and the inertia of tradition. James Baldwin's *Go Tell It on the Mountain* (1961) makes the negro's point imaginatively, and his two volumes of autobiographical fulmination, *Notes of a Native Son* (1955) and *Nobody Knows My Name* (1961), put the same point with stark logic: 'the South will not change—*cannot* change—until the North changes'. Baldwin reports with candour and almost balletic logic on the ubiquitous ghetto from which Ralph Ellison's *Invisible Man* (1952) cannot escape. Unlike Richard Wright (*Black Boy*, 1945; *The Outsider*, 1953), Baldwin has faith in Portia's rain, but not much in Europe as a refuge. The problem, the guilt and the remedy are American only. As Baldwin says, in *Nobody Knows My Name* (presumably because he is invisible), in his address to the white man,

> No one in the world—in the entire world—knows more—knows Americans better or, odd as this may sound, loves them more than the American Negro. This is because he has had to watch you, outwit you, deal with you, and bear you, and sometimes even bleed and die with you, ever since we got here, that is, since both of us, black and white, got here—and this is a wedding. Whether I like it or not, or whether you like it or not, we are bound together forever. We are part of each other. What is happening to every Negro in the country at any time is also happening to you.

From that wedding the negro can now look back to his own

Israel: Africa, the reconstructed homeland from whose newly acknowledged power the negro writer may gain the same sense of corporate belonging as the Southerner gets from rituals. (Wright's *Black Power*, 1954, the dynamic tract he composed after visiting the Gold Coast, makes a similar point.)

But it would be unfair to Baldwin to specify him as a distinguished writer on negro themes alone. His *Another Country* (1962) is a tragic, strident and ardent novel which owes something to Dreiser and Farrell but gets off the ground under its own unflagging power. What Baldwin does with a clique of the lost in and around Greenwich Village is so forceful and penetrating that he has to be reckoned among the most promising of the best. To what he shares with Céline he needs only to add something of that spiritual abandon we find in, say, Wolfe and to some extent Isaac Singer, whose *The Slave* (1962), the fourth of his novels to be translated from the Yiddish, transforms seventeenth-century Poland into a middle-Europe of the spirit and the wanderings of Jacob, the blond Jewish slave, into a profoundly moving parable. Both Baldwin and Singer have the unique ability to transcend racial and futile prejudices; they write of man in general, indignantly seeking his own cosmic significance.

Among the ritualists, and especially those who present negro-white confrontations in shocking terms, Lillian Smith is outstanding. She knows her region and can make its horrors and paradoxes live meaningfully in the popular imagination, as her best-seller, *Strange Fruit* (1944), showed. But, knowing well, she tends to explain over-well—perhaps because she deals with the Shallow South rather than the Deep South. Her best novel, *One Hour* (1960), is swollen with the often inconsequential reveries of the narrator, David Landrum, Rector of All Saints, Windsor Hills, a town in Virginia. Landrum, caught between pastoral care and devotion to two friends upon whom public hatred unjustly falls, sinks into complicated meditation. In the end he gets into a brawl, but almost without knowing it. He realizes that he, no less than an unreasoning mob, sees what he wants to see; that is the book's theme. But Miss Smith's decision to exemplify that theme in the narrator blurs the action needlessly.

In his own wordy, dot-ridden way Landrum describes the crisis brought about by a trivial incident. One Monday afternoon an eight-year-old named Susan goes wandering into a dark, disused store and there encounters Mark Channing, a brilliant young cancer-researcher who, returning from buying Cokes, has strayed into the store on a boyish impulse. Thinking himself alone he makes use of the urinal, turns around, and Susan, child of quarrelling parents, sees a partly unzipped, tall, thin man. She runs home, talking of rape—a word she has picked up from her mother who was once chased by a negro youth. Before long, against all reliable evidence and the pleas of the narrator, the town begins to ostracize Channing and his wife. Atavistic appetites demand blood. Channing's career crumbles: he is eased out of a public lecture; a crank releases his laboratory animals; a poison-pen letter brings about the death of his son; and his highly imaginative wife begins to lose faith in him and turns to Landrum, who has adored her for a long time. Susan's parents withdraw all charges, but persecution goes on. The laboratory janitor talks of sinister experiments with the sex of mice and extends his fantasy to include the changing of whites into negroes. Finally, after the Channings have gone for good, a mob burns a cross on their lawn and dynamites the house. The young clergyman is left with an anguished sense of failure and a knife-wound in the hip.

The mob's wild urges counterpoint the obsessions of individuals. Susan's mother dreams of rape; Landrum, who lost a leg in the war, dotingly attributes his physical and spiritual regeneration to Channing's wife; she once had a Lesbian affair that haunts her; Channing's mother died of cancer. These people trap themselves in a net of interrelation; they also punish themselves into incoherence, thus becoming as irrational as the mob. Landrum significantly regrets 'the fragmented quality of human awareness'; to him 'we're all in pieces and overlapped'. Only too true of this novel. Massive themes, grouped like monoliths, cast shadows through the decent-seeming town and the narrator's mind.

As long as Miss Smith writes of her region, her turgidities seem less idiosyncratic than symptomatic. The love-affair in *Strange Fruit* tells us much about the kind of community which has lynchings; and *Killers of the Dream* (1949), her 'experiment in the joint autobiography of a person and her region', personifies without sentimentality or tedium. But her rambling autobiography, *The Journey* (1954), is full of *longueurs* and commonplace astonishments at commonplace discoveries. When Miss Smith writes for herself, or about herself for (it seems) her friends, she writes tamely and often tediously. Her most inspired manipulations of language take place only when she is so possessed by her ethos that she has no time to set (as in *One Hour*) a clergyman talking endlessly and other characters devouring, dumbly as rabbits, books of philosophy. She errs in thinking intellectual is the opposite of trivial or funny the opposite of serious.

With Truman Capote (1924–) we reach a scrupulous aestheticism which, nevertheless, rarely lapses into the gaudy, meretricious Gothic of such novels as Speed Lamkin's *Tiger in the Garden* (1950). Capote, as well as being fastidiously articulate, shows a mastery of the colloquial equal to Ring Lardner's and a surging, Falstaffian appetite for listing objects: Dolly, in *The Grass Harp* (1951), 'put a foot-high pot of coffee on the stove and pushed a pan of biscuits into the oven; and the oven, opening, would let out a hot vanilla fragrance, for Dolly, who lived off sweet foods, was always baking a pound cake, raisin bread, some kind of cookie or fudge; would never touch a vegetable. . . .' Those who reprove Capote the prose voluptuary ignore this kind of rapt, childlike savouring of the physical world. The lists ballast him; their unmanipulated quality counterpoints his more exquisite runs in which technique is as important as truth-to-life. 'I believe', Capote has said, 'a story can be wrecked by a faulty rhythm in a sentence.' He looks for a final effect which silences the imagination and satisfied 'laws of perspective, of light and shade'.[1] And it must be conceded that, relishing as he does the storied ethos of the South, Capote disciplines his panache extremely well.

His weakness is people. His people, from the intensely aware adolescent boy of *Other Voices, Other Rooms* (1948) to the whimsical, wistful Holly Golightly of *Breakfast at Tiffany's* (1958), are somewhat invisible, more than somewhat contrived. It is as if he regards his characters as stage-effects: even the people in *The Grass Harp*, the love-seekers and the gracehopers,

1. *Paris Review* (Spring–Summer 1957).

show an alarming talent for taking off their lives and hanging them up like coats just when we are getting interested. Holly Golightly, for instance, lives for her little retreats into Tiffany's 'lovely smell of silver and alligator wallets'. Then Capote supernaturalizes them, galvanizes them. He responds too acutely to horror, misery and dementia to leave them in the possession of ordinary people; he likes to detach a state of mind and fantasticate it in prose of unobtrusive but unflagging beauty. This is a pity, for he excels at exposing the weird in life's mundanities; he does not need an exotic world to deal with. So far, however, that is precisely the world he has dealt with, as if every day had to be Christmas and all intensity short-winded.

Capote's type of child's wishfulness reappears in William Saroyan (1908–). *Papa You're Crazy* (1958) is a series of conversations between the narrator and his ten-year-old son: they feed on beans, drive about in an old car and chatter about everything— mostly things boyish. We see the narrator through the son's eyes just as, in Capote's most vivid writing (which does not include *Breakfast*), we find perceptions cleansed of all adult flavour. It is a method which, in Saroyan, suggests insouciant evasiveness; in Capote, the uncompromising boredom with adult explanations which he reveals in such statements as 'The "message" of a story should be after all the story itself'. Saroyan's dexterity, always threatening to produce an art of pure cachinnation or smug hymn, is of the chummy sort; Capote, just as deft, achieves intimacy, not chumminess, and never tells us so. Saroyan's antiwar novel, *The Adventures of Wesley Jackson* (1946), is a warm, selfconscious thing, quite unequal to the nature of war—whether to the criminality of war's farce or to the anonymous bestiality of mass conflict. It is hard to conceive of Capote's attempting any such thing; his view is too myopic for the thorough presentation of large themes.

It is obvious why the South is so rich in stylists and fantasists. Its essence is melodrama and display; so much that is winning and engaging alongside the segregation war assists compensations into being. And such writers as Capote, McCullers and Tennessee Williams, having nothing vast to say, and choosing not to say minor things vastly, have turned the South into pageantry and rhetoric. They have internationalized the superficies of it (in much the same way as P. G. Wodehouse, A. G. Macdonnell as well as Henry James and Ivy Compton-Burnett have internationalized some aspects of English society). They have exploited the South's novelty, whereas the Faulkners and Caldwells have found novelty not just on the surface but deep in the springs of that ethos's characteristic passions. No wonder such writers as Capote seem determined to exchange thea dult's organized, stereotyped account of things for the child's untutored and unguilty originality. Fable has grown with nightmare, and some of the most spectacular, excited and superficially exciting American novels of recent years have been imaginative refusals.

Outstanding among such exercises in the bizarre are John W. Aldridge's *The Party at Cranton* (1960), in which an ex-poet from (of course) the South lords it for a while over the Cranton campus and finally disappears, after a sexual misadventure, wading into the scummy river. As well as a Rose Macaulay-Mary McCarthy glitter of claws, Aldridge achieves a gorgeous urbanity: contorted sentences, no talk, plenty of self-conscious similes and a general effect of calculated blur, all make *The Party* seem a verbal prank, a lavish aberration. But aberration is of the essence. Similar exercises include James Agee's upsetting *A Death in the Family* (1957), a novel methodically cinematic and packed with relentlessly collected, slightly twisted detail; James Purdy's brilliant probings of innocence corrupted and respectability; and Anais Nin's *Seduction of the Minotaur* (1961), in which a divorcée, landed up in Mexico, supplies an obbligato reverie to the events of her new exile.

Agee's novel mixes flashback with the point-of-view method, sets the boy Rufus in the foreground but keeps him mystified for much of the time. The method is complex because Agee, omniscient narrator as he is, wants to work his way into characters who are at varying distances from Rufus; and the resulting dispersal of creative effort makes the novel read as if things simultaneous are being forced into succession. In *The Nephew* Purdy applies his involved, brooding style to a character, the nephew, whom we never see; and the result is as baffling as *A Death in the Family* is distracting. Purdy's previous books, *Colour of Darkness* (stories, 1957) and *Malcolm* (1960), gave slightly demented accounts of the horrors, tendernesses and unclassifiable mysteries beneath conventional surfaces. *The Nephew* is a piece of Nabokov: a manifest realism continually quivering under the pressure of the ineffable (which seems the intended effect) and of the vaguely earnest (an effect both accidental and unfortunate). There is so much that is merely hinted at—grand or foul—that one gets irritated, as by Penn Warren's deliberate mystifications (and, in his worst novels, *Band of Angels*, 1955, *Wilderness*, 1961, his melodramatization of them in the white heroine who has some negro blood, and is sold as a slave, and Adam Rosenzweig, the crippled outcast Jew). And the baroque manner seems, for once in something of Purdy's, gratuitous: a cover-up, not the natural consequence of apprehending a theme intensely. The prose is about itself, and so takes Purdy back to Capote and McCullers, both of whom he seemed to beat, in the stories of *Colour of Darkness*, at their own game. Somehow, when he becomes unallusive he reveals a heavy, gauche touch which ruins his most poignant scenes. His best writing occurs when his temperament has engulfed his themes, not when he is adding style to them. Anais Nin, sometimes a slovenly and exiguous writer making her style live up to an occasion—dulcet for adultery, diamante for death—writes well when she forgets to try to do so. She can write a subtle, melodic prose marred only by a habit of excessive anaphora.

My main point here, however, is these writers' preoccupation with device and their discontent with realistic drawing: there is always something extra which they must try to articulate or suggest. And these twin emotions often make them confuse the literal with the insufficient. It is not that, like Tennessee Williams, they desert a theme's power for the merely bizarre (a 'Field of Blue Children', a one-armed male prostitute, a young doctor with 'an awful flower [which] grew in his brain like a fierce geranium'); or that, like Richard Wright at his most wilful, as in *The Long Dream* (1958) which has adultery in an undertaker's parlour, lynching with mutilation, and the dismemberment of a dead dog, they become impatient with language and use violence as ideogram, at the same time omitting ideograms of gentleness. Or that they are addicted to the flashy or the savage, or tempted by the medicated cascade of such a prose as Erskine Caldwell's. They are just after the impossible, a commodity which the

American novelist has usually captured in the form of myth: that is, not realism and not expensive texture, but structural patterns of immense comprehensiveness—harking back to such allegorical works as James Branch Cabell's *Jurgen*, 'A Comedy of Justice' (1919), *Figures of Earth* (1921) and Christopher Morley's *Where the Blue Begins* (1922) and *Thunder on the Left* (1925) and Henry Roth's Joycean *Call It Sleep* (1934).

Janet Burroway's *Descend Again* (1960) explains itself. Set in Arizona, with some graphic desert scenes, it tells about an orphan schoolmistress and her very brief love-affair with Toad Emerod, after which she descends again, pregnant, into Plato's cave of prisoners. Robert Lewis Taylor's *A Journey to Matecumbe* (1961) brings Huck Finn up to date. Down the Mississippi flees Davey Burnie, with his uncle, into the Everglades and so to the Florida Keys. Like its predecessor, *The Travels of Jaimie McPheeters* (1958), this novel resumes the idiom and knockabout of Twain's yarns, but also fattens out the atavism with Swamp Elixir, floggings, crowbars, a fleeing belle and much documentary stuff. After this, the three Arcadian protagonists of Arthur Miller's *The Misfits* (1961), set in Nevada, seem to be going in tedious circles. But the novel does communicate, as does Jack Kerouac's *On the Road* (1957), something of a vanished America: an America, august and without gas-stations, which reappears when you hunt mustangs to provide cat-meat or roll on wheels across the continent at night. The Flood in *Doctor Sax* (1959) may be intended to induce similar exaltations, although the style, itself flooded with banal adjectives ('great', 'wild', 'saintly') and pointless inventions ('up-fluge', 'ookeries'), gives us too much of the same thing. Sax himself, the Zombie in a French-Canadian boy's adolescence, is both Evil, 'fading, choking, mad, maniac, caped, green-faced', and W. C. Fields. He eventually champions the Good against the Castle on Snake Hill, a wizard and the World Snake. Finally, a giant Bird descends.

At his best, Kerouac writes deliciously about boyhood games and escapades (playing marbles, baseball; fisticuffs) and also about older attempts to regain these unselfconscious excitements (*The Dharma Bums*, 1958). But he overlays everything with myth as if he were trying to be a picaresque Spenser or an Homeric Aesop, and sets too much store by spontaneity of the kind studied, as boyish overflow, in *Doctor Sax* (1959). All very well for a boy to falter before resorting to adult language; but the sleepy-eyed jumble called *Book of Dreams* (1961)—'I mean smot flock blanket bot smot rot ran sea'—is less 'Revelations of the loose mind in Essence connection' than futile verbal doodling. On the elation of movement he is convincing; he bounces one into empathy.

On the painful grind of having to keep on the move, Glendon Swarthout's *They Came to Cordura* (1958) is eloquent: heroism is in every footstep. It is also in the vastness of area in Edna Ferber's Texas and Alaska novels; in the loneliness and imprisoned past of old Tom Scanlon, only inhabitant of the ghost town in Wright Morris's *Ceremony at Lone Tree* (1960); in the failed lawyer-failed farmer who, in Julia Siebel's second Kansas novel *For the Time Being* (1961), goes out at night on to the prairie with his telescope while his blinded wife bakes the bread of life; and, in the thought ('Imagine getting all this for nothing!') of Seymour Levin who in Bernard Malamud's *A New Life* (1961) stares at the night sky, at the cattle and forests of the Pacific Northwest. Levin is a New Yorker, a drunkard and a teacher. Like Roy Hobbs in Malamud's *The Natural* (1952) and Frank Alpine in *The Assistant* (1957) he is a tragi-comic Prometheus, both victim of circumstance and heir to all the stars: Dick Diver as well as Jay Gatsby, and embedded in a tender, flexible prose which sharpens the realism while setting up allegorical reverberations of Chekhovian wistfulness.

Malamud's lonely protagonists have many siblings in recent American novels. Lone man confronting the cosmos knows that the veneer of civilization cannot protect him; so truth, as in Paul Bowles's *The Sheltering Sky* (1949) and Edward Newhouse's *The Hollow of the Wave* (1949), seems always metaphysical. Bowles's Sahara and Newhouse's Utah desert cave (a possible bomb shelter for World War III) chasten the individual, freely reasoning man no less than the ideological absolutes of liberalism and refurbished Calvinism chasten John Laskell, the humanist hero of Lionel Trilling's thoughtful, sane novel *The Middle of the Journey* (1947). But Trilling's hero is liberal and imaginative as well as disturbed; he has the sense and the sensibility to adapt to our own times the feet-on-earth, head-in-heaven view of Pico della Mirandola: 'an absolute freedom from responsibility—that much of a child none of us can be. An absolute responsibility—that much of a divine or metaphysical none of us is.' The main virtue of Trilling's novel is its presentation of a metaphysical point in strictly social terms: 'significance' does not obtrude; on the contrary, we have to elicit it by patiently fingering the narrative's texture. Trilling (1905–), who has always shown a fine sense of the edifice of his own ideas, here gets to grips with the fabric of society; and the only allegorizing is that in the novel's title.

The ultimate, fruitful irony of trying to be responsible is that identity has to depend on a fitful intercourse between uncertain people seeking to define themselves by recourse to other uncertain people. Small wonder the stereotype is cherished; after all, it reassures and consoles. So does a feel, a breath, of the settled Old World as presented, for instance, in the revised translations of Nabokov's Russian novels. *The Gift* (1963) deals with a young Russian writer living in Berlin and groping about among old, honoured certainties, but also evokes his father, an entomologist who goes trekking across Central Asia. The one image is exotic; the other is obliquely American. Nabokov can achieve this double appeal because his soul (or whatever it should be called) is marinated in experience, and that is why he can strike, as in *Pnin* and *Lolita*, to the essence of modern America without condescending. In this he is rare; few other American novelists have his universal resources, his basic confidence in particular ethical and aesthetic standards. His sophistication is a state of mature incapacity for being surprised whereas the sophistication of such writers as Warren, Marquand and McCullers is cautious and shuffling: they forestall surprises by making resolute inductions whereas he has known it all already and knows it will keep on happening. He works by ear; they work by formula. The one way is empirical, the other noumenal. And the ghost in the background is lost innocence for them, absurdity for him. Theirs, finally, is the sophistication that protects innocence; his is the sophistication that retains of innocence only its complete humility when confronted with increasing knowledge. His notion of identity is balance whereas theirs is tied up with assertiveness.

III

The war novels of 1914–18 depict suffering individuals rather than meaningful examples of what Norman Mailer has called 'a bunch of the dispossessed'. Dos Passos's *Three Soldiers*, Cummings's *The Enormous Room* and Hemingway's *A Farewell to Arms* are much more idiosyncratic than, say, John Hersey's *Bell for Adano* (1944) and *The Wall* (1950). Exploring a small Italian town under American occupation and the 'papers' of Moach Levinson, the Polish intellectual, Hersey concerns himself with communal fates (just as he does in his documentation, *Men of Bataan*, *Into the Valley* and *Hiroshima*). The predicament of mankind attracts him more than individual misfortune does; and, not surprisingly, it is the integrity of groups and the strength of traditions which he finds reassuring—not the heroic individual feats we find in Malraux, Hemingway and Silone. For him, man alone simply does not count. So too, for the generation which grew up during the depression, turned pacifist and then suddenly became painfully sensible of the instability of everything, war was a national chore: an interruption and an assininity.

Norman Mailer's *The Naked and the Dead* (1948), developed from a story called 'A Calculus at Heaven', and complete with its 'Time Machine' device, offers a microcosm of futility. Ten men, according to Mailer, here exemplify 'man corrupted, confused to the point of helplessness'. He has said that the novel is symbolic, not realistic; and the mountain, like Hersey's bell and wall, is certainly meant to symbolize, whereas the peacetime army-camp in James Jones's *From Here to Eternity* (1951) amounts to nothing more than itself: it *is* the 'system'. Yet, once again, the view is communal, as well as being confused, emphatic and bitter. Prewitt and his cronies are just as helpless as Mailer's ten survivors, just as morally sapped by the depression years. Irwin Shaw's ambitious, episodic *The Young Lions* (1948) traces three careers from New Year's Eve 1938 to the end of the war, but overdoes the attack on anti-semitism. The whole, with its three protagonists—Austrian Nazi, Broadway stage manager and young Jew—is sometimes stiltedly allegorical, sometimes like an

equation with the terms known. For all its massiveness of conception, *The Young Lions* hangs together less well than John
Horne Burns's *The Gallery* (1947), a series of character studies
set in Algiers, Casablanca, Fedhala and Naples. *The Gallery* is
both mordant and sensual, so much so that Burns predominates
over his characters; their idiosyncrasies are less personal than
thematic, and the final effect is of disorganization.

Just as episodic, Alfred Hayes's *All Thy Conquests* (1946)
presents Rome through three Italians and two Americans, in
alternating episodes, and his *The Girl on the Via Flaminia* (1949)
through a young American soldier who misuses Lisa, an Italian
girl, and eventually loses her at the very moment when his first
access of human charity lands him in a redeeming confusion. But
even he, compared with Hemingway's lieutenant in *A Farewell to
Arms*, is more of a Daisy Miller type—the alien misfit—than a
specific person. The American-at-War appears *en masse* in James
Michener's *Tales of the South Pacific* (1947), which, after Thomas
Heggen's *Mister Roberts* (1946), is the most desultory of the war
books.

For a patient, sedulous study of a military community, James
Gould Cozzens's *Guard of Honor* (1948) is hard to surpass. It is
all there: in three days at a Florida air base in September 1943,
a microcosm of the war, of war; of the military mind and of
military mindlessness. The characters live and squabble in a
meaningful framework; it is a novel of ideas, Cozzens's eleventh,
and the first to get him noticed. The Cozzens case, finally writ
large in *By Love Possessed* (1958) and probably damaged by that
novel, is curious. Gifted at dialogue, a master plotmaker and
scene-setter, he wrote well in an old-fashioned, solid way until
By Love Possessed, in which he not only became prolix and
parsonically lyrical but peeled psychological onions with all the
selfconscious, involved gravity of a Meredith. The gravity of
tone congeals like gravy: 'Ah how wise, how sure, how right, was
that genius of the language whose instinct detected in the mani-
fold manifestings of the amative appetite (however different-
seeming; however apparently opposed) the one same urgent
unreason. . . .' And so on: the idiom is Arthur Winner's, but is
offered in the lump, without reflective analysis. Which amounts
to the kind of verbal freewheeling that the strict Cozzens of *The*

Just and the Unjust (1942) and even *S. S. San Pedro* (1931) never allowed himself.

We notice, again, the aggrandizing tendency of American novelists, whether dealing with society, war or love. They inspissate in order to counter the cosmos. The bigger the novel or the vaster the corporate entity explored, the solider becomes the human protest. The novelist feels an inordinate need to identify himself with the public—something which Hemingway's generation never considered. The cult of raw experience and the cult of comprehensiveness have, between them, spawned more gratuitous violence than is symbolically useful and more thin epic than is meaningful. The motives are wilful, popularistic; the sort which led Herman Wouk from *The Caine Mutiny* (1951) to the spongy pretentiousness of *Marjorie Morningstar* (1955).

Similar motives animate an endlessly transcribing O'Hara or James T. Farrell. To attack America, as Mencken did, sustained by his faith in European standards, is no longer possible. To attack it from a Russia-cherishing standpoint, as Dreiser did, is difficult, to say the least. Yet to espouse modern America seems unthinkable. The intellectual novelists—from May Sarton (*A Shower of Summer Days*, 1952; *Faithful are the Wounds*, 1955) and Trilling to Mary McCarthy and Harvey Swados—converse among themselves. The stylists, from Capote and McCullers to Frederick Buechner, Vance Bourjaily and Gore Vidal, elegantly expose the bumptious mundanities of the air-conditioned nightmare. It is not the super-American they neglect so much as the all-American. After all, His and Her private planes, air-conditioned hearses, mink-wrapped weekend shoppers flying from Houston to Paris, all give the stylist or the panache-monger a good start.

Instead, the intelligent (not necessarily intellectual) novelist has begun to create snide, aphoristic versions of *caveat emptor* addressed to the public pummelled by the mass media. In Britain these media sink down through horizontal strata; in the United States they spill across perpendicular divisions of ethnic and cultural origins. In America, then, comprehensive statement is easier than it is for such English writers as Alan Sillitoe, Anthony Powell and Angus Wilson, who all keep to their elected strata. As Norman Mailer has said: 'There are really no such things as types in America, and as a result an American writer has to spend a good bit more of his time in defining his characters down to the section in which they live.' But American advertising, for that reason, is classless; British is not. Hence such trenchant anatomies as Ira Wallach's *The Absence of a Cello* (1960), J. D. Salinger's *The Catcher in the Rye* (1951), with its scatologer-Huck hero who wilts away from all that is phoney (including even such genuine phoneys as Holly Golightly), and Richard G. Stern's *Golk* (1960), which amounts to a modern horror-story, aimed at TV, along lines established by Kafka and Nathanael West.

Tracts against the gulling of people abound and include tracts on the ruining of adolescents. Salinger's *Franny and Zooey* (1961) shows children sold to a radio quiz-show; John Hersey's *The Child Buyer* (1960), John Updike's verbally dizzying *Rabbit, Run* (1960) and James Leo Herlihy's *All Fall Down* (1960) sketch out the nightmares and Frankensteins who attend upon the child's and adolescent's soul. Such cautionary tales dramaturgically rehearse some facts of modern life; they also remind the American reader what lies outside the soft cocoon spun for him by advertisers: malevolence, disease, death, dementia and so on. In *The Kenyon Review* (Summer 1949) Hannah Arendt suggested that the modern novelist is really 'a poet whose main concern is judgment and not reporting, and as a philosopher who wants not just to portray the course of events but to discover and demonstrate logically the laws of movement governing the "disintegration of values" '. Such poetic-metaphysical intent permits of social observation and also permits all kinds of quaintness, distortion and acerbity.

In Philip Roth's portraits of Jewish-American bourgeoisie, *Goodbye Columbus* (1959) and *Letting Go* (1962), resignation is peppered with alarming laughter; in Edward Albee's play *The American Dream* (1961) the tone is rebarbative against the sweet idyll of the Decent Average Family; in Norman Mailer's *The Deer Park* (1955) the bravura rutting damns itself and yet seems to have given Mailer the pleasure of writing lewdly (almost on the moraine of Edmund Wilson's *Memoirs of Hecate County*, 1942). The rebel, in fact, still wants to be accepted: as a traditional kind of rebel—which of course he cannot be. There is no pastiche in genuine rebellion; only the itch to damn and be damned. Constant change still sends thoughtful novelists back to the old

Dream: A. B. Guthrie's *The Big Sky* (1947) and *The Way West* (1949), Ross Lockridge's *Raintree County* (1948), Sinclair Lewis's *The God-Seeker* (1949), Michael Straight's *Carrington* (1960) and John Barth's ribald, fecund historical novel, *The Sot-Weed Factor* (1960), all testify to an unsettled society's craving for the reliable old dreams, the old fulfilled epics. Lack of faith in present social arrangements explains much of the nostalgia, violence and trifling-with-footling in the American post-war novel.

Avoid, disrupt, deny: these are the aims and reflexes which endear, say, Faulkner to the intellectually feuding French; which account for American pre-eminence in the unjudging thriller and crime novel (Hammett, Chandler, Spillane); which respond to the stock biography of modern America: the Gilded, Progressive and Jazz Ages, the Depression and the War, Korea and Cold War. After the death of Thurber, there are few who can laugh without being arch or bitter: Peter de Vries (too often meretriciously slick), Ludwig Bemelmans, the subtlest verbal cartoonist of all, Max Shulman (aim erratic, however), John Cheever (suburbia is hell, nor am I out of it). Louis Kronenberger's *A Month of Sundays* (1961) digs into the lunatic world of Serenity House, a psychiatric clinic, and in fact makes caricature the norm. The result is laborious rather than funny. Robert Graham's *The Annals of Logan* (1961) is the usual anti-organization novel, but written in verse, with each character being given his own typographical pattern.

After Philip Wylie's *Generation of Vipers* (1942) no analysis of the quality of American living could be both vitriolic and dazzling without seeming a pastiche. Anthony West's *The Trend is Up* (1960), about the First-Million-Before-I'm-Thirty mentality, is sombre and convincing but perhaps too determinedly against the materialism whose coltish joys fizz and spill throughout Jim Kirkwood's jaunty melodrama *There Must be a Pony* (1960). Wallace Stegner's Sabrina Castro, rebelling in *A Shooting Star* (1961) after 'twelve years of decorative nothing' as the wife of a dude doctor, carries expiation to the ironic end of rescue by Angry Young Man. Sloan Wilson's *A Sense of Values* (1961) fixes on Nathan Bond who created a nationally syndicated cartoon figure called Rollo the Magnificent: not, this time, grey flannel suit but grey flannel mind. Divorce looms, but so does a happy mending. The best parts of this overlong cautionary tale (with its preface's thanks to 'a fine editor') concern the miseries of being a success. Of the dedicated failure undertaken by the Beats, Bernard Wolfe's *The Magic of Their Singing* (1961) gives a scrupulous, fantastic account worthy of the man who wrote, among other novels, *The Great Prince Died* (1957), about Trotsky's assassination. His phantasmagoria of mambo, hip, orgy and 'Being vs. Coming' is both dramatic and vivid: probably the most perceptive novel on this theme. Glendon Swarthout's campus queen vacationing in Florida in *Where the Boys Are* (1960) luridly exemplifies another kind of failure, has affairs with a tiro-tycoon, an Ivy-Leaguer and a pop-singer. Finally pregnant, she becomes a contradiction: machine made fertile—a far cry from the cohorted parturitions, weanings, separations and reunitings of Evan Hunter's four women in *Mothers and Daughters* (1961). In this umbilical extravaganza (by the author of *The Blackboard Jungle* and *Strangers When We Meet*) even life's renewal becomes mechanical. The women either have their Visitor or get the woollies out again; that is life.

Novels such as Hunter's have drawn attention from such skilful, unobtrusive reporting as Daniel Fuchs's trilogy of Jewish life in Brooklyn (*Summer in Williamsburg*, 1934; *Homage to Blenholt*, 1936, *Low Company*, 1937), reissued in 1961. To Fuchs there is no innocence for adults: the butcher upstairs asphyxiates himself; a freebooting whoremaster perishes; a butterfly gets wafted into a subway train. This is the fault of everyone, even of the immigrant children, for whom (perhaps?) there have to be butterfly symbols. Altogether more Dickensian, Edwin O'Connor (*The Last Hurrah*, 1956) creates an engaging comedy of humours (*The Edge of Sadness*, 1961) around an octogenarian bird-lover, masquerading as Sire Vinegar, and an ex-alcoholic priest. Where O'Connor excels in zest, Shirley Ann Grau (*The Hard Blue Sky*, 1956; *The House on Coliseum Street*, 1961) presents pain (rejection, abortion) through an evocative verbal mist which both magnifies and distorts. As the emotional weather changes, Human and Gargoyle loom up or recede like Darby and Joan until mental collapse is complete.

Of the miscellaneous futility of comfort, security, conformism and piety the mid-century American novel makes a great deal, and of the old stand-by—the power to beguile of the national romance, the history and the dream matching each other—makes much less. One is tempted to say that *Lolita* typifies a new attitude in which illusions play a minor part and which feels European; not so much disillusion as a waning enthusiasm that makes some sacred cows seem laughable.

I mean an attitude already identified in its extreme versions in what I have said about the English and the French novel: defying time and cosmos through distortion, chronicle and fable, which is what we find in Faulkner, O'Hara and Hemingway, in Caldwell, Marquand and Wolfe. The American novelist now seems closer than he was even ten years ago to a European train of thought which goes something like this: against faith in fraternity, charity and self-sacrifice (as recommended by Cary, Myers, Lawrence, Malraux, Camus and Sartre) the following views emerge: other people are objects because man (a) is self-engrossed or (b) wants others to be too reliable or (c) cannot stand others' volatility and so pretends it does not exist or (d) empathizes too much to dare to respond at all or (e) thinks everything but art is absurd or (f) thinks everything is futile, art included. The spaceman in his whirling capsule is only the ad-man writ large in Cold-War language, and many American writers seem to find the American experiment—always far from perfect and suffering much of the time from being conducted in divine perfection's shadow—gone sadly wrong. An increasing number of novels deal with insanity, resort to the metaphor of the mental ward and embark on a progression we can document easily in the French novel, not to mention the German and Italian.

It amounts to this: the world of things is indifferent to us, and if we think it reflects our moods we delude ourselves; the world of people is alien too, and our happiest experiences (say, 'love', so-called) occur when we insist on interpreting to suit ourselves; to be honest is to incur social hatred and cosmic disadvantage; all we can do is try to define ourselves to ourselves (absurd, but the illusion is helpful) through virtuous commitment or *actes gratuits*; but in the long run, self-defining is Man-defining, an act of unheroic pensiveness we are justified in rejecting in favour of aestheticism, hedonism, destructiveness, despair, vegetating, violence and suicide. Losing faith in their ability to restrict technological inventiveness to virtuous purposes, men have reacted violently; and in America, where the hostile or indifferent universe was always conquerable, especially by the innocent, the national experiment seems too far advanced to justify further anthems about its promise. Instead, the end-product is visible and hard to alter. Wolfe celebrated a growing country, an expanding concept, whereas Kerouac's picaresque records a daunting *fait accompli*. It becomes harder for the lyrical novelist to mimic the endeavours of the pioneers—to extol power. For power, in the hands of the mass-media at home and, internationally, both cause and consequence of an unwanted and uncomfortable rivalry, has lost its glamour, and America, vexed by Red China still and by Cuba, may well prompt its novelists into twin extremes of scathing documentary and escapist fantasy.

Voluptuaries of fantasy abound, distorting the everyday and conventionalizing the bizarre. Kenneth Patchen's *Journal of Albion Moonlight* (1941) typifies the mode and Henry Miller's *The Colossus of Maroussi* (1941) has something of the mode's bombinating audacity. The private vision is almost all, whether drug-induced as in Alexander Trocchi's *Cain's Book* (1960) and William Burroughs's brilliantly scabrous *Naked Lunch* (1959) or the fruit of derangement as in Ken Kesey's *One Flew Over the Cuckoo's Nest* (1962). There are many elaborately urbane meanders through Weirdland and Night-town. John Knowles translates a boys' school into unlyrical Kakfa in *A Separate Peace* (1960). In *The Moviegoer* (1961), Walker Percy chokes a stockbroker hero with decent attitudes. David Stacton, a prolific stylist and master of aphoristic Grand Guignol, refurbishes the legend of the Duchess of Amalfi in *A Dancer in Darkness* (1962), and Joseph Heller, in *Catch 22* (1961), creates a shambling, apocalyptic war satire about an Air Force captain persecuted because he is sane. John Barth, author of *The Sotweed Factor*, is less known for the scalpelling nihilism of *The End of the Road* (1958) and the precise dementia of *The Floating Opera* (1957). Ralph Ellison's *The Invisible Man* resorts a good deal to the phenomena and pressures of nightmare. The hero of George P. Elliott's *David Knudsen* (1962) is a victim of radiation sickness, and Elliott presents him as 'an outside member'. Other novels which rely on illogic, horror, macabre or beserk paraphernalia are Allan Seager's *Equinox* (1943) and *Death of Anger* (1960), and John Hawkes's vivid, mannered surrealist exercises, *Charivari* (1947) and *The Cannibal* (1949).

We look back to Melville's terrifying *Encantadas* and note the vitality of all this neurosis compared with the debility which increases between Salinger's illustrious *The Catcher in the Rye* and *Raise High the Roof Beam, Carpenter and Seymour an Introduction* (1963). The most ingenious verbal artists of all, John Updike (*The Poorhouse Fair*, 1959, *Rabbit, Run*, 1960, *The Centaur*, 1963) and Hortense Calisher (*False Entry*, 1961, *Textures of Life*, 1963) seem to retreat into cocoons of cool, daedal felicity, and it is to the new surrealists that one looks for an animated, unrefined vision. Not that the more established novelists are out of action; they are not. Saul Bellow, for example, after the brilliant, relentless *Dangling Man* (1944) and the aridity of *The Victim* (1947), objected to attempts to make work 'durable through form' and dreamed up Augie March. Since then he has turned to phantasmagoria, and *Henderson the Rain King* has much in common with the work of Burroughs, Barth and Hawkes rather than with that of Nelson Algren and William Styron: Bellow's latest heroes, Henderson and Herzog, live in the world of everyone else but also among objects that have no attitude to man at all.

The United States has no Robbe-Grillet, but it has some writers just as bleak in spirit and others, such as O'Hara, whose very cataloguing suggests man's inability to make sense, justice or decency out of anything. This is private man considering his predicament abstractly because he belongs to society rather than his society to him. No wonder that, deprived of the American dream, which did for him what class-games do for the English and metaphysics for the French, the American novelist is tempted to become a disdainful, articulate observer, disclaiming responsibility while thinking up, like the novelists of post-war Western Germany, something worth believing in. Evasive fables, in both instances, are the only other recourse.

PART FOUR

Other Countries

Two Germanys

> But the essential and typical national differ-
> ence is the social spirit of the French work,
> the mythically primitive poetic spirit of the
> German work. . . . At the turn into the twenti-
> eth century and in its first third there takes
> place generally something like the formal
> and intellectual breakthrough of the German
> novel into the sphere of European interest.
>
> (THOMAS MANN)

I

GERMAN writers mythologize easily and naturally. Even a
modern novel of tenacious realism will often broaden out into
prophecy, anagoge, *Märchen* and pattern; and the reader advances warily into a storming replica of the twentieth-century
German experience, all paradoxes and extremes. No wonder that
the German miracle—from cautery to resurgence—is written
about apocalyptically as a feat of spiritual pioneering in a provi-
dential saga similar to the American Dream. The world of such
novels as Hesse's *Der Steppenwolf* (1927), Ernst Jünger's *Heliopolis* (1949) and Mann's *Der Zauberberg* (1924) is a world of too
many possibilities. How could one expect an unmixed genre from
the nation which all too readily has reached and tampered with
the human limits? Atrocity, hubris, genocide, purge, messianism,
decimation and prostration precede humble pie, occupation,
partition, subsidy, nihilism, fingers worked to the bone and
supremacy eventually regained. Mythologized megalomania
treats the surfaces of life as both a respite from thought and as

the evidence of destiny. What scope and what pitfalls for the heirs of Mann and Kafka!

The major German novelists of the mid-nineteenth century are, for the most part, observers of the social pageant: Jeremias Gotthelf describes farming communities, Gottfried Keller the Zürich bourgeoisie, while Raabe, Stifter and Storm apply their microscopes to small segments of the social surface, and Fontane achieves something of Balzacian sweep. These novelists exemplify a tradition which continues in Thomas Mann and such densely documenting writers as Doderer (*Die Dämonen*, 1956), but which in neither of those authors quite holds its own against another tradition going back to the allegorical fantasy of Grimmelshausen's *Der abenteuerliche Simplicissimus*, Wieland's *Agathon*, as well as *Wilhelm Meister*. It was therefore inevitable that Nietzsche and Freud should have tilted the novelist's imagination away from observable daily realities towards an intoxicating, inexhaustible subjectivity. When Johann Buddenbrook dives into the writings of Schopenhauer, and his son submits to Wagner's dionysiac crescendos, they both sense a liberation, their sudden participation in the flux. And, of course, to German predisposition of this kind and to intellectual fashions which intensified it, history conveniently added war, restrictive National Socialism and defeat: the very experiences to tempt an imaginative German even further into himself.

We have to fortify ourselves, then, for a sea-changing realism; we have to be as willing as the hero of Rilke's *Malte Laurids Brigge* (1910) to accept as natural the supernatural's invasions of the daily world. Almost from the Neo-Romantic period at the turn of the century, German novelists have used a fractured mirror to reflect a disintegrating world; and it is not unfair to suggest that the same mirror, in the hands of German power-hunters, accounted in large measure for the disintegration, between 1914 and 1945, which German writers were already so well equipped to record; when, of course, they could speak out at all.

We have to do with a national tendency and its part in, its response to, a calamitous European experience. Faith in the stability and perdurable nature of the material world is, naturally enough, rare in the modern German novel. Instead, an almost insane longing for apocalypse and a frantic sense of man's precariousness obsess the novelist. In his *Beschreibung eines Kampfes* Franz Kafka (1883–1924) broods on 'the things which sink around me like a fall of snow, while for other people even a little liqueur glass stands firm . . .'

Unfortunately for the disciples of Nietzsche who condemned Wilhelm Meister's final decision to serve the community as a surgeon, who readily evolved a libidinous aestheticism to console themselves with, who preferred anarchy to the moral training exemplified in the *Bildungsroman* or novel of personal development, there were limits. Twin humanisms emerge from twentieth-century literature, the one exiguous and aloof, the other avid and inquisitive. Both seek to defend and extol cherished human attributes by either elimination (see C. P. Snow against the English novel of sensibility) or such a compassionate attentiveness as the idea of 'presence' advanced by Marcel, Buber and Brunner. This idea has been advanced by theologians mostly, but it is possible to entertain it seriously without subscribing to any particular theology.

Even realistic intellectuals, after tortuous ratiocination has failed to make received religion possible for them, embrace a philosophy of the village barber. Once they have exultantly discovered such constants as man's inchoate yearning for fraternity, they are as serene in their complicated sententiousness as the orthodox in their theology. Such was the humanism of Gotthelf and Stifter. And again, the fastidious, hermetic aesthete turns eventually to an exalted notion of the simplest things, such as the blue flower which enraptured Novalis. In other words, outgoing humanism or withdrawal depends on banalities—charity or flowers; and it is this that the German novelist, lacking moral conviction, but longing for ravishing spiritual experience, cannot face. The world is not intense enough for him; but equally as for Thomas Mann, mere moral intensity is just as unsatisfying as sterile aestheticism. Mann's Tonio Kröger laments that 'Feeling, warm, heart-felt feeling, is always banal and unusable . . . . The Artist is finished as soon as he becomes human and begins to have feelings.' Tonio himself tries to be human and ignore his feeling of separateness; but that is a rare effort among the heroes of modern German fiction. Nihilism and violence is all that remains for the individualist who finds art too inanimate. At his most virtuous he produces something like the rapt pragmatism of Expressionism; at his worst, the brutal, inexplicable world envisioned by Kafka in elemental images. The cold, unimpassioned manner of Stendhal in *La Chartreuse de Parme* (1839) is an early version of the unethical aestheticism which haunts the protagonists of Thomas Mann. The unbending aestheticism of Stefan George's *Blätter für die Kunst* constantly implies a disregard of humanitarian standards; the cult of pure art is not unrelated to the cult of the pure German, and the stern dedication of the aesthete to that of the dedicated creators of a Buchenwald.

Disintegration—of the Empire, politically and socially—is the theme of Bernhard Kellermann's *Der 9. november* (1920), a representative not highbrow novel which portrays the suffering poor, the corrupt sybaritic rich and the wholesale maiming of soldiers. As the war draws to a close, notes of revolt, radicalism and nihilism complete the passionate indictment of a depraved society. Kellermann's novel has much in common with Andreyev's *The Red Laugh* (1904), Barbusse's *Le Feu* (1916), Vicente Ibañez Blasco's *The Four Horsemen of the Apocalypse* (1916), Dos Passos's *Three Soldiers* (1921), Faulkner's *Soldiers' Pay* (1926), Ramón J. Sender's *Pro Patria* (1929), as well as with Erich Maria Remarque's *All Quiet on the Western Front* (1929). But there are other German novels, not all of the first quality, which are hard to parallel, in other literatures, for their apocalyptic, morbid approach. Rudolf Brunngraber's *Karl und das 20. jahrhundert* (1933) deals with a young Austrian who commits suicide thirteen years after the war ends. At odds with the universe, he finds no provision made for self-respect. It is the world of Kafka, the world in which Hans Fallada's bewildered young bookkeeper, Johannes (*Kleiner Mann—was nun?*, 1932), averts tragedy by relying on his wife's love and Willi Kufalt (*Wer einmal aus dem Blechnapf frisst*, 1934) commits robbery in order to return to the security of gaol. In Ernst Glaeser's *Der letzte Zivilist* (1935) Johann Bäuerle returns from America with a fortune, only to encounter Naziism, the suicide of idealists, and despair. He once again leaves Germany. The main character of Alfred Neumann's *Der Held* (1930) finds that the authorities will not even let him confess to murder, thus depriving him of martyrdom and confining him to guilt and mental breakdown. Altogether more gruesome, Leo Perutz's *Der Meister des jüngsten Tages* (1923) mixes morbid introspection, black magic, murder and epidemic suicide into a Mann-like allegory set in modern Vienna. But perhaps the most vivid allegorical figure of all is the young 'orphan of Europe' in Jakob Wassermann's *Caspar Hauser* (1908): only seventeen, hardly able to talk or walk, and able to remember only his solitary confinement, he is finally assassinated, a pathetic piece of flotsam destroyed by uncaring cosmic machinery. Another of Wassermann's novels, *Christian Wahnschaffe* (1918), is a fitful panorama of industrial society in decay; Christian Wahnschaffe, son of a captain of industry, eventually seeks the gutter, prepares to become (like Wilhelm Meister) a doctor but suddenly vanishes, still seeking a fruitful self-immolation.

To these semi-allegorical novels we should add Lion Feuchtwanger's *Die Geschwister Oppenheim* (1933), about a Jewish family disintegrating under Hitler; Frank Thiess's *Der Leibhaftige* (1924) in which Caspar Miller, while thinking himself a success, gradually degenerates until he heads a peerage of pimps and runs a high-class Venusberg; and Bruno Traven's *Das toten Schiff* (1930) in which an American sailor, stranded in Antwerp, picks his way across Europe and eventually joins a ship which the owners are having sunk for the insurance. Down in the stokehold of the doomed vessel, he symbolizes wasted life and evokes Kafka's 'K' in demonstrating that the 'Castle' or 'Grail' is perhaps something commonplace: as commonplace as charity.

For Thomas Mann (1875–1955) that perception came with the defeat in 1918. Shedding his faith in Imperialist standards—and especially in romantic conservatism—he supported the Weimar Republic and the principles of social democracy, at the same time exchanging the directness and robustness of his early stories and *Novellen* for a method more intricate and didactic. His is the intellectual's version of the themes we have just noticed in middle-brow novels, and his particular achievement was to combine Dostoevskian profundity with Biblical or Teutonic myth. His search for values leads him from diffident intellectualism to the simplistic Hans Castorp who, in *Der Zauberberg* (1924), matures until he can confidently assert love and charity against evil and death—whatever the cost. The hero of *Joseph und seine Brüder* (1933–43) is more of an outsider, a man of flair who realizes, upon being put into the well, that he must be shrewd too. And shrewdness begins to pay. But Mann, hinting at a world-sadness all of his own, points to Joseph's lively self-interest, hardly that of the guileless visionary in the myth which Mann genially shuffles about.

The mood of *Doktor Faustus* (1947) is very different. Mann takes another artist-figure, a musician, who cannot adapt himself to society like Joseph or, like Tonio Kröger, vaguely trust the larger hope. Adrian Leverkühn denounces and rebels; his religious teachers dote on demonology, and his own love of music (as Mann sees it) leads him towards the devil; away from everyday reality whether social or political. It is noteworthy that Mann presents music as a German vice and links it to both Leverkühn and the devil through venereal disease. Everything makes for the hubristic artist's isolation: the devil prevents him from loving; the pox ensures his being a pariah, and Adrian's only two breaches of his pact with the devil come about through contact with the Swiss, whom Mann sets up as a model. Finally, after watching his little nephew die of cerebro-spinal meningitis, Adrian collapses at the keyboard. The novel is a tract against Goethe and Nietzsche, against instinct and aestheticism. Adrian epitomizes the man without values, almost without qualities. 'Your life is to be cold,' the devil tells him. And yet, surely, Mann is a little muddled: he presents Beethoven's last piano sonata as an example of Teutonic libido destroying the discipline of form, and yet damns the coldness and barrenness of formalism.

In fact, of course, Mann himself was powerfully drawn to art's aloof, icy disciplines: his own world had vanished; chaos had supervened; the music of mysticism had taken over. His difficulty was that, recognizing as he did the nature of German excesses, he had to argue for an antidote, for a colder discipline than he wished upon himself. Therefore Adrian, the complex personification, is an unconvincing sandwich of hyperbole against a nation and Mann's infidelity to his true self. It is almost certainly impossible to personify a nation in a figure antithetical to oneself (but not quite) without getting confused; and what there is of the disciplined Mann in Adrian Leverkühn prevents us from regarding the personification as a person or as a clear statement. Such theoretically inspired confusions typify the German novel of our time, and Mann's next work, *Der Erwählte* (1951), blithely mixes piety, Popery and incest in highbrow rebuke aimed, it would seem, at Adenauer's Christian rebuilders. *Die Betrogene* (1953) takes us back to the period after 1918. Rosalie von Tümmler, the sentimental matron who succumbs to a brash young American, misinterprets the signs of Nature. Her haemorrhage is no second spring but the result of womb-cancer; but it is, plainly enough, Mann's interpretation of a supposedly resurgent German bourgeoisie. This violent allegory suffers from the same cerebral dispassionateness that handicaps Leverkühn, as if Mann had come to identify even compassionate emphasis with what he called 'chaos-bearing anti-reason'. *Felix Krull* (1954), however, is a radiant, rattling comic novel begun during the *Der Tod in Venedig* (1913) period, but never finished. Picaresque and urbane, this novel resumes most of Mann's earlier themes in frivolous mood. Disease, sexuality, music, growing up: Felix negotiates them all breezily, shallowly, as he schemes his way onward and upward. *Felix Krull* is not a revoking coda, but it does make one wish that Mann's intensities were not so solemn, his levities so shallow and his colours almost always primary.

But before we blame Mann for compartmentalizing, we have to acknowledge that German literature has always dealt in the homogeneous. The idyll tradition of the eighteenth and nineteenth centuries has survived intact, largely because Arcadia and Utopia merged together into the kind of inward pastoral longed for by disillusioned moderns. Also, in the 1930s and after, it was dangerous to be topical; so the novelist had to present his view as insignificant news from nowhere; indict through analogues only. As Hans Carossa (1878–1956) said, the German writer in the totalitarian state 'was compelled either to be silent or at least to pass over in silence very essential phenomena of the contemporary world . . . he appeared either as provincially limited or as false'. But Carossa's autobiographical volumes, from *Eine Kindheit* (1922) to *Der Tag des jungen Arztes* (1955), deal in simple, honoured formulas to which, in his account of life under the Nazis, *Ungleiche Welten* (1951), he lovingly recurs. He writes of the dry summer of 1947, studying the routine of an old Bavarian couple during one day. It is a moving story, rich with longing for the endurance of human kindness.

Hermann Hesse (1877–1962) began as a regionalist but, after denouncing national military policy in 1914, began to express his dissatisfactions in myth and fantasy. *Demian* (1919) and *Der Steppenwolf* (1927) argue, through a smooth prose darkly, for an outgoing spirituality, while *Narziss und Goldmund* (1930) contrasts life-tasting with asceticism; the dilettante's miscellaneous sympathy is preferred, and *finesse* over *géometrie*. In *Das Glasperlenspiel* (1943) Hesse predicts a Utopia in which an élite called the Castilian Order manipulates the beads, the philosophers' stones, in accordance with 'the quintessence of intellect and art, the sublime cult, the mystic union of all the separate members of the universe of letters'. All is sanity and light; the ivory tower is all-powerful; intellect prefigures beauty and beauty faith, while mathematics leads through music (very much the opposite of what it is in Mann) to mystical experiences. But Josef Knecht, head of the Order, is 'Servant' to Goethe's 'Meister' and, in rebelling against the Order where Meister submitted to the 'Society of the Tower', accuses the Order of remoteness from life. (One thinks of Swift's Academy of Lagado.) Before he can return to the world as a kind of intermediary, Josef is accidentally drowned. Obviously the delicate algebra of such a novel is not to be tried crassly against known quantities; sufficient that cold cerebrality and the out-of-touch aesthete stand rebuked. But these formulas lack the life of even Mann's personifications, and the book's popularity in Germany tells us a good deal about German literary tastes. The abstract is, for Hesse, a mode of the elegiac; it means an approach to a realm of ideal forms and not, as for less exacting tastes, the loss of interesting instances, material circumstance and personal peculiarities.

The bucolic nostalgia of Ernst Wiechert (1887–1950) is easier to share. Technological civilization affronts him, as militarism does, and the pastoral norms of *Das einfache Leben* (1939) sustain him through two major works, *Die Jerominkinder* (1945–7), set in darkest East Prussia, and *Missa sine Nomine* (1950). Both novels seek to explain the presence of evil: the first through a young country doctor who returns from the First World War and watches 1939 gradually creep up; the second through three brothers uprooted by the Second World War. One farms; one devotes himself to displaced persons; and the other tries to recover from four years in a concentration camp. Wiechert proposes no remedial plan; men either adjust or go under; and the main problem of life is to decide how adaptable the human heart can be without becoming perverted. His writing is some-times hysterical, sometimes unimaginatively discursive; but his fervour just about carries one through to sympathy with his Tolstoyan kind of Christianity. But it is Albrecht Goes (1908–) who, in two *Novellen, Unruhige Nacht* (1949) and *Das Brandopfer* (1954), makes Christian points the most unforgettably. An army chaplain tells of the Russian campaign; a butcher's wife, serving meat rations, suddenly realizes the horror of Nazi exterminations.

Goes counsels forgiveness but Ernst Jünger (1895–), one of the most isolated figures in modern German literature, has preached reform of the élite: the apex of the triangle, not its base. Clinical, persuaded of logic's power, he epitomizes all that Mann regarded as Leverkühn's punishment. 'To sacrifice oneself for a faith', Jünger has written, 'means to reach one's maximum, irrespective of whether that faith is true or false', and his main concern is not with adjustment but with 'an ultra-human reality' beyond and within us. He sets modern problems in a mythic world and illustrates, in fact, the German habit of abstracting and then packing the abstraction with details picked from the original instances. The result, as in *Auf den Marmorklippen* (1939) and *Heliopolis* (1949), is a meticulously described super-reality poised in the mental empyrean. His theme is aristocracy *versus* dema-goguery; privilege *versus* plebs; in fact, the age-old feuds con-ducted in an increasingly well-equipped laboratory. In *Auf den Marmorklippen* the *Oberförster* (plebeian demagogue) has things his own way over the aristocracy, but the Mauretanians in *Heliopolis* stand in no danger from the grasping *Landvogt*. In pursuing this social counterpoint ('two great races, each with a wholly different conception of happiness') Jünger sets aside all notions of fraternity, charity and 'presence'. Conflict is inevitable so long as there is life; what matter its degree? His is, perhaps, the callousness of the statistician, the military planner, the clinical botanist (all of which Jünger is). The aristocrats in his novels have sensibility in plenty but little sympathy. This is important, for sensibility does not always develop into sympathy; and we often excuse a person whose extreme sensitivity to the sufferings or joys of others almost destroys him and compels him to be callous or indifferent. A man, we say, has his own troubles: not all men can, or should, participate in the troubles of others. And to participate in the joys of others is often the most exacting labour of all.

It would be generous and perhaps just to excuse Jünger on these grounds. A sensitive man who dare not be compassionate, he evolves an attitude from which all human response is banned. He advocates total mobilization, a process which alters the world to assuage a private embarrassment. He has no instinct for the *via media*. He cannot vacillate. He needs an extreme, and one that is simple and consistent. Neither his sense of history nor his feeling for life is complex enough. His imagination outruns his sense of reality. He invents extremes which justify his own apathy. He describes man's condition as tragic, and then excludes himself from the human condition. He has immense will-power; he has used it in forging a vigorous and impressive myth of modern life. And much in the world which is vicious and intractable has been coerced into that myth:

> It is enough to look at this life of ours in its full unleashed vehemence and in its pitiless discipline, with its smoking and glowing hunting-grounds, with the physics and metaphysics of its transport, its engines, planes, and cities of millions, in order to divine with a feeling of horror mixed with lust that there is here no atom which is *not at work*, and that we ourselves are deeply involved in this process.

He has enough ingenuity and enough will-power to invent a myth, but not enough maturity and balance to control it. *Feuer und Blut* (1926) and *In Stahlgewittern* (1942) are frightening documents rather like Barbusse tinged with Blake. But they come more under reportage than under myth-making. It is in such later works as *Auf den Marmorklippen* and *Heliopolis* that the narratives assume the stature of meaning, and begin to offend by their presumptuous obloquy. But Jünger is to be commended for having tried to remedy the stagnation into which literature has been compelled by the Pastoralism-or-Silence dilemma in poetry and by the Realism-or-Gentility dilemma in the novel. His mythology is raw and intricate. It represents the teeming ant-life of industrial towns, the mushroom-white faces of the workers; the taut men who move switches in the silent control-rooms of power-plants; the high-speed fliers who see no reason for not attempting even greater speeds; the tomb of the mine; the stark paraphernalia of colliery and factory; the close coffin of the battle-trench. All this is the *Werkstättenlandschaft* (work-shop-zone), dominated by the despotic *Oberförster* and his Mauretanian freebooters. Marina is a tranquil lake; but tran-quillity and serenity in this myth are always thwarted. There are huts full of corpses and speared skulls. At the research-centre in *Heliopolis* experiments are conducted on living patients; love is always between fugitives, and happiness is clandestine.

Such, one would like to say, is not an accurate version of life as we know it. Jünger flaunts his concocted nihilism with all the dead jargon of the fanatic: 'Only the utter disintegration of the old structure makes it possible for there to appear the reality of another field of forces.' This is a sombre travesty of sombre events; but he thinks such ideas will help to displace what he considers a dead humanism. Yet it is possible to feel that the stagy reverberations of the word *Zersplitterung* (disintegration) give some kind of a game away. Perhaps he is merely toying with a literary idea. But his logic, or what he offers as rectilinear thinking, is grimly perverse. If humanism is dead, then he must crusade for whatever had the power to kill it. If wars destroy progress and develop out of progress, then wars must be made vast enough to engulf everything. What is to be rejoiced about is our ability *to conceive of completeness*. And nothing is more complete and consistent than nullity.

Prophets are, nevertheless, always offering patterns; and novelists and even historians often act like prophets. A work such as *The Dynasts* is really a ponderous guess: these things may not be thus, but otherwise. So, Jünger, who in *Über den Schmerz* (1936) wrote off pain as irremediable and inescapable, retracts his assertion and tries to make it less of a fiction. Not everything goes on in the deathly realm. Some institutions still serve the people. Pain is not ubiquitous, and surgical indifference not always necessary. *Besuch auf Godenholm* (1952) and *Gläserne Bienen* (1957) present, respectively, not the life-conflict but dejected ex-soldiers trafficking with a Norwegian wizard and an ex-calvary officer contemplating a job at a mechanical-toy factory. But the bees are artificial and artificial human ears are floating on the garden pool. The officer, however, needs money, just as the soldiers need faith; so he takes the job, even though it entails his subjection to mechanized artificiality. The machine age wins. The wizards and tycoons exact obedience and keep us ticking over while we calculate the life-price. The pity is that so original, deep-reaching and up-to-date a novelist as Jünger should write a prose so repellently lapidary. His clever verbal tiling, covering so many German skeletons, proves his unwitting honesty, but at the same time insulates the reader from his talk of 'hope' in much the same way as a rough-and-ready zest for life alienates us from his cult of death. But his warnings about the role of the mere *Arbeiter* (Worker) cannot be ignored; nor can his performance, typifying as it does the modern German novelist's peculiar temptations and skills.

II

Jünger's interest in botany is one aspect of a wider movement which contrasts the bucolic unfavourably with the urban and technological. All the same, his botanical studies awaken him to the minute detail of an insistent universe and draw him into fatalism. Jünger, less obviously than Carossa and Hesse, presents reality by appearing to discard it. Utopia iconoclastically accuses and Arcadia, as found in Otto Heuschele's *Musik durchbricht die Nacht* (1956) and Hanna Stephan's *Der Dritte* (1952), rebukes: the disruptive forces of war, industrialism and political greed drive man back to Nature, at once returning him to animality and freeing him of neurosis. Bernt von Heiseler's *Apollonia* (1941) shows love in a rural setting and his *Versöhnung* (1953), set in a Bavarian country estate, opposes Lutheran Christianity and the whole spirit of pride in countryside to the Nazi doctrine of force. Once again, disintegration of an old order sends the novelist back to the familiar, silent, undiscriminating tyranny of the land

and the weather. The difference is between a chosen regime and an inflicted one, and we have only to consider (as Heiseler does) the nature of Nazi persecution to understand why Germans have come to regard the countryside as a free zone akin to a utopia.

Chaos is the theme of Oskar Maria von Graf's *Die Eroberung einer Welt* (1948): virtuous government somewhat improbably restores order after a hypothetical third world war. Much more grandiose, and possibly more acceptable, *Stern der Ungeborenen* (1945), by Franz Werfel (1890–1945), anticipates life as it will be in 100,000 years' time. Werfel, who was prominent among the Expressionists and (unfortunately) is best known for *Das Lied von Bernadette* (1941), has much in common with H. G. Wells, Orwell and Aldous Huxley. His timid new world, set in California, is secure and well run but hermetic, like that in Forster's story 'The Machine Stops'. It is continually threatened by the modern savages who so far have been shut away, in reservations, like American Indians. But the savages prevail and the over-delicate civilization crumbles: a fine instance of Jünger's point concerning implacable Nature, and a stark reversal of the bucolic idyll. Werfel's amorphous prose suggests, in itself, a chaos not quite tamed. A similar novel, Hermann Kasack's *Die Stadt hinter dem Strom* (1947), deals with life after death; everyone lives underground and in accordance with a highly developed etiquette. The hero, Robert Lindhoff, is the only man alive beyond the river; an orientalized Kafka character, he is a protest against material prosperity, cold reason and the gaudy ballyhoo typified in Kasack's more vigorous but less profound novel about Hollywood, *Das grosse Netz* (1952). Walter Jens's *Nein, Die Welt der Angeklagten* (1950), in which the future world-state has organized mankind into three estates of animality, is a directer *1984*; and his next novel, *Der Blinde* (1951), about a middle-aged man who suddenly goes blind, creates a moving metaphor of man's efforts to adjust to immutable conditions. His other novels are much less arresting, largely because he is not covertly writing philosophy: *Vergessene Gesichter* (1952) and *Der Mann, der nicht alt werden wollte* (1955) deal respectively with retired actors and the academic world. These two novels have an oddly trivial air and the writing seems tired, as if Jens had nothing much left. His antithesis is Arno Schmidt, a mordant and gnomic stylist, fond of the role of seedy Diogenes and of the journal form. His acerb *Leviathan* (1949) describes a train journey from Berlin in 1945; the route is eastwards and towards death. Time and again in the German imagination, lightly undertaken journeys conduct the traveller into limbo or metaphysical doom. For Schmidt, life is a cheerless conundrum. The ex-soldier in *Brand's Haide* (1951) takes what spiritual aliment he can from the food-parcels his ex-mistress sends him from America. Why, Schmidt seems to ask in his *Aus dem Leben eines Faunes* (1953), should *not* Allied bombing eliminate the fatuities of German provincial life? Once again the pessimistic absolutism of Jünger reappears, but Schmidt's sardonic turn of mind prevents his work from being portentous. His satires deserve to be more widely read.

Stefan Andres has specialized in presenting political themes in vast images of epic associations. *Wir sind Utopia* (1942) deals with the Spanish Civil War and shows a monk re-entering the world in pursuit of a civic ideal. *Die Hochzeit der Feinde* (1947) probes into relationships between France and Germany; *Ritter der Gerechtigkeit* (1948) deals briskly with Mussolini and *Die Sintflut*, an uneven trilogy, shows the rise of a Nazi, Moosthaler, his eventual assumption of complete power and his persecution of dissident minorities. Time and again Andres saves himself from being dreary by giving full scope to an almost Dickensian gift for hyperbole and inflation: *Die Reise nach Portiuncula* (1954), for instance, confronts us with a middle-aged brewer on holiday in Italy, revisiting the scene of an old love-affair. It is a theme which could lead to both grossness and whimsy, but in Andres's hands it leads to neither; on the contrary, the novel is larger than life in being intensely thoughtful beneath an arabesque surface.

Other German novelists have followed along lines summed up by Ernst Kreuder, who in *Die Gesellschaft vom Dachboden* (1946) sets the members of a secret society discussing means of asserting imagination against the bourgeoisie, alleged realists and highbrow sophists. Their motives are hearty but the resulting slapstick (Laurel and Hardy and Chaplin being the avatars) is dismally thin. Kreuder's next novel, *Die Unauffindbaren* (1948), resumes this theme of slack pleasure-seeking in the story of an estate-agent who leaves his Sunday afternoon routine and gets involved in a series of bizarre adventures which have a strongly surrealist flavour. Kreuder manipulates his topsy-turvy world adroitly and delicately, and H. M. Waidson in *The Modern German Novel* (1959) has suggested an interesting parallel with Henry Green and L. P. Hartley. But the writer evoked by Kreuder's most powerful novel, *Herein ohne anzuklopfen* (1954), is the T. S. Eliot of *The Elder Statesman*: the characters repine, retreat, elect to vegetate rather than submit further to, or urge onwards, the pandemonium of modern civilization. Kreuder's concern with innocence and retreat reappears in the work of a much more dynamic novelist, Hans Erich Nossack, whose *Nekyia, Bericht eines Überlebenden* (1947) uses the unknown region between death and reincarnation as a metaphor of Germany's post-war period. The narrator is the only survivor of his own society, and the world in which he moves is a phantasmagoria based on a national nightmare. Hamburg is bombed in the supposedly factual reports of *Dorothea* (1948), and the black marketeer personifies death. In *Spätestens im November* (1955), however, the industrialist whose wife leaves him for her writer lover is the incarnation of death-in-life: the writer and the wife, who are eventually killed in a car-accident, know something of genuine life, which is the life of the spirit sketched, once more, against an antithetical business world, in *Der jüngere Bruder* (1958).

Gottfried Benn (1886–1956) was both a highbrow charlatan and a lavish stylist. His *Der Ptolemäer* (1949) has a beauty-specialist for hero and world-weariness for theme. The New Germany is developing into a barren maze of concrete, cars and regained luxuries. Religion is a fool's game, like technology, and the only truly comfortable people are the recluse and the crook. The former is better if he happens to be an artist: 'Blow the world as if it were glass, like breath from a pipe.' Through art, said Benn, we can still control the civilization we have allowed to get out of hand. In spite of his nihilism and his voluptuary's fingering of futility, Benn makes a sharp verbal impact, proving his point about the glassblower at the same time as explaining the pointlessness of all else.

Elisabeth Langgässer (1899–1950) wrote an early novel, *Proserpina* (1932), about a child of five poised between good and evil, which displays her fondness for dualisms as the structural basis of semi-allegorical novels. *Das unauslöschliche Siegel* (1946)

deals with a Jew who turns Roman Catholic and spends much of
his time in the role of cultivated idler, seeking high-class oblivion.
He walks all the mazes of futility, gradually succumbing to vivid
dementia, but is eventually redeemed by grace. An earlier novel,
Der Gang durch das Ried (1936), had advanced a similar theme:
a young man runs away to the Foreign Legion, ends up in a
mental hospital and finally returns to his childhood haunts. All
of Elisabeth Langgässer's novels entail a journey through the
Valley of the Shadow and a redemption. Her main fault is her
tendency to reproduce the characters' wanderings in the structure;
she seems to think any digression an enactment of her point.
In *Märkische Argonautenfahrt* (1950), for instance, a band of
people travel from Berlin to a monastery in quest of some kind of
grail. The prose is mannered, the Catholic emphasis unrelenting,
and the whole reads like Graham Greene crossed with Faulkner.
Her characters know much of sulphurous sin and inward fester-
ing, but their visions (or intuitions) of the divine calm them
down.

Journeys abound in the modern German novel: usually
journeys home. Disintegration and mental incoherence are the
themes of Werner Warsinsky's first novel, *Kimmerische Fahrt*
(1953), and also qualities of the writing. Time and again we see
the German imagination probing inwards, hoping to achieve
some integration with which to face the disordered post-war
world. Heinz Risse's *Irrfahrer* (1948) sets an ex-prisoner of war
in the same flaccid, shattered post-war world, and Willi Heinrich's
Die Gezeichtneten (1959) watches over the return of yet another
soldier. In this novel Heinrich deserts the incandescent war scenes
of *Das geduldige Fleisch* (1955) for the sedater ethos of post-war
Nuremberg. Heinrich is the boom's muckraker, the Suetonius of
the new-rich moguls who got away with infamy or turpitude and
now ride in sleek Mercedes, dreaming of the *Herrenvolk*'s next
millennium. They either pay the blackmailer or keep him in gaol
on indefinite remand. Into their world of muffled conscience,
well-fed piety and busy obesity comes a former soldier, Hergett
Buchholz, just released from a Siberian prison-camp.[1] Clumsy,

1. Cf. Erich Landgrebe's *In sieben Tagen* (1955) and Gerd Gaiser's *Eine
Stimme hebt an* (1950), in both of which returning soldiers are movingly
portrayed.

emaciated, shabby and resentfully sincere, he returns to his voluptuous ex-wife and a desultory, futile love-affair with the daughter of a crypto-Nazi *Landrat*. But Buchholz is too much of a misfit to convince women or hold a job: he takes his emotional bearings from his family home in Ilmenau, now in the Eastern Zone. Gradually, in his bewildered and idealizing mind, Ilmenau becomes an image of lost Eden; and in a pathetic and desperate attempt to cross the frontier he brings about his own death. Ilmenau, source of regeneration, is unattainable: the crooked *arrivistes* and smug power-seekers have no time for it. The plight of unparadised Man moves them not at all, absorbed as they are in the mundane gratifications of the *Wirtschaftwunder*.

Rich in unobtrusive allegories, savagely vivid in its denunciations, tender but never mawkish in portraying alienation, this novel fuses several genres. There are no incongruities. The bouncing farce of *Landrat* Schneider and his wife ('those two-hundred-pound mounds of flesh')—his petty fornications and her passion for layer-cake—supplies gross counterpoint to the record of Buchholz's spiritual progress. Heinrich does everything possible to balance indictment with allegory, to ensure the one's completeness and ballast the other with the unmitigated ordinariness of everyday life. *Die Gezeichtneten* is an energetic parable—a piece of Sinclair Lewis documentation informed with a Wyndham Lewis acidity. The flashbacks are relevant and unforced, and there is one brilliant scene in which the drunken *Landrat*, standing with Buchholz in a deserted open-air amphitheatre outside Nuremberg, orates with Hitlerian hysteria from the very spot where the lost leader himself had stood. But most impressive of all is Heinrich's ability to make us see faces and physiques: each character is seen through the eyes of several others; and much care goes into the attaining of this synoptic effect. The result is Babylon anatomized, its bad heart dissected, integrity banished like the *Steppenwolf* and the national mania shown renascent.

The book communicates both shame and hatred without ever seeming reiterative or snivelling. It is a positive document, saddening, but respectful of liberal and humane ways of living; and from it emerges a final vision rather like Brueghel's 1559 drawing, *Allegory of Hope*. Brueghel's characters too act under compulsion, meshed in a temporal, seasonal and nurtural web;

and Nature is his remedy too. (Buchholz's vision of Ilmenau is of a refuge both pastoral and simple-featured; nothing could be farther from the manic rush of the German technological recovery. Buchholz is, in fact, in the line of descent from Werther; Ilmenau derives from Weimar and Utopia.) Harmony with Nature outstrips and transcends all obsessions. Heinrich's version of Hope is rather grim; but Buchholz transcends his wasteful death and seems to linger in the mind, dominating like a ghost the grotesque cartoon of the lumpish, new German democracy.

The other novels of Heinz Risse, whom I mention above, recall Kafka and specialize in incongruous mixtures of genres. His first novel, *Wenn die Erde bebt* (1950), belongs in the same category as Johnson's *Rasselas*. As in *Rasselas* itself, there is a personage who predicts the future; Risse's hero works in an insurance office and refuses to place his gift at his firm's command. During the earthquakes, people become charitable to one another; but afterwards they revert to their usual spiritual meanness. *So frei von Schuld* (1951) is a similar kind of tale about a modern Job who, after disaster upon disaster has unfairly fallen upon him, wonders what hope there is except in returning to thoughtless animality. *Belohne dich selbst* (1953) is a fable which epitomizes the argument of *Dann kam der Tag* (1953) about an old man who tries to burn down his own factory in remorse for a life of success based on insincerity. Risse's best writing occurs when he takes the trouble to pack his didactic pattern with the stuff of contemporary life. He is as much a novelist of manners as of man in the abstract.

Altogether more Conradian (and even reminiscent of Thomas Wolfe), Hans Henny Jahnn (1894–1959) attempted a pageant of the archetypal wanderer. His *Fluss ohne Ufer* (1937–50) is about the stream of life and of consciousness-in-life. His hero, Horn, knocks about the world as a sailor, his conscience seared by a catastrophe at sea; he has been trying to forget (like the heroes of Elisabeth Langgässer) and eventually turns to music, spurred on by a pianola in a down-at-heel South American hotel. Obsessively detailed and staccato, Jahnn's writing controls and ties down the sea-swell of his theme: his blend of *Bildungsroman* and *Künstler-roman*, of Jünger-like resignation and surrealist violence, brings about one of the most enthralling, most morbid modern German novels.

Time, the river, can be firmly conceived of only as past and future; the present is a hypothesis, a mere line. The past yields mythologies; the notion of the future provokes visions of utopia; and in both instances time is malefic. Hermann Broch (1886–1951), an Austrian and an admirer of Joyce, commended Joyce's ability to create a subtle microcosm of the human condition. Where Jünger is driven into absolute attitudes, Broch strives to be comprehensive: to forge a timeless image which implies everything. His trilogy, *Die Schlafwandler* (1931–2), embodies its didacticism in a trio of contrasting men—in much the same manner as Irwin Shaw's *The Young Lions*—and suggests the passage of time by concentrating on three periods. But, periods notwithstanding—and they cannot withstand time at all —Broch moves naturally into the stream-of-consciousness technique. The whole world is thus made interior, put within one character's possession, and so becomes implicit in everyone's private symbolism.

It was logical that Broch should, in *Der Tod des Vergil* (1945), fix upon the Roman poet's last eighteen hours and attempt to suggest them through a colossal interior monologue. Dying Vergil, losing faith in his work and discussing with Augustus, is a representative figure of the same intensity and extent as Mann's Leverkühn. For Broch, art is by no means everything: what counts in life is charity, awareness and 'presence'. *Die Schuldlosen* (1950) rebukes the Stephen Dedaluses, the Meursaults and Hemingway's numbed sensitives; *Die unbekannte Grösse* (1933) argues the futility of seeking knowledge for its own sake. Life, in Broch's novels, is dynamic, epitomized in the beating heart which is also vulnerable and susceptible, as *Der Versucher* (1953) shows. A religious fanatic stirs up an Alpine village until a ritual murder takes place. The basic story might have come from Erskine Caldwell, but the writing is complex and the symbolism heavy. Elemental forces keep betraying man's intelligence, and metaphysical impulses keep distorting the mere narrative. Broch has to be read for his massiveness and lyricism, but he too often attempts transcendences which are beyond the verbal medium.

Even vaster metaphors have been constructed. Robert Musil (1880–1942), in his 1600-page *Der Mann Ohne Eigenschaften*, first published as a whole in 1952, deals with a new Faust: a

'Man without Qualities', a man who lives for himself only. Ulrich, the hero, emerges against a backcloth of neo-Dostoevskian extremists: men of divided heart; a society hostess with a passion for soul (and later for sexology); a highly strung young wife infatuated with a killer; mystics, amoralists and aesthetic brahmins. The pageant of Austrian society is prodigiously detailed without coming alive; it is a scientist's tabulation of phenomena. Musil's main interest is in typifying various social attitudes, whether moral or political; and the work as a whole is like an aromatic harness-shop with horses blatantly not in evidence. A comi-tragedy of humours, it writes the obituary of Yesterday's Arrangements and of military élites. Musil claimed that he wrote for people who do not exist—at least until they have read him. He worries endlessly about why things are not otherwise instead of as they are, and succumbs to the lure of hypothesis: surely, thinks Ulrich, there is possible a new morality attainable through mysticism and mathematics. But history drives inexorably on, leaving Ulrich high and dry, a high-minded anachronism casting around for an ideal harness. Musil is difficult reading, but he certainly spells out the consequences of undue scepticism mixed with German perfectionism. It is interesting to study the seeds of Ulrich's perfectionism in the twisted psychologies on show in Musil's novel about a boys' boarding-school, *Die Verwirrungen des Zöglings Törless* (1906). To Ulrich, it seems, having no qualities and no commitments is better than developing bad ones.

A third Austrian novelist, Heimito von Doderer (1896–), makes the same points as Broch and Musil but much less apocalyptically. He is interested not so much in attitudes or ideas as in individuals, and his main concern, in his two principal novels, is to celebrate the quality of lives lived—however many modern impediments there are. Doderer is like a witty rubberneck strolling along. *Die Dämonen* (1956) is as much a comedy of manners as an indictment of mechanized living, while *Die Strudlhofstiege* (1951) complicatedly interweaves two periods of time as a prelude to *Die Dämonen* and microscopically studies Major Melzer's progress from meek diffidence to social assurance. Doderer mingles meandering with switchback, meditation with comic extravaganza, momentous event (the burning of the Palace of Justice in Vienna in 1927) with literary selfconsciousness (two mutually mocking narrators), and lubricious gusto (one character makes a sexual study of fat women) with demonic possession. All in all, a potent synthesis more vivid and detailed than Broch's, more 'life-enhancing' than Musil's. Doderer's disapproval of modern society neither prevents him from laughing nor causes his laughter to be nihilistic. If an Austrian precariousness continually reminds him of the skull beneath the skin, of the beast beneath the brain, an unfussing mundanity keeps him steady and devoted to the immediate present. He is strongly against fantasies and visions, but just as strongly in favour of such an ostentatious sensibleness as that recommended by C. P. Snow; and this down-to-earthness makes him of all the modern Germans the most graphic, wide-ranging and least bloatedly metaphysical specialist in microcosm.

Doderer's delight in social surfaces can be found in the work of other, less ambitous novelists who engage in philatelic reassurance or documentary nostalgia. Max René Hesse (1885–1952), in his *Dietrich Kattenburg* trilogy (1937–50), probes and reports in the orthodox manner of the *Bildungsroman*. His hero Dietrich grows convincingly up in the presence of the awkward, old bourgeois, military traditions. The novel creates no appetites which it fails to satisfy, and it is typical of a tradition which includes Johannes R. Becher's episodic *Abschied* (1948), Anna Seghers's proletarian novels, the best of which are *Die Toten bleiben jung* (1949) and *Transit* (1944), about German refugees; and the social realism of Alfred Döblin's *Berlin Alexanderplatz* (1929), which employs the interior monologue, and *November, 1918* (1939–50), a tetralogy about the Berlin revolution.

German documentary novels usually exhibit twin emotions: near-incredulity at the ordinariness of life after catastrophe, and baffled fascination because vast national manias suck their power from ordinary lives. Kasimir Edschmid's *Das gute Recht* (1946) studies a family during war, and *Der Zauberfaden* (1949) the artificial-silk industry. Hermann Kesten's *Die Zwillinge von Nürnberg* (1947), apart from some facile ironies of plot, convincingly portrays two contrasting careers against the events from 1918 to 1945. In this novel, as in Edschmid's *Das gute Recht*, there appears the familiar writer-artist figure: the man apart who becomes morally implicated in a national crescendo. He senses the futility of war before the event, whereas that other recurring

German figure, the returning soldier, comes back a misfit and therefore evolves attitudes to match. And, of course, in the post-war boom, the Künstler-figure once again shrinks from bumptious industrialism; the old national momentum piles up while prosperity is assumed to be its own justification. It is not surprising that such writers as Jünger think in terms of 'process' and automatons. After heroic nihilists electing to let the war-process have its way with them, there come the heroes of national resurgence; and the whole idea of 'process' eliminates notions of responsibility.

These points are made, not always intentionally, by the best of the war novels. In Alexander Lernet-Holenia's *Mars im Widder* (1941) an Austrian officer similar to Julien Gracq's pensive sensitive in *Un Balcon en forêt* is borne along in the invasions of 1939. Heroic necrophilia on the Russian front is the theme of Erich Landgrebe's *Mit dem Ende beginnt es* (1951). The Lutheran pastor in Kurt Ihlenfeld's *Wintergewitter* (1951) meditates on suicide and stoicism, as does the journalist conscience-figure in the same author's *Kommt Wieder, Menschenkinder* (1954), in which Ihlenfeld writes at his most densely philosophical. Much more superficial, Dieter Meichsner's *Weisst du warum?* (1952) is about a fanatical German remnant in the Bavarian Alps; it might have come from Hemingway whereas *Die Studenten von Berlin* (1954), set in the last days of the war, attempts a complex social image but fails to control its mass of material.

No account of war-reportage should omit Hans Werner Richter's boldly drawn *Die Geschlagenen* (1949), *Sie Fielen aus Gottes Hand* (1951), the latter being notable for its portrait of the helpless and homeless in a D.P. camp, although the portrayal is more cursory than that in David Rousset's *L'Univers concentrationnaire*, and globe-trotting flashbacks (which distort *Du sollst nicht töten*, 1955) keep everything rather superficial. Richter shows little of the psychological and spiritual penetration of Luise Rinser's *Mitte des Lebens* (1950), a moving account of a resistance heroine, or of the picaresque-satirical mood conspicuous in Rudolf Krämer-Badoni's *In der Grossen Drift* (1949), or of the intellectual sharpness of *Die Insel hinter dem Vorhang* (1955), the curtain is the 'iron' one. But even Richter is subtler than Erich Maria Remarque (*Im Westen nichts Neues*, 1929; *Arc de*

Triomphe, 1946) and Hans Hellmut Kirst (*Null-acht-fünfzehn*, 1954–5). Theodor Plievier (1892–1955), on the other hand, makes few concessions to popular taste in his almost bureaucratically documentary trilogy *Stalingrad* (1946), *Moskau* (1952), *Berlin* (1954). But the O'Hara-like cataloguing is redeemed by auto-biographical lunges and apocalyptic set-pieces.

Naturally enough, the German is torn between a marvelling close scrutiny of the facts and an attempt to generalize them (both blurring and commanding them). The documentary-*versus*-myth dilemma also invites resolution through the historical novel. Werner Bergengruen, for instance, in *Der Grosstyrann und das Gericht* (1935), presents his attack on *ad hoc* justice through a potentate of the Italian Renaissance. *Am Himmel wie auf Erden* (1940) shows sixteenth-century Berlin expecting a second Great Flood—an interesting contrast with Stefan Andres's *Die Sintflut*. Which is remoter from modern times, Bergengruen's old Berlin or Andres's unplaced region, it is hard to say. Both are metaphors, but Bergengruen's is the more facile and the less portentous, perhaps because he excels at the *Novelle* and short story and prefers surfaces to depth. His most persuasive fables (persuasive as fables only) are *Pelageja* (1947), related almost in the manner of *The Old Man and the Sea* by a shipwrecked sailor, and *Das Feuerzeichen* (1949) about the suicide of a recluse. Bergengruen's imagery—cavalry officers, nineteenth-century Russia, courtly courtesies and displaced aristocrats—celebrates a defeated way of life but, in doing so, also partly defeats itself by depriving the novels of emotional claims other than those of plot and tension.

Gertrud von Le Fort, on the other hand, is not so anxious to lament the passing of a social code: she unsentimentally, without glibness or blithe arabesques, finds historical parallels: a Carmelite nun during the French Revolution (*Die Letzte am Schafott*, 1931), the Thirty Years War (*Die Magdeburgische Hochzeit*, 1938), Guelph and Ghibelline feud (*Die Tochter Farinatas*, 1950). Most of her *Novellen* have historical settings, but in *Gelöschte Kerzen* (1953) she combines ancient and modern with bewitching poignancy, just as in *Am Tor des Himmels* (1954) she combines the story of Galileo with a modern air-raid. In fact, whether she is refurbishing Pontius Pilate (*Frau des Pilatus*, 1955) or the persecution of the Huguenots (*Der Turm der Beständigkeit*, 1957), she almost always achieves an ideal of unevasive analogy. Some-times, as in her major work, *Das Schweisstuch der Veronika* (1928–46), she over-insists on the right-mindedness attainable only through religious orthodoxy. But, usually, like Pilate's wife, she shows how to unite individuality and spiritual certainty without losing the power to open one's heart.

When events move as quickly and violently as they have done in Germany since 1920, many writers are reluctant to commit themselves to vast projects; and one of the most intriguing phenomena in post-war German literature has been the vogue for brevity—for *Novellen*, short stories, sketches, parables and short fables. This is not the place to explore in detail the many fine examples of these forms, of which Mann's *Mario und der Zauberer* (1929) is a prototype. But mention must be made of Wolfgang Borchert (1921–1947), quick, deft and mercurial in this genre; Ilse Aichinger (who also wrote a moving novel about a Jewish girl, *Die Grössere Hoffnung*, 1948), and Gerd Gaiser, whose novels *Das Schiff im Berg* (1953), *Eine Stimme hebt an* (1950) and *Die sterbende Jagd* (1953) are rather laboured and over-ingeniously pretend to blurt things out. Heinrich Böll, some of whose works have been translated into English, ignores the pre-war world and constructs an actuality of neon and ruins in accordance with his view that reality is what we make it. After two war novels, *Der Zug war pünktlich* (1949) and *Wo warst du, Adam?* (1950), he developed subtler, less 'either/or' attitudes in two novels about family life: *Und sagte kein einziges Wort* (1953) and *Haus ohne Hüter* (1954). Once again, ineluctable processes (war and post-war regeneration) dwarf average man: against the world of *Machtpolitik*, bombers, treaties, overcrowding in bombed buildings, seedy poverty and barren wealth he has little chance. The steel, concrete and glass superstructure of the German Miracle impress Böll not at all, whereas love at sight (experienced by the previously humdrum mechanic in *Das Brot der frühen Jahre*, 1955) is a transfiguring illumination. Böll writes an illus-trious vernacular, is at his sharpest and least fanciful in his short stories, and, through regarding 'reality' as our own private inter-ference with an established order, achieves truth in fantasy without becoming whimsical. This cannot be said for many German novelists of the previous generation.

In summary, we notice the pervasive *Bildungsroman* tradition growing even stronger because of calamity's impersonal disregard of individual lives, and a consequent fondness, among the older generation of novelists, for the occupations of man in privacy: abstract speculation, interior monologue, self-defining and world-evaluating. Surrealism has become merely a useful technique in an all-out effort to make sense out of life, to 'make new' the supreme patterns or myths which confer power because they make life seem predictable. As Robert Musil's Ulrich says:

> Most people are in their fundamental relationship to themselves narrators. . . . They like the orderly arrangement of facts in sequence, because this makes it look like a form of necessity, and they feel somehow protected in the midst of chaos by the impression that their life has a 'course' to run.

Of such inward certainty and public incoherence German novelists are still writing a good deal. Jünger, for instance, even finds inevitable destruction reassuring: a fixed fact—or at least a fact he will fix in his own imagination. But the craving for an absolute is paralleled, among the younger novelists, by a preference for Hemingway-type adventure stories and slightly adjusted social photography. Inner turmoil has almost always, in modern Germany, found its analogues in society; so all kinds of celestial cities, Uranopolises, *Urbes Beatae* and fictive regions (both physical and metaphysical) have been invented for the purpose of mythologizing reproof and despair. We have only to study the Swiss novelists—say, the mildly rebellious Robert Walser (1878–1956), Alfred Kübler (whose main work is the long, staid and stable *Öppi*, 1943–51) and Kurt Guggenheim (*Der Friede des Herzens*, 1956)—to see the differences and to appreciate the *planche de salut* offered the novelist by a stable society. Even Max Frisch's *Stiller* (1954), for all its deliberate debunkings of the Swiss way (sensible, hygienic and minor), misses the extravagance of Jünger, Hesse, Jahnn and Kasack, to mention only a few. The Germans, like the Americans, inherit myth-mindedness and easily become grandiose while seeking to relate minutiae to a grand pattern. It is not straining things to see in the renewed popularity of the *Novelle* not only the youngest Germans' impatience and sense of impermanence, but also their repudiation of the heroic décor which characterized an older generation of novelists and, most of all, the old Germany itself. At its most impressive, the modern German novel affirms that while cataclysm and calamity impersonally ignore individual man, it is not man's job to impersonate calamity. The youngest novelists and exponents of the shorter prose forms stress nothing so much as the need for men's 'presence', one to another, whether facing disaster, recovery, materialism, persecution, wolves, rivers of death, malign magicians, time's uncounted clocks or the devil himself. And the person who stands most severely rebuked is the *Künstler* wherever he tries to close his heart against his fellows.

Western Germany in the post-war period suffers still from paralysis by guilt. A committed humanism bravely exposing its chin is the last thing we find; after 1918 it was different, and the '*engagement*' of such writers as Werfel, Becher and Ernst Toller was similar to that recently undertaken by Sartre, Camus and, rather longer ago, André Malraux. It is hard to spot the political affiliation of modern West German novelists, conservative or socialist; such matters have palled into comparative insignificance, so much so as to remind us that the Second World War cut off the Germans completely, whereas the previous war, for all its cataclysmic impact (the first war of its kind), did not sever all lines of European cultural communication. The post-1945 German is a severed head who has not even, as the French have always had, a tradition of disputatious over-concern with social and political issues. Sartre's arguments with Camus, for instance, have no parallel in West Germany even now (allowing for the time-lag), and never have had. A Thomas Mann, trying to make up his mind, cannot argue publicly. In *Buddenbrooks* (1901) and his early *Novellen* he exposed the necrophilia beneath the vainglory of Imperial Germany, but in 1914 sided with bourgeois *Kultur*. Even in that weird tract of 1918, his *Reflections of a Non-political Man* (a title no Frenchman could have arrived at), he stuck to his anti-democratic position and, in *A Sketch of my Life*, describes this book as 'the last great retreat action, fought not without gallantry, of a romantic bourgeoisie in the face of the triumphant "new" '. All the same, the Mann of *Von deutscher*

Republik did break through, far enough to attack Nazi romanticism and to write, during his exile in California, *Doktor Faustus*. But Zeitblom-Mann *versus* Leverkühn-Mann (dull democrat *versus* spectacular Teuton) remains an imperfect contest because Mann never quite deserted the bourgeoisie: Brecht did. And we have to consult Mann's letters to Paul Amann, the Austrian Jew, to see the full torment which Mann went through while trying to justify his 'patriotism'. Amann, writing from the bloody front, rebukes Mann's 1914 chauvinism, and Mann writhes.

The example is revealing because the self-questioning that Mann pursued in those letters, even while he was composing *Reflections*, was private; had to be private. And things were easier then than in the thirties. Even so early, Mann typifies the isolated, shut-in German, more interested in the religious aspect of politics than in platform details. Immediately after 1945 the pent-up urge for humanitarian commitment burst out, and Wolfgang Borchert, now an almost mythical figure, is typical. The situation was extreme: it was not a matter of *which* programme but of re-establishing valid values, and this during the mental pandemonium of guilt and the physical epic of merely surviving. Salvage, not innovation, was the theme. After all, Germany was in foreign hands, and compromises were obligatory. It is revealing, therefore, to find Heidegger proposing not a philosophy of action or a basis for humane politics, but philosophy without results, not even metaphysical, yet an end in itself. This is the application to philosophy of aestheticism: art for art's sake, the attitude castigated in Britain by C. P. Snow and in France by Sartre and Camus. Compared with such a professional French philosopher as the late Merleau-Ponty, Heidegger is hermitic, his system hermetic. And Heidegger's view squares with Gottfried Benn's assertion that 'Works of art are phenomena, historically ineffective, without practical consequences'. This is like Nietzsche refurbished by Stefan George; and it leads us at once to the other side of Benn's proposition: if what you do has no consequences, or, rather, if what you do in art and philosophy has no consequences in history, then you are not *responsible* so long as you devote yourself to art. What, then, of what *does* happen in history? That is beyond our control: that is the process, the unending cycle of Nature which persists, no matter how we tamper with it. Man is a part of Nature, like the silkworm and the fox.

This is the rationale of Jünger's zoological and botanical writings in *Strahlungen* (1949), his diary during wartime. Jünger, a devout right-winger after 1918, resembles the Malraux who became the most fervent of Gaullists after 1945. Both, for similar reasons, now fix on the impersonal processes of the cosmos: on recurrences, cycles and patterns. Jünger, writing on East and West in *Der Gordische Knoten* (1953), is as far from 'presence' as Malraux is when dwelling on the 'humanity' in his 'imaginary museum'. In fact, Jünger, Heidegger and Mann, in their respective ways, are typically German intellectuals in that they protest against the secularization of culture. After the medieval empire disintegrated, German intellectuals built nihilism into their world-view, and evolved such essentially German ideas as the difference between 'state' and 'nation' and that between nature and spirit. It has never taken much to precipitate them into metaphysical evasion, aesthetic abdication and nihilistic destructiveness, and these, of course, are habits and attitudes which the Second World War provoked in abundance and which the division of Germany perpetuates. Man, separating himself from Nature, creates chaos; therefore man returning to Nature as a mere item in the catalogue sheds all guilt and responsibility. It is as if the modern German writers have turned their national history into a metaphor: the Germans' error, displayed time and again, was to have assumed the initiative and, deludedly, to have believed themselves to blame for a cataclysm which would have come about in some other form. Man's only freedom, his only possibility of superiority within Nature, is mental, and his physical misadventures are his penalty for attempting too much. In fact, the German tragedy has come to be interpreted as Nature's own injunction to man to enclose himself in a mental garden: to avoid looking directly at the facts of war or of its aftermath; to think in general terms (like Kafka, who died in 1924 and so knew few of the facts). The only novelists to deal directly and confidently with recent events have been the religiously orthodox (Goes the Lutheran, Böll the Catholic) and the older ones (Gertrud von Le Fort and Elisabeth Langgässer, both Catholics). The same extremes apply and fail to communicate: Mann's

Leverkühn-Zeitblom dilemma reappears as wildly imaginative inwardness and mundane matter-of-factness. As we have noticed, such a Swiss rebel as Frisch is fortified by what he attacks, for his target is fixed and sanctioned. The modern German writer, on the other hand, in the Western Zone at least, is undermined by having nothing to object to except a resurgent materialism which only drives him further into himself.

III

In the German Democratic Republic, still 'Central Germany' to its revisionist inhabitants, the writers who have remained or entered are, presumably, 'committed'. We might expect some *esprit de corps*. With something to hold to, the novelist should be able to make some confident (even if unsatirical) statements; and certainly such novels as Anna Seghers's *Die Toten bleiben jung* honestly investigate the Nazi phase. In 1949, however, the Deputy Prime Minister, Ullbricht, pronounced rules for writers along much the same lines as the Russian Proletkult proposed in 1920 (and especially the 'Old Guard' extremist group). But whereas the 1920 Proletkult movement tolerated the non-political 'Serapion Brothers' whom Trotsky called *poputchiki* ('fellow-travellers'), Ullbricht's edict permitted of no deviation; and Anna Seghers's dutiful story *Der Mann und sein Name*, dealing with the period immediately after the end of the war, made the best of the new order: her main character, an ex-S.S. man, gradually develops into a correct communist. All the same, in spite of Anna Seghers's mature approach and her boldness in tackling a theme usually avoided in West Germany, the narrative has no punch. It is more a judicious parable than a thorough probing of a man bent on self-correction.

A similar inertness and diagrammatic quality characterize Bodo Uhse's *Die Patrioten* and Willi Bredel's *Die Enkel* (1956), both written as if ideological conformism (including post-Nazi denunciation of Nazidom) exempted a novelist from being aesthetically meticulous and licensed him to indulge himself so long as he operated within the approved pattern. This is the other side of inspiration; where communist faith sustained these novelists in exile, it now prompts them to slacken their literary muscles. Away, they become indignant; back home, with their own elected creed in complete ascendancy, they relax and do as they are told. There is a world of difference between writing as you feel because you are the only person who wants that, and doing so in the full knowledge that, while you do it, you are doing the approved thing. That is the difference between Anna Seghers's *Der Mann und sein Name* and her passionate masterpiece *Das siebte Kreuz* (1941). Above all, authoritarian prescription dismisses style and technique as light matters, whereas, of course, these are the outcome and resort of individual temperament. You cannot prescribe style without proscribing honest literature and you cannot minimize it without stultifying the literary impulse.

To some extent this was realized after the first Five-Year Plan was inaugurated in Russia in 1928; at first, the Russian Association of Proletarian Writers outlawed authors who failed to treat of the Plan, but by 1932 Gorky managed to get the Association dissolved. Similarly, after the tide had come and gone several times more, the 1954 Second Congress of Soviet Writers began another fight against planned literature and ostentatious Socialist Realism, but ended with the usual lame communist uplift avowal in the Fourth Congress of German Writers: 'Only the methods of Socialist Realism can today depict all that is new in life and express the power of the new man to change his environment. . . .' Ilya Ehrenburg's plea for intuition, his heterodox novel *The Thaw* and Pomeranzow's articles on literary integrity all fanned on the aesthetic rebellion, but to little purpose in East Germany.

It must not be forgotten, however, that the best East German writing belongs to a tradition which, in the late thirties, appeared in John Lehmann's periodical *New Writing*. The names, most of them forgotten, are Brecht, Seghers, Kisch, Kantorowicz, Petersen, Kurella and Leonhard. These authors, famous or forgotten, built on foundations laid by Heine, Herwegh, Büchner and Freiligrath, and strengthened in the twenties by the political satire of Tucholsky, Kästner and Erich Weinert. Then, from the objective group which called itself 'Neue Sachlichkeit' (New Reality), there developed about 1930 a proletarian movement, almost the antithesis of Expressionism. In 1933 all this went underground, and the writers concerned became a closely knit group for as long as they survived. Twelve years later they were hopelessly dispersed: Tucholsky and Toller had committed suicide; Mühsam and Ottwalt were killed; some, such as Regler, Weinert and Renn, fought in Spain and then found themselves in French camps; Becher went to Moscow; and Brecht for the first time became known in England and France. Not all of the backlog survived, and many works were less fortunate than Hans Fallada's *Der Trinker* (1950), found and deciphered after his death in 1947. Some writers settled in the West and others (Feuchtwanger, Graf, Remarque and Heinrich Mann) stayed away altogether. Finally, after four and a half years of military government, things settled down only to be stirred up again by the June 1953 rising and the events of 1956. In 1957 the party cultural congress once more proscribed 'decadent' Western forms (as extolled by such as the German-minded Hungarian, Georg Lukács, and Professors Ernst Bloch and Hans Mayer of Leipzig). The desiderata were reportage and 'agit-prop', conspicuously missing from such periodicals as *Sonntag*, *Neue deutsche Literatur*, *Sinn und Form* and *Aufbau*. Lukács, insisting as ever on the paramountcy of aesthetic criteria, was roundly condemned. (One of his judgments labelled and dismissed Arthur Koestler as a 'little superficial journalist'.) According to the *Kulturpolitiker*, the danger was outside influences, not mediocrity.

Obviously the East German novelist has his troubles in a world full of soldiers and policemen, devoid of thrillers and Whodunits, clamped (although erratically) by *Kulturpolitik*, isolated from West German nihilism and the Proust-Joyce tradition, and just as strait-jacketed as the West Germans are disorientated. A few fine works have emerged: Strittmatter's Joyce Cary-like novels, *Tinko* and *Der Wundertäter*, Anna Seghers's novel about the division of Germany, *Die Entscheidung* (much more human and down-to-earth than Jünger's *Der Gordische Knoten*); Ludwig Renn's *Morelia* (about his period at a Mexican university), *Der Spanische Krieg*, *Meine Kindheit und Jugend* and *Adel im Untergang*. But Renn's *Krieg ohne Schlacht* lacks confidence and becomes a stale exercise in ideological cant. Hans Fallada's last novel, *Jeder stirbt für sich allein*, is vastly superior: it movingly and chasteningly shows a middle-aged Berlin working-class couple against a spineless inert public.

But novels about the war, the Nazi débâcle, the camps, about
exile in Mexico and Switzerland, about the Spanish Civil War,
are now beginning to be seen as evasions of the local scene.
Arnold Zweig's additions to his Grischa series have become
mechanical; and such novels as Bruno Apitz's *Nackt unter
Wolfen* rake over the war ashes to little new purpose. It would
seem that what can be said about life in Russia's Germany is not
worth saying. The Federal Republic is not interested, anyway.
None of the authors who stayed on in Nazi Germany has had any
crucial formative influence; none of the non-communist exiles
returned to Germany; the petty-bourgeois, like the Nazi rem-
nants, flourish again. Both Germanys, in fact, have their respective kinds of barrenness: in the East, regimented *Kitsch*; in
the West, except for the youngest writers, revulsed rationalization.

The main hope lies with such of the indignant young as Franz
Schonauer, author of *German Literature in the Third Reich*,
Siegfried Lenz, Hans Magnus Enzensberger and Christian
Geissler. For older generations, in both Germanys, everything is
the fault of the politicians: the Germans still want to shunt off
their consciences, grievances and responsibilities; they embody
themselves in a leader and then pretend that part of them is no
longer under their own control. But if anything is being achieved,
it is in the West. Gottfried Benn's laconic musings continue to
influence the younger writers. Alfred Döblin's *Hamlet* (1957),
about a war-wrecked Englishman returning home, brilliantly
manipulates flashback and soliloquy and goes deep into the
disturbed hero's obsessions without getting obscure. Gertrud
von Le Fort's *Die letzte Begegnung* (1959), about power, makes
Mme de Montespan and Mme de la Vallière vibrate with modern
pertinence, and Uwe Johnson, a man of profound moral intelligence who left East for West in 1960, has produced a quasi-
Faulknerian masterpiece, *Mutmassungen über Jakob* (1959),
about an East German railway-switchman's mysterious death.

In 1959 Günter Grass published *Die Blechtrommel*, presenting
Nazi Germany from the viewpoint of a deranged dwarf, and
Heinrich Böll, in *Billard um halb zehn*, produced one of the most
concise novels of the decade, covering within the space of one
day in 1958 three generations of one family. Böll's use of
interior monologue and flashback is brilliantly functional, never

exhibitionistic. Gerd Gaiser, less Dickensian than Böll, has written a new satire on the *Wirtschaftwunder* called *Schlussball*, and a second, 'Neue Sachlichkeit', seems to be developing in the calm, carved narratives of Hans Bender (*Wunschkost*, 1959) and Rolf Schroers (*Im fremder Sache*, 1957). Siegfried Lenz's first novel, *Es waren Habichte in der Luft* (1951), has a Baltic wartime setting, but his most recent novels hammer at the new getting-and-spending Germany (*Der Mann im Strom*, 1957; *Brot und Spiele*, 1959).

In most of this there is hope. But it is to be hoped that the case of Wilfred Schilling will not be repeated: his novel *The Fear-Makers* (1959) could find no publisher in Germany until it had been anonymously published in England and Holland. It will serve as a conclusion because it looks hard at German society and sets a firm foot on a difficult road which the Federal Republic has pretended does not exist.

The Fear-Makers is a dramatized tract on the vendettas initiated by surviving Nazis. Alfred Link, the journalist hero and martyr, once belonged to the German Underground; in 1945 he played a minor, almost secretarial part in the rounding-up of war criminals, two of whom were robbed and beaten up by his associates. Eleven years later, in collaboration with other well-placed ex-Nazis, these two have him arrested on a trumped-up charge of robbery-with-violence. Much of the novel is devoted to discussions which Link has with a fellow-prisoner and the good-natured but bovinely imperturbable gaoler, Grimm. Eventually, after Link's wife has consulted a variety of corrupt or pusillanimous officials and advisers, the charge is quashed—a small but only temporary victory against the cohorts of dormant sadists and active cynics. Shelving the idea of escape to Switzerland, Link carries on in the belief that his kind is needed, and awaits the next move of a corrupt judiciary and its associated fear-makers. The novel's end is abrupt and grotesque, half fable, half nightmare: the only supportable consummation to this weird, Kafka-like rite of claustrophobic innocence and deluded self-sacrifice. A squad of seemingly innocuous locals execute a bemused but calm Alfred, who dies 'having stood firm in our lost cause'. His supposed offence: treason. Alfred Link, for the sake of the German people, embraces both charge and sentence.

Here is the rationale of a haunted nation. The novel has some unforgettable episodes: in one, the criminals are made to exhume their victims from a mass grave; a G.I. and his German girl-friend come strolling out of the countryside right into the middle of the ghastly process. We are made to see the growth of an unholy and degrading union between prisoner and gaoler—like that between tortured and torturer searingly described in Henri Alleg's horrifying account (in *La Question*) of his torture by French soldiers in Algeria. Alfred Link, alone in his cell, hemmed in during exercise by either riff-raff or other and resigned political prisoners, begins to yearn for trial, even injustice—anything rather than being left to rot, etiolated and dumb, on endless remand. His humanity begins to fade and crumble.

But much of the story we have to picture for ourselves. If we enter sufficiently into Alfred Link's predicament, as we probably do into that of Kafka's 'K', we illustrate the theme for ourselves. The book's main force is expository but, thanks to a wealth of poignant aphorisms, some scaldingly articulate tirades and the suffusing horror of such scenes as the exhumation, there is not an unprovoking moment. It is rather as if Malraux had combined the starkness of the cell scenes in *Le Temps du mépris* with the passionate oratory about human survival in *Les Noyers de l'Altenburg*. The modern German novel is slowly setting about its proper business. It is our duty to read, and our good fortune to be able to shake our heads about the significances of, a German novelist who has to fight his own anonymity. Such novels as *The Fear-Makers* help to break down the hermetic shell of German litera-ture and philosophy. They begin to work, although obliquely, at the same level and for the same purpose as, say, Bertrand de Jouvenel's *Power* and *Sovereignty*, which inquires into the nature of 'political good' and seeks to define a moral and philosophical basis for Western political institutions. When such inquiries are made openly in Germany, in the Federal Republic at any rate, the débâcle will be over. Of any similar efforts in East Germany, there are the condemned writings of Lukács, Bloch and Mayer; and, beyond these, not much public sign at all.

Unfortunately, however, few novelists tackle the moral prob-lems of war or of peace; the emphasis is on technologies which, while complicating life, distract man from moral complications. And such compartmentalization reinforces the prevailing interest in the isolated man who is safer in the uncommitted 'abyss' of himself than in the hurly-burly of the *Wirtschaftwunder* or in honest rediscovery of the recent past. The lack of a *national* Press inhibits the impulse to reach out, and the absence of a truly national capital makes for mental partitioning. Kafka's outlines attract the young, as do generalities of time and place. The young novelist prefers self-expression to documentary, and keeps his work closer to poetry than to sociology: he has become the aesthetician of archetypes, the connoisseur of inwardness, the shuffler of the impersonal stage properties variously called 'totalitarianism', 'the politicians', 'society' and 'the others'.

Böll is one of the few novelists with accurate total recall (historically speaking), and Doderer, through the periodical *Wort in der Zeit*, has attacked 'the utopian or trans-real novel'. But the West German novel, for all its disdain of bourgeois materialism, for all its hostility to newly regenerate Germany, remains middle-class in atmosphere and averted from the working-class themes exploited by the Nazis. It was Hugo von Hofmannsthal who accused the Germans of being unable to face the present, 'be it the epoch, or the moment'. It is the Swiss, Max Frisch, who, in *Tagebuch* (1946–9), has argued for the very thing which the Germans lack: 'a feeling of responsibility'.

> It has been precisely the Germans, who have never lacked talents and minds that felt themselves to be above the demands of the everyday. . . .

To the German novelist the everyday is fearsome—which it is not (not quite) to such writers as Amis, Sagan and Salinger. Compared with their work, much modern German fiction is fanciful, philosophical amnesia. The Germans, up to now, have been too busy forgetting and shelving to let the novel do its traditional work of social analysis: work which, one suspects, they will not much longer evade. The signs are promising: Wilfred Schilling's Alfred Link proudly accepts an unjust death-sentence, and, in Günter Grass's brilliant phantasmagoria, *Die Blechtrommel*, Oskar Matzerath willingly makes his own atonement by accepting the guilt and sentence for a murder he did not commit. Such allegories are eloquent of a spiritual rehabilitation long overdue. Certainly, the rest will not be silence.

Italy

I

THE development of the novel in Italy, from Manzoni (1785–1873) onwards, demonstrates some vicissitudes of realism. Manzoni himself, in *Discorso sol romanzo storico*, demolished the principle of the historical novel even though *I promessi sposi*, set in the first half of the seventeenth century, made the widest and most successful appeal of any Italian novel then in print. Martyrdom, he eventually decided, could have a satisfactory outcome not only in the next world, but in this; and his peasant lovers, Lucia and Renzo, had the same unrestricted appeal as the exoteric prose style of Silvio Pellico's *Le mie prigioni* (1832). In fact it would not be fantastic to see in Manzoni's honesty about and care for the underprivileged the seed of modern Italy's association of realism with socialism. (We are perhaps only now beginning to acknowledge that realism is a method just as applicable to affluence as to poverty.) Lucia and Renzo, contrasted with the Cardinal Federigo Borromeo and the Innominato, look forward to the wide and sentimental appeal of Edmondo De Amicis (1846–1908), especially his *La vita militare* (1868), to Luigi Capuana (1839–1915), who before Pirandello combined psychological probings with realism in *Il marchese di Roccaverdina* (1901), and of course to the *verismo* (truthfulness) of Verga. And if the eventual, thorough honesty of Verga (and of his successors Pirandello, Svevo, Carlo Levi, Giuseppe Berto, Pier Paolo Pasolini, Elio Vittorini and Vasco Pratolini, not to mention the film-director Luchino Visconti) seems too humdrum—as nearly all socialist realism is humdrum—out of indignant concern, it may reasonably be argued that De Amicis, Capuana and D'Annunzio overworked the vein of extravagance.

De Amicis preferred the lachrymose, especially in *Cuore* (1887), in the story *Dagli Apennini alle Andi*, and his long novel about the ocean voyage of illiterate immigrants, *Sull' oceano* (1897). De Amicis declared himself a socialist in 1890 and thenceforth mixed the sentimental custard even thicker; but he did at least care, like Manzoni, for the idea of linguistic unity. Capuana, who championed Zola and revered Balzac, never quite conquered a shallow fondness for weird effects: with him, naturalism was a repertoire of arresting gimmicks, which it was never for his fellow-Sicilian Verga. Psychology constantly leads Capuana into the occult and the pseudo-scientific. Most of his effects are meretricious and wild, as in *Le appassionate* (1893) and his quasi-clinical first novel, *Giacinta* (1879).

D'Annunzio (1863–1938) is even more extreme; his first novel, *Il piacere* (1889), deals in wanton melodrama and *orribili sacrilegi*; *L'innocente* (1892) defends *perversione sadica*, and such other novels as *Il trionfo della morte* (1894), *Il fuoco* (1900) and *Forse che sì forse che no* (1910) create hot-house permutations of carnality, sensationalism and supermanship. His characters live at the tops of their voices or at least at the tops of voluptuary, incestuous whispers. It is no wonder that, in the work of later novelists, disgust is glum, prosaic, and passion joyless. Another novelist who worked the same vein was Alfredo Oriani (1852–1909), a decadent vulgarian whose most pernicious efforts were *Memorie inutili* (1876) and *Al di là* (1877). It is customary to commend Oriani's eventual self-reform, his eventual choice of sober attitudes and serious themes; but, austere and balanced as he is in *Matrimonio e divorzio* (1884), he for the most part merely exchanged the extravagance of decadence (obscenity and pagan licence) for the extravagance of colonial messianism: sweetness and light to be achieved through African bloodlettings. His militarism, forcibly expressed in *Fino a Dogali* (1889) and *La rivolta ideale* (1908), is sickly stuff and, like D'Annunzio's cult of voluptuous heroism, anticipates Mussolini as well as explaining why some modern Italian novelists associate extravaganza with oppression and therefore refrain from panache altogether. Antonio Fogazzaro (1842–1911) too, for the hectic and almost wilful spirituality of *Malombra* (1881), belongs with D'Annunzio and Oriani, although not for his Manzoni-inspired and temperate best novel, *Piccolo mondo antico* (1895), which achieves a lambent comic touch absent from the work of both Verga the earnest realist and D'Annunzio the earnest fantast. Like Capuana, Fogazzaro dabbles in the occult, but that is only one element in a rather muddled *œuvre*: the sequel to *Piccolo mondo*, comprising both *Piccolo mondo moderne* (1901) and *Il santo* (1905), reveals too many conflicts in him. A grandiose mysticism, which is to prompt social reform, wars with a hyperbolical naturalism, and these with a lyrical sensuality that consorts oddly with his anxious social concern. But he is neither lax nor pessimistic and his neurotic resolve to be hopeful anticipates the doomed Pavese.

As Italy united, the regions and their dialects came to the fore. Matilde Serao (1856–1927) many times over described the complexity of Naples, and especially well in *Il paese di Cuccagna* (1891) and *Evviva la vita!* (1909). Her work has a Hogarthian accuracy, a teeming sense of the city's fertility, whereas Grazia Deledda (1871–1936), recording the solitudes and fastnesses of Sardinia, achieves the kind of cosmic drama (and melodrama) we have noticed in the American novel. She is expert in emotions, in how they wreck ancient and honoured routines. *Elias Portolu* (1903) is a moving, intense account of the return to Sardinia of an ex-convict, and her work in general is every bit as emotionally massive as Verga's without his grinding insistence. Her carefully planned studies of rural brutishness and peasant tenacity, especially *Il vecchio della montagna* (1900) and *Marianna Sirca* (1915), introduced a new world to the reading public, as it were making even more elemental—in the context of the land's tyranny—the material and spiritual backwardness so beautifully and tragically exposed, in more urban terms, by Emilio de Marchi's neglected *Demetrio Pianelli* (1890).

II

As the nineteenth century closes, social awareness emerges unsteadily from the blather of furtive historicism and gaudy rapture. But the poor, asking as in Ada Negri's poems for 'peace, work and bread', stimulate writers to a socialism that is too lavish, sometimes pathetic, sometimes preposterously reverential of dialect and even productive of a new aestheticism which finds in squalor the chance of a new style. Not until Mussolini has gone does Italian social realism become unembarrassed; as the art of the cinema matures, calling upon a wider audience than even Pellico and Manzoni, so does the novel settle down, with the most accurate portrayal always on the side of the angel's left wing. And it is Verga, the advocate of impersonal realism, who at once inspires the new realism and remains a standing rebuke to its political tendentiousness. But we can hardly wonder that an Italian novelist, inheriting Manzoni's rejection of the historical, turning to Verga, then studying the poverty (before and after Mussolini) of much of the nation, should choose a commenting, socialist realism. After all, between the arrival of D'Annunzio and the end of Mussolini, Italians had their fill of the flamboyant; and with the Christian Democrats apathetic about the arts, in contrast with the example of Gramsci who could found the Italian Communist Party without disdaining the matter of beauty, there was little choice. So, risking the possibility of socialist-realist rhetoric (which they could risk because they had seen the literary and political rhetoric of D'Annunzio, Oriani and Mussolini), the Italian novelists committed themselves politically.

With Giovanni Verga (1840–1922) we see genuine social concern gradually working its way to the surface. His early novels have little to commend them: his romanticization in *La storia di una capinera* (1871) of a young nun in love is just as tediously romantic in its tearful way as *Tigre reale* (1873) and *Eros* (1875) are in their defiant naughtiness. In such novels as these Verga was creating oubliettes for his subjectivism and, unwittingly, preparing himself for his great effort at impersonal realism. *Nedda* (1874), which he called a *bozzetto siciliano* (a Sicilian sketch), shows the way he would eventually go. His theme is the arduous life of a young peasant girl; her mother is sick and money is scarce; Nedda goes off to make a little money, but in the meantime her mother dies. Nedda then becomes pregnant to her lover, who also dies, soon to be followed by the new-born child. Such a story is the essence of the mature Verga, at the opposite pole from his Milan erotica; and gradually, as Verga returned in spirit and person to his native Sicily, he found his way into a massive prose orchestration of his favourite theme: being defeated by life. The motto he chose for his Sicilian novels tells us all we need to know: 'I Vinti', the conquered; and this is the thesis the novels support. It is the personal quirk in his mightily impersonal *œuvre*.

In the introduction to *I malavoglia* (1881) Verga announced his intention: to 'study' without evasion 'the flood of human progress', the human role as flotsam and debris. Man may think he has power, but in the long run he has none; he may assume responsibility, but the fault ultimately is not his; he is born for defeat, and social standing exempts him from nothing. In fact 'I Vinti' was to pursue the victim theme up the social ladder: *I malavoglia* deals with Sicilian peasants, *Mastro-Don Gesualdo* (1889) with bourgeois avarice, and *La Duchessa de Leyra*, *L'onorevole Scipione* and *L'uomo di lusso* (the planned but never written next three in the series) were to present life's victimizations on the upper rungs. Verga constantly fed his own perceptions and feelings back into his characters, almost as if he wished the reader to exclaim 'Look, no driver!'. Yet, at the same time, he seemed to think nothing real unless it was unfortunate: only bad luck is real, which is just as bad as Croce's interpreting the 1939–45 war as a breach in the flow of Spirit. Because man is doomed to calamity anyway, Verga does not take the trouble to attribute blame: in *I malavoglia* the usurer Crocefisso strangles the helpless family, but Verga regards him as merely one of several agents who might have been chosen for the same purpose. As in the German novel, we sense the refusal of local responsibility and see the attribution of ultimate responsibility to a malign universe. The same is true of the social pageant in *Mastro-Don Gesualdo*: there are sins and misdemeanours galore, but no moral commentary and not always even enough insight into motives. Verga, like Faulkner and some of the younger French novelists, offers a fictional world which we have to interpret—as we interpret daily life—for ourselves. But, while such an illusion may be something of a novelty, it fails us when we recall that art comes into being to do more than recapitulate the sum of human trouble. This is not to ask art to encourage but to ask the artist to remember that art gives us a sense of achievement only when we are allowed to recognize it as *art*. Art which pretends to *be* life is just as vain as art which offers a world in which all is wrong or all is well.

Manzoni dismissed the past, in theory at least; the futurists belligerently asserted the present; and such sober, thoughtful novelists as the mature Verga, as Luigi Pirandello (1867–1936) and Italo Svevo (Ettore Schmitz, 1861–1928), could hardly make themselves heard during the spectacular commotion made by D'Annunzio, Papini, Marinetti and the rest. Pirandello finds the present disenchanting and deepens our sense of calamity not by offering Verga-ish catastrophe but by constructing images of all that is temporary. He is obsessed by life's apparently un-planned, mercurial nature: strip us of the poses, roles and respon-sibilities we assume, and where are we? What is our identity? It is contextual and multiple, or it is as nothing. Verga watches and reports the hammer-blows; Pirandello, just as determined to be a camera, does X-rays and secretes microphones. His art is encephalographic and almost surreptitious, in some ways comparable with that of Virginia Woolf (for subtle and tactful overhearing) and that of Camus (for its eventual discovery, beneath the veils of illusion and multiplicity, of life's hard absurd-ity). He responds sharply to both flux and fixity, finally to emerge with positive reassurances after a prolonged examination of the role of our unconscious and the discovery that identity is the act of resisting arbitrariness. In this respect he differs from Svevo who leaves life, as he finds it, an unpurposeful blur. But both Svevo and Pirandello examine Papini's futuristic drive to tear away from life 'the meretricious veils of habit and convention' and find it destructive. Svevo holds to his pessimistic routine-mindedness; Pirandello, comparing the fleetingness of life's surfaces with the volatility of the spirit, ultimately decides that man's *personae* are part of man's nature and are prophylactic against '*la vita nuda, la natura senz' ordine apparente*' (life naked; Nature without apparent order).

Pirandello has something of Forster's sense of the fertile muddle: at first he finds the muddle, as Svevo does, abortive, but his dialectic compels him to prize the divine spirit wherever and however he finds it. Even the mundanity and pettiness of daily life cannot quell the miracle of life's incessant self-renewal. The relativism of his essay, *L'umorismo* (1908), laughs at man's categories, and his views on identity are much the same as those advanced by Lawrence Durrell and Nigel Dennis. 'Reality' can never be other than what we think it is: the play *Così è, se vi pare* (1917) shows his drift.

The force of illusions was his constant theme. His main problem was that the simple Sicilians of his stories in *Amori senza amore* (1894) and *Il carnevale dei morti* (1921), to mention two volumes only, were not the ideal vehicles for such metaphysical specula- tions. Since such personages cannot explain themselves without getting out of character, they have to be manipulated; in con- sequence the stories are too demonstrative and the novels, offering him more room, are operatic. Mattia in *Il fu Mattia Pascal* (1904) acquires a new identity accidentally and Rocco in *L'esclusa* (1901) blindly drives his innocent wife into the very infidelity for which he believes he is punishing her. It is all a little too neat, like Vitangelo's discovery, in *Uno nessuno e cento- mila* (1926), of his nose's peculiar shape: let Vitangelo think what he will, Verga's iron fate will defeat him in the long run. Only the very rich can change the shape of their noses, and as for a lopsided nose derided by one's wife—well, that just con- firms the Verga-Hemingway view that 'they' always get you somehow in the end.

Pirandello's themes do not so much emerge as blurt out. They pummel. And it is only in the historical novel *I vecchi e i giovani* (1913) that things are done in tertiary and secondary colours. But this pageant of Sicilian life during the nineties drags and clots. As far as Pirandello the novelist is concerned, we have to take blurting grotesquerie if we want vigour or prepare to be bored if we want social panorama. The novel was too indirect for his purposes and tempted him to expose his own person too much, thereby confronting him with the problem of his own identity and role before he even started. To Verga's only-the-bad- is-real we have to add Pirandello's thinking-makes-it-so. Both talked of objectivity yet neither achieved it, for only fate could be objective. Verga's wilful fatalism and Pirandello's wishful thinking both expose their own inadequacy and inaccuracy. But we can hardly infer this as part of either novelist's deliberate intention. Verga was too much tempted by absolutes, Pirandello by the excitement of exposing the defenceless nerves. So Verga seems wrong because his *cavalleria rusticana* pretends to a realism no one can achieve and offers a philosophy corresponding to that impossibility: like Ernst Jünger, he adapts life to his philosophy but cannot even present that life's exact, complete nature. And Pirandello, obsessed by incertitude, comes to rely on life's very unreliability.

Svevo is altogether less Procrustean. When he sent a copy of *Una vita* (1892) to Paul Heyse, the German novelist, Heyse responded with cautious praise and asked why Svevo wrote about such insignificant characters—the clerks, functionaries and minor officials among whom Svevo spent his days. But those characters, both the funny and the forlorn ones, pulled strongly at Svevo, and the hero of his second novel, *Senilità* (1898), is a Triestine office-worker: once again Heyse expostulated about insignificance; the novel flopped, and Svevo concentrated on his job with a varnish firm. From then on, until 1922 when he drafted his third novel, *La coscienza di Zeno* (1923), in a fortnight, the only literary events in his life were his interest in psychoanalysis and James Joyce's interest in him. But this novel too fell flat and Svevo had to wait three years before Valéry Larbaud and Benjamin Crémieux read it and began to get him known: Svevo was then sixty-three. Apart from the short *Una burla riuscita* (1928), there is a play together with a group of short stories: it is a slight enough body of work for all the comment it now excites, but it appeals nowadays for special reasons.

In the first place Svevo is honest: honest about forlorn, aging men unable to cope with young mistresses, about young men too timid to spurn marriage to the wrong girl, about all the varieties of backsliding, place-keeping, clock-watching and crisis-cowardice. He excels at depicting the maladroit and the fumblers, uncomplex affection and the reprisals which (in their minds only) functionaries enact against bosses. In other words, Svevo masters the unheroic. His first two novels are exercises in the manner of Flaubert, say; but *Zeno*, untidy and almost incoherent, makes its point ('The natural law does not entitle us to happiness; it prescribes, rather, wretchedness and suffering') through an original mixture of hilarity and glumness. The prose is far from mannered; in fact it has the flatness and everyday quality of such English writers as William Cooper and Kingsley Amis who both, as

C. P. Snow has pointed out,[1] derive something from Svevo and from William Gerhardi's *The Polyglots*. It is hardly surprising that the attempt to portray hapless, baffled people fumbling in a haphazard world should have given rise to the prose of inconsequence, of no surface glitter and small dignity: for such purposes it is the perfect prose and, in Svevo's hands, becomes also a satisfactory vehicle for interior monologues by characters who verge on the Dostoevskian when not having a snigger at the silly mystery of it all. Svevo's sure grasp on the tawdry, the small-time and the faint-souled sets him apart from Verga (to whose heroics his views on 'natural law' superficially relate him) and Pirandello (who cuts and dries more answers than Svevo thought necessary).

Una burla is Svevo at his most lugubriously comic, and *Zeno* is his best analysis of bourgeois self-seeking in a meaningless world of drifting phenomena where whimpers outnumber bangs as small lives fizz up and peter out. And, ultimately, this is what disappoints us in Svevo: his world is all worry, sighs and wry acquiescence—too few steps to get him as high as the Dostoevskian altar to which he aspires. Anyone wanting fire, power and intensity will have to turn back to Verga and D'Annunzio or forward to Pavese, Silone and perhaps Moravia. Verga and D'Annunzio come together in that they modify the world: the one adapts it to an absolute, the other intensifies it into a gaudy riot. Svevo and, to a lesser extent, Pirandello try to present it as it is, counting on the shock of recognition rather than on a pleasing reconstruction: like the girl in Katherine Mansfield's story, 'The Garden Party', they end up exclaiming 'Isn't life—isn't it. . . .' and cannot quite articulate the rest.

Yet our dissatisfactions are based on the notion of a world in which things go as we want them to: efface that notion, take this world as it is, and we have grown up. A great deal of the best modern Italian fiction tries to do just that, especially through charity and social realism. The chimaera-world of D'Annunzio and the Futurists still haunts Italian writers, and the hermetic (*ermetismo*) movement in poetry illustrates a major temptation. Of the most interesting novelists, Cesare Pavese (1908–1950), successful, admired, a man of profound human sympathy, adjudged himself a failure in his intimate life and found that fact

1. In *Essays and Studies*, Vol. 14 (1961), pp. 7–16.

paramount; and Ignazio Silone has put charity and his fellow-men before all orthodoxies and formulas without getting laxly idealistic. Silone discerns and defends an invincible compassion: in his own words,

> . . . something more stable and more universal than the mere compassion of Albert Camus. It is founded, in the last analysis, on the certainty that we human beings are free and responsible; that we feel the need of reaching out to touch the inmost reality of our fellow men; and that spiritual communion is possible.

Alberto Moravia, on the other hand, arguing that 'Men have been victimized by their technology. . . . To them the sexual act is the only natural act left', has defined narrowly and grown to depend upon a sexual hell almost as boring as that of Henry Miller. False gods—whether political, aesthetic or mystical—always tempt the honest man into self-denial and only the severest realist, like the severest escapist, survives.

These remarks might serve to sum up—if one can summarize gradually assembled anguish—the diary of Cesare Pavese, *Il mestiere di vivere* (1951). Its pages reveal a mind which is perpetually falling down steps, unable to profit even from its own highly sophisticated irony. It is possible to make fun of the person who takes himself, as we say, too seriously. There is a tough and right reasonableness in making such fun. But sensitive people keep on developing or being born; and, discipline themselves as they may, they think too precisely upon each event.

Pavese, acutely, fatally, sensitive tried to set up a code for living, a code which would be implemented at some vague time when the interpretation of life was done. As if such a time would come at all. It is as if he strives through generalization to awaken a dormant principle; as if he never quite believes what people say, but uses words as divining-sticks over ancient ground. The trouble, perhaps the tragedy, is that while he is deciding how to live, he has to go on living, so that his facts change while he surveys them, and his resolutions and insights are always out of date. There is a mode of self-observation in which a sensitive thinker asks himself where he is landed by his meditations; and has to answer that everything is its own reason, and must remain so until he accepts a traditional dogma. Life goes on, to no noticeable end, self-perpetuation being its purpose, while the majority of people relegate their conscience to the sphere of the wistfully inoperative. The conscience which would terminate life ends up in assent or self-destruction.

There is, in abstract, no reason for suicide. But a personal evaluation of the state of things is always unique. It is always adequate to the person concerned; but it cannot be laid under contribution and reshaped into a maxim. Thus the conscience of a Pavese is, in the last analysis, a private affair. There can be no uncontroversial description of the human condition. Pavese, obsessed by his inability to communicate effectually, reminds one of Camus, who says in *Actuelles II*: 'The time of sedentary artists is over. But we must avoid bitterness. One of the temptations of the artist is to think himself alone, and it comes to the stage when people hoot this at him with quite shameless delight. But he is nothing of the kind.' Pavese, whose increasing obsession with suicide exposed truths never to be of use or comfort to himself, expressed his own longing for being present to others. It is to be seen, then, that happiness is inseparable from the gift of the self to others:

Does not the man who sacrifices himself do so to ease the suffering of another? Which amounts to saying: even if I myself suffer, provided that the others do not, all is well. . . .

That is Tolstoyan. We might have expected such assertions from the author of *Tra donne sole* (1950), for which he received the Strega Award two months before his death. The Rosetta of that novel, like Rosalba in *Il diavolo sulle colline* (1949), finds suicide the only way out. Yet even in those instances his quiet mastery of emotion disguises the import of his narrative (the reverse of Pirandello's procedure). Only in his Diary is he explicit, and even there a *sprezzatura secca*, a dry disdain, curbs the vatic expansiveness: 'The only creed worthy of respect is compassion—charity to one's neighbour. The teaching of Christ and Dostoevsky. . . .' And, compassionate as he intends us to think him—whether he is dealing with peasants (*Paese tuoi*, 1941), betrayed girls (*La bella estate*, 1949), a crippled boy (*La luna e il falò*, 1950), or various types of prisoners (as in *Il carcere*, 1949; *Il compagno*, 1947) and Resistance workers (*La Casa in collina*, 1949; *La Luna e il falò*)—he as often as not transposes the heaviest onsets of emotion into symbolism and maintains the role of 'an onlooker who watches things greater than himself take place'.

He had learned a great deal from the American and Elizabethan writers he served so meticulously and imaginatively as translator. From Melville, Sinclair Lewis, Sherwood Anderson, Dos Passos, Gertrude Stein and Faulkner, as from Shakespeare, he culled a technique of mythic indirection while rejecting their respective involuntary excesses. He cannot be called any kind of realist; rather he is the brahmin of an ascetic art—'Artists', he said, 'are the monks of the bourgeois state'—and he spent much of his time embellishing and decorating his major motifs. At his best, this ensures an arresting quality such as we find in his beautiful, haunting novel about the post-Resistance period, *La luna e il falò*; at his worst, as in *Il diavolo sulle colline*, about some young boys who fall in with a wealthy drug-addict, it leads him into enamelled aimlessness and allows the futility-theme to sap the vitality of the narrative itself. There was not an emotion in him which did not incite him to cultivate its opposite—especially an animal gusto (' "savage" things') which rebounded upon him when zestful participation, principally through relationships with women, led him only to inert self-loathing. Admiring Balzac, Flaubert and Stendhal, he aimed at objectivity not least because it implied his being uninvolved. He wanted, so to speak, a tower both invulnerable and open to every current of life. It was an impossible requirement, of course, and this is why he writes so movingly about trapped people: trapped not by their conscious efforts so much as by accident—wealth, corruptness or neurosis—and attempting to break out simply by increasing the pressure on themselves until something gives. Inward explosions are not the easiest things to describe, and Pavese handles them so vividly because, like Stendhal, he thinks readily in images of prison. The trouble is that when characters disintegrate inwardly, it is the body itself and not relationship (whether to people or to cell-walls) which is the prison. And Pavese, in an act which meshed his literary preoccupations with his private life, proving all his points with irrevocable emphasis, escaped on 27 August 1950.

What crippled him was his intractable temperament when confronted with the assumptions and needs of women. He was too complex emotionally to achieve the simple bliss he wanted. Like the school-teacher hero in *La casa in collina*, he lurks in the hills while contending forces—partisan, Fascist, German and Allied—settle the country's fate. There were more on Pavese's side than he thought, and there will surely be many capable of responding to the symbolic import of his life and work.

Compared with 'Ignazio Silone' (Secondo Tranquilli, 1900–) Pavese seems decadent and self-obsessed; and were it not for Pavese's emphasis on compassion (which is Silone's too) the name D'Annunzio would be relevant. In fact Pavese's neuroticism was just about as unselfish as neuroticism can be, and his compassionateness was just as spontaneous, just as dryly resolute, as that we find in Silone. Both men felt strong sympathy for the peasants of Piedmont and the Abruzzi respectively, and both took shelter among them, Pavese from 1943 to 1945 and Silone in the years before 1930 (when he broke with the Communist Party) and his elected exile (until 1944) in Switzerland. Consequently the theme of return to the native province is strong in both writers, implying a return to the source, a renewal of humanity and the shedding of poses.

Where Pavese tends to be cynical, Silone arrives at the irony of severe devotion. Pavese can be aloof, as has already been said; Silone, still not appreciated as he deserves in Italy, is always down-to-earth; and his earth grows politics. Italy, he has always said, must save itself from within, not through outside intervention. And this Mazzini-like conviction bears the same relationship to Silone's realism as his ethics to his politics. For Silone, whom everyone so readily pigeonholes as a 'political' novelist, deals in his own kind of mystagogy: what he cannot prove affects him just as profoundly as what he documents. His novels are based as much on 'presence', epiphany of one kind or another, and earth-ecstasy as on principles of political action. For him art is not a haven but an antenna or a weapon. For him no introverted verbal fussiness; his concern, and therefore also his kind of prose, is raptly practical: to remedy the felt loss of the presence of God by various permutations and mergings of such attitudes and activities as fellowship, compassion, trustfulness, public service, 'presence' and moral duty. His characters travel the vexatious maze between spiritual desolation and a mundane sense of belonging. Where Pavese's *Il mestiere di vivere* recalls other meditations on suicide, such as Donne's *Biathanatos* and Camus's *Le Mythe de Sisyphe*, Silone attempts a voracious humanism which fastens on human virtue, and has—to be fully understood—to be seen against the background of our century's twin humanisms, one exiguous and aloof, the other avid and inquisitive. The first is personified by Stephen Dedalus, the second by the picaresque hero. After all, if *Civitas Dei* gives way to a defensive or a compassionate heresy, and thinking people return to medium simplicities or create new Temples of Art, or (like Malraux and Pavese) try both, a void has to be filled, whether with systems or myth, whether with what Swift called 'auto-suggestion' or with defiant imagination. The sense of nothingness, of loss, prevails, and has to be conquered.

The typical picaresque here offered by Silone presents the humanist experiment at its most vigorous. He strives, through all kinds of human encounter, to acquire the necessary *planche de salut* or even a comforting illusion; and the method he selects is combative, open-hearted and haphazard. In so far as he is a picaro, he is also a saint. Like Pietro Spina in *Pane e vino* (1937) and *The Seed beneath the Snow* (1942, first published in English), he returns from exile, from mountains of lunar and perhaps lunatic theory, to the facts of everyday poverty. *Pane e vino* throbs with the rhythms of life and the excitement of discovery, whereas the sequel is a more selfconscious piece of literary artifice, mixing realism with symbolism. But, over and above literary merits and shortcomings, these novels together with the widely acclaimed *Fontamara* (1933), another study of Abbruzzese peasant life, expound a noble yet realistic view of man's possibilities. The supreme experience is the sudden perception of something worth living for, worth dying for. This perception is not confined temporally or doctrinally; but its occurrences often determine the whole structure of the novel. It is presented as an epiphany, suffusing the picaresque progress; and, taken together, the various epiphanies suggest something like a secular grail.

Silone, always an admirer of Camus, goes beyond fraternity to talk of 'the intimate reality of others', of *fiducia* (trustfulness) not *fede* (faith), of companionship's literal, almost sacramental burden: the taking of bread together. In *The Seed beneath the Snow* Pietro Spina, who eventually (like Berardo in *Fontamara*) confesses to and dies for a crime he has not committed, tells how the deaf-mute Infante learns to say the word 'bread' and 'companion'. 'Cumpaani', murmurs Infante, seeing mice hunting for crumbs. This episode, which takes place in the stable where Spina is hiding, evokes the moving hovel scene between the same characters in *Pane e vino*: Spina, disguised as a priest, sits a whole evening with Infante at the door; they smile occasionally at each other; there is no talk; when Spina coughs, Infante fetches him a blanket. That is Silone's typical antidote to the assorted imbecilities of modern politics and the vogue for nihilism. Such episodes epitomize not only Silone's whole ritual of return (to one's people and oneself, to *amicizia*, simplicity and selflessness) but also his two-fold inquiry into life's basis: love and common sense. 'You have', says Giuditta to Rocco in *A Handful of Blackberries*, 'the sadness of one who set out to go very far and ends up by finding himself where he began. Didn't they teach you at school that the world is round?' This is the folk-wisdom, the folk-morale, symbolized in the same novel by Lazzaro's trumpet: 'It's a way of calling out to each other, being together and giving each other courage.' Back we go, in Silone's novels, to fundamentals at once comic and miraculous and, it must be admitted, sometimes dull, as in *Il segreto di Luca* (1958).

The complement of such communal love is Pietro Spina's question 'What is man?' That is exactly the question substituted at the last moment for 'The eternal elements of art', the topic for discussion at the colloquy in Malraux's *Les Noyers*. Walter Berger, the host and moderator, has just learned of his brother's suicide, and his consequent shift to apparent basics is a promise of epiphanies to come. In the same novel German soldiers end up carrying gassed Russians—another epiphany of buried virtue. Such incidents, carefully presented by Silone, Malraux, Camus and Faulkner in defiance of what Camus called 'the wine of the absurd and the bread of indifference', and carefully avoided by most modern German novelists, give the lie to berserk relativism. There *is* continuity of human virtue across the ages; there *is* something noble in man, which we can see at first hand, as well as something else, also noble, which we can approach only through art. The picaresque saint—be he lecher, *juge-pénitent*, adventurer, damaged priest, *shaman*, political opportunist or rebellious peasant—is precisely not of plaster. And Silone's contribution to this discussion is what sets him above Pavese: not for his elated, simplistic paganism but for sustaining the part of charity against so many enemies and so many aesthetically effete ways out.

We are sent back to Stephen Crane's story 'The Open Boat', in which the universal power produces an absurdity conquerable only through 'the subtle brotherhood of men . . . established on the seas'. The picaresque saint (the title of a comparative study by R. W. B. Lewis) is an implicated transcendentalist who rebukes both the excesses of aestheticism and the wilful austerities of the plain school: Malraux's dithyramb, Faulkner's elaborate lava and the politicist mind-game of Camus, as well as the emotional shallowness, the verbal thinness of Gerhardi-Cooper-Amis knockabout, and French *chosisme*. Furthermore, although it may be thought that Silone's type of charity, endlessly insisted on, is dull, it is not necessarily duller than a series of smouldering young French bottoms or a Jim-crack concatenation of tame words. In an age which believes Virginia Woolf and Joyce wrote in much the same kind of prose, it is worth emphasizing that so trite-seeming a notion as Silone's *fiducia* can elicit good prose from its exponents, whereas the gaily conceived *School for Dictators* (1938, first published in English) fades damply away.

It is unfair to assume that a Silone without a political cause is a Silone without a cause at all. His quest is, and always has been, religious, ethical. If his technique seems old-fashioned, not cinematic enough, that has nothing to do with his beliefs about man. He refrained from the post-war technical stampede just as he did from the stampede in politics. His mastery of the ridiculing detail —'Chay-doo' for 'Duce'—is direct, manichean and clever. No abstractions, no formulas: you betray neither your fellow-man nor yourself for any formula or dogma—not if you are 'honest'. This is the theme of *La volpe e le camelie* (1960), in which Daniele, a mechanic, maintains a secret outpost in Switzerland for the Italian anti-fascist underground. Daniele, happy with his farm and daughter to care for, finally loses everything because his daughter falls in love with a Fascist agent. But, in its oddly shallow way (shallow as some of Camus's *novellas* are shallow), this is a religious not a political fable; love proves more capable than ideology of provoking self-sacrifice—even from a Fascist. Silone's concern with 'honesty' (as in *honnête homme*) amounts to the specification of conscience as a form of grace, or at least of the 'daily' grace which protestantism dispensed with in the sixteenth century, leaving only 'saving' grace. In this context Silone's religious emphasis is clear, especially when we remember that the Christian Democrats are little interested in culture, that socialist realism has pre-empted most worthwhile Italian novelists, that since 1950 Silone has been affiliated with no political party. Against absurdity he ranges the robust physical presence of the soil, the power of conscience and of ridicule. Because his view is fundamentally religious he is not unflaggingly solemn, and *La volpe e le camelie* has for hero not one of his usual peasants (*cafoni*) but a fairly prosperous farmer, and is set not in the Abruzzi but in Switzerland. The writing, like the argument, is plain, formal and discreet. Silone's position is similar to that in which Svevo found himself before Larbaud and Crémieux took him up. Silone's best work, having appeared in English but banned from Italy, had little chance while the latterday D'Annunzios of the Liberation period revelled in extravagance. Something of a misfit and anachronism, in some ways almost English, he was not oblique enough or gaudy enough; and, worse, he reappeared in Italy as the very personification of wise rebuke, still noting the neurosis and the fear of nothingness beneath 'these gay Italians'. An uncomfortable revenant indeed, and the more discomfiting for readers of all nations the more they ponder on what he has done, written, and how.

Silone's regionalism has many echoes, the most moving and eloquent one being Carlo Levi's *Cristo si e' fermato a Eboli* (1946), in which Levi recalls his exile in the malarial wasteland between Apulia and Calabria: ' "Christian" ', he says, 'in their way of speaking means "human being". . . . They at least live for better or for worse, like angels or demons, in a world of their own.' Poverty is stubborn there and Levi's picture of it relentlessly precise. Once again we are obliged to interpret Italian realism as a religious metaphor; just as it is humanitarian—in such documentaries as Danilo Dolci's *Banditi a Particino*, *Inchiesta a Palermo*, Rocco Scotellaro's *I contadini del Sud*, *L'uva puttanella*, Leonardo Sciascia's *Le parrocchie di Regalpetra*, Giovanni Russo's *Baroni e contadini*, the early films of Rossellini and de Sica, most of the films of Fellini and Visconti, and Pasolini's own *Accatone*—so is it metaphysical and allegorical, especially in such novels as Elio Vittorini's *La conversazione in Sicilia*, Pavese's *Paesi tuoi* and Giuseppe di Lampedusa's brilliant, terse and sardonic *Il gattopardo*. Lampedusa's novel of 1860 Sicily, with power slipping from landowner to bourgeois, won especial force from the publication, about the same time, of a report on Palma di Montechíaro, the Sicilian town in which most of the novel is set. The conjunction of Lampedusa's elegiac urbanity and the report's cool enumeration of squalor provoked an outcry. Again, Carlo Levi has published a collection of articles on Russia, *Il futuro ha un cuore antico*; *if* the future *has* an ancient heart, then so has present squalor a long genealogy and an indefinite spiritual significance for the thoughtful.

Yet realism leads nowhere; it just leads to the accumulation of quasi-evidence; it offers no sense of control, of power or of interpretation. Under the Fascist regime, realism yielded to the hermetic, and angry writers cast their indignation in allegorical form. It is therefore sad that post-Liberation novelists either retrogress into allegory, obliquity, *ermetismo*, having tired of repeating themselves, or keep hammering away. Ultimately, as the best Italian writers have realized, the truth of things is spiritual not sociological, religious not political; and in these very realizations lies a temptation to argue the impossibility of total realism against the possibility of a realistic style. The outcome is, as we find in the films of Visconti and Fellini, in the novels of Pavese, Moravia and Vittorini (*Erica*, *La garibaldina*), that personal vision twists actuality and realism becomes increasingly identified with reports and documentaries. The novelist shunts off the reportorial role and takes his stand on the power of anagoge, and we see an increasing amount of what one French critic,[1] apropos of Stendhal, calls '*décor mythique*'. Just as Salvatore Quasimodo can win the Nobel Prize for injecting social realism into his previously

1. Gilbert Durand, *Le Décor mythique de 'La Chartreuse de Parme'* (Paris 1961).

hermetic poetry, just as he and the painter Guttuso can argue for
the figurative and realistic against the private and the abstract
(always, of course, with communist emphasis), so can aestheticism tempt in the form of diluted D'Annunzio: cinematic tricks,
wild fantasy, exaggerated gaiety, apocalyptic inwardness and
trompe d'œil of all kinds. Perhaps even *chosisme* may emerge as,
after Verga and Pasolini, the kind of realism most suitable for
novelists afraid of being unwittingly subjective.

'Alberto Moravia' (Alberto Pincherle, 1907–) has not advanced
far beyond the sullen realism of his first novel, *Gli indifferenti*
(1929); though he has widened his range of characters to include more than the shallow apathetics and pessimistic self-
inquisitors who recalled Svevo, Pirandello and the unenthusiasti-
cally D'Annunzian heroes of Frederigo Tozzi (1883–1920), whose
best novels, *Tre croci* (1920) and *Il podere* (1921), explore the
tedium in the so-called pursuit of pleasure. Moravia's most recent
novels merely repeat the demonstrations begun in *Gli indifferenti*,
resumed in *Le ambizioni sbagliate* (1935), and turned into thematic clichés in *La romana* (1949) and *L'amore coniugale* (1951).

For Moravia there are two discoveries: the adolescent's sudden
discovery of his body's potentialities, beautifully and tersely expressed in *Agostino* (1944) and *La disubbidienza* (1948), and the
fairly experienced young adult's discovery of tedium, loneliness
and futility, all ground into the now familiar Moravia dust of
'indifference', 'contempt' and 'boredom'. In his suicide letter to
Adriana, in *La romana*, Mino says, 'the character I ought to have
been collapsed' and refers to 'a mysterious interruption of the
will'. Moravia's characters do no forget their ideals; they simply
run out of will-power, lose resilience, and cure one affliction only
by acquiring another. A third discovery, of which Moravia has so
far written little (only in *La ciociara*, 1957),[1] is of the possibility
of regeneration. In much the same way as the worldly brutally
strip the innocent of cocooning optimisms, so—eventually—do
they have to strive back towards innocence and inexpert open-
ness. On the one hand, in the story 'Inverno di malato' Moravia
shows a sensitive youth being brainwashed by a worldling until he
is driven to attempt a futile seduction: this in a T.B. sanatorium,
where spiritual malady and tuberculosis run in parallel. On the

1. English translation: *Two Women* (1958).

other hand, in *Gli indifferenti* Carla longs to achieve 'a new life'. But her muted echo of Dante's *Vita nuova* only presages her failure.

Moravia's characters nearly always fail: indifference, equivocation, pusillanimity, loneliness and lassitude beset them endlessly. His world has no moral or creative tension; his men are insignificant manikins, wryly resigned, his women bovinely limited. He is the peeping Tom, anxious, but not desperate, to catch a glimpse of God; but all he reports is a perfunctory Eros shuttling between dismay and satiety. The erotomaniac empties himself: both he and those who study him notice a mystery that 'recedes [as Moravia puts it] backwards into a less accessible zone'. Only in *La ciociara* does a gleam of regeneration appear: Cesira, the mother, finds in the story of Lazarus an incentive to 'the compassion we owe to others and to ourselves'. 'Grief', she says, 'had saved us.' That could be a new starting-point for Moravia: not an acquiescent sadness but a sense of outrage violent enough to provoke new life. From such a position he might be able to discern truths about the sharing of pain, the value of suffering and the gesture of self-sacrifice. Both Dostoevsky and Silone resort to the Lazarus theme, but both develop a faith by energizing the kind of world-sadness Moravia leaves inert.

The trouble is that Moravia is much more resourceful in depicting the disconsolate boredom of the helpless than in divining the springs of self-renewal. When he goes deep, as in *La conformista* (1952), probably his most relentless and least meretricious novel, he tends to prolixity, marking time on repeated explanation rather than supplying extra, intimate evidence. The unwitting self-degradation of an ingenuous youth becomes a line produced at the same angle. Once we know the angle, we can dispense with repeated emphases: the same is true of *La romana*. One cannot help wishing that Moravia, obviously a moralist troubled by human turpitude, could illustrate the basis of his reproofs as vividly as he illustrates corruptness. As it is, we need more about the possibility and the potential of will, even if written from a personal standpoint; there comes a point at which the cataloguing of evil seems an indulgence, not a caution. Moravia gropes towards the charity recommended by Pavese and Silone, but he has, for the most part, been caught up in the morbid and grotesque. Like the Tozzi of such early novels as *La*

zampogna verde (1911) and *La città delle vergini* (1913), he seeks
the perverse and the flashy with a growing sense of guilt, with his
mind rather than with his heart. His work continues to suffer
from the Fascist ban on books which were realistic about morals
and social decay. Just as there have always been people unable,
ever, to reclaim themselves spiritually, there are others who can.
One does not ask Moravia to falsify by always providing uplift
endings, but one does not want the opposite either. So far, he has
failed to achieve an image of life's mixed nature. He is with Verga:
it is too easy to apply the formula of any one novel to the others,
and eventually we have to judge him according to two extremes.

One is that of the simplistic insister who finds life too predictable; the other is that of the super-sophisticate who cannot
be surprised because he is familiar with everything and therefore
works in glib formulas. (A similar case on a less ambitious level
is Françoise Sagan.) In some ways he is still the young Pincherle,
ill with tuberculosis of the bone in the sanatorium at Cortina
d'Ampezzo, carefully solving life as if it were an equation intended
to meet the grandiose aspirations of lonely, upset boys. Not that
people are not as brutal, insensitive and crude as he paints them;
they are. But the other aspect of the human, which Pavese and
Silone discover without exaggerating it, rarely appears in Moravia.
As a result, even his satire is more negative than is necessary or
usual: *La mascherata* (1940), for instance, impales the amorous
naivety of a dictator without separating excusable human out-
goingness from a corruptness which seeps out from one man to
blight a nation.

In his short stories Moravia shows some fondness for characters of low social status; and their robust practicality is a reproof
to his well-to-do neurotics. He has not gone as far as Silone; he
does not spend his time on characters who hope regardlessly but
rather on those who despair after a limited review of the facts.
And he is a long way from embracing folk-wisdom: his versions
of sexual and urban distress are meant to conjure up (if anything
at all) sexual and urban remedies. The husband in *L'amore co-
iugale*, for example, secludes himself and his bride only to find
the ways of the countryside upsetting. Moravia's characters are
best qualified to perpetuate their own problems in the lives of
others; not to help themselves or to comprehend the nature of

personal responsibility, the human obligation to resist interpreting oneself as a pawn. The sensitive such as Agostino has to
accept the facts of insensitivity without losing heart. Or so we
infer: in fact, Agostino seems fated to fail. Life, as Pavese saw,
will not stand still while we interrogate it. Moravia's main interest
is in emotions and their private release, so much so that his
characters' contact with everyday reality is intermittent and to
some extent symbolized in his use of Roman argot.

La noia (1961) confronts us with a familiar Moravia type:
Dino, a rich painter of abstracts, develops erotic mania in a last,
desperate effort to involve himself meaningfully with anyone,
anything. But he discovers that he can possess his mistress's body
only: her essence continually eludes him until he tries to kill himself by driving his car at a tree. It is only while convalescing that
he realizes how despair has quickened in him a new appetite for
living. Partly regenerate, he is no longer bored, which means only
that he is ready for new pain of his own making. Finally we have
to ask how representative Dino is; how meaningful to how many
readers. This glum, brittle novel alienates us, as so often with
Moravia, through generalizing from a trivial character at the same
time as omitting necessary circumstantial detail. These people
have no shadows, not only because they are—for all their lustfulness—insubstantial, but also because Moravia permits them no
relationships with the clutter of ordinary life. His world is as
personal as Verga's, as idiosyncratic as D'Annunzio's; and it is
hard to see how, while pretending to be objective, he can make his
statements carry much authority. If hell is inward, then where is
heaven? So far Moravia has resorted to objective disregard when
even theoretical happiness has been implied. He will surely have
to show more of himself if he is to be regarded as anything more
than an indefatigable raker of ashes and embers. After all, fires
have burned and not all of them by courtesy of mental hell.

III

Elio Vittorini (1908–) has translated a good deal of English and
American literature into terse Italian, some of the authors being
Poe, D. H. Lawrence, Faulkner, Hemingway, Saroyan and, one

to whom he pays especial tribute, Daniel Defoe. His first novel, *La conversazione in Sicilia* (1939), is a simple but far from simplified account of a young man's brief return to his birthplace; it won the praise of Hemingway and Robert Penn Warren but, compared with Vittorini's later works, seems rather thin and exiguous although composed with evident love. After *Uomini e no* (1945), a patchy and undistinguished novel, came *Il sempione strizza l'occhio al Frejus* (1947), translated as 'The Twilight of the Elephant', and then *Il garofano rosso* (1948), which had been written between 1933 and 1935 and which with unmawkish tenderness follows a young love-affair against the background of Fascist Italy. The young man is attracted by Fascism and the nearer he gets to it the more blatant does the movement's nihilistic bravado become: the ghost of D'Annunzio is evoked and damned, as in Moravia's *La conformista*.

Vittorini's tenderness is that of a virile temperament which abominates violence but does a great deal of private, mental infighting with itself, as *Le donne di Messina* (1949), *Erica* (1956) and *La garibaldina* (1956) reveal. Erica lives with her mother and father in a teeming tenement; when she is fourteen her father leaves to work on the mountain roads, taking the mother with him, and Erica stays behind to care for the two other children. Rarely has poverty been handled with such disciplined compassion: Erica, lonely and harassed, creates a world of her own based on need and service. She chats to the coal and the fire, sometimes threatens both, while the other people in the tenement set a daily cacophony of comment ricocheting up the sounding-tube of the tenement's internal walls. Eventually Erica runs out of supplies and turns, as we knew she would, to prostitution—without heroics or self-pity and without quite realizing the nature of her decision. This is a much defter, tighter work than Verga's *Nedda*, with which it has much in common. But Verga could not have conceived *La garibaldina*, in which a weird old woman who claims to have known Garibaldi buttonholes a young soldier going on leave. She takes his part against pompous officials, boasts of her lost beauty, her well-married daughter, and promises the soldier a prince's welcome when their train gets in. Of course, she has been romancing; the soldier discovers that she is a notorious local crackpot, but he has also discovered her perky self-esteem, her faith in people in their own right and the harmless charm of innocence. Erica sacrifices herself to gain *minestra* for the children, and the *garibaldina* offers herself on the altar of a past flamboyance. When something is lost, something is always found: we are close to Silone's *fiducia* and emancipated from Verga's grim pattern, as from Moravia's despondent boredoms. Vittorini distils from reality an essence which is palpable and disturbing yet peculiarly unforced and factual. His emotional range is wider than Moravia's and, one suspects, his main conviction that of human worth, however disguised and puzzling that worth may be.

Riccardo Bacchelli (1891–) shows something of this conviction in such historical novels as *Il diavolo al Pontelungo* (1927), about Bakounin's nineteenth-century experiments in socialism, and *Il mulino del Po* (1938–40, in the periodical *Nuova Antologia*) which spends two thousand pages on successive generations of one family from Napoleon to 1918. Bacchelli began by writing lyrically, in the poet's way of *Dr Zhivago*, and he generally relies on intensity of feeling to engage the reader. This is one reason for his output's rather viscous, unexciting quality, while another reason is his scholarly disinclination to make lively narrative out of his synoptic view of cyclical time. *Il diavolo* is the briskest by far, and even that has mannered flourishes which recall *Il filo meraviglioso* (1910). Another novel, *La città degli amanti* (1929), is a *jeu d'esprit* about a city for lovers, built by an American business man, which the lovers cannot stand. And *Lo sa il tonno* (1923), a satirical extravaganza on the tunny-fish, shows him labouring out of his depth. Bacchelli is at his best in the slow-moving, history-savouring chronicle such as *Il mulino* or, rather shorter, *Oggi, domani e mai* (1932), a novel which is academic in the worst sense because the personifications capture his own imagination so little, not to mention the reader's. He is an acquired taste, too reliable and too fond of theorizing to bring history as alive as Lampedusa does in *Il gattopardo*, although both have in common a fondness for set, mannered pieces often a paragraph long. And Bacchelli's *Il rabdomante* (1936) reveals him once again as fonder of considering than of telling.

'Curzio Malaparte' (Curzio Suckert, 1898–) is a much more animated performer. Born of an Italian mother and a German

father, he was one of the earliest members of the Italian Fascist
Party, founded in 1919. Under Mussolini his literary career
flourished, although his independent spirit got him five years of
confinement on the island of Lipari from 1933 onwards. He has
always claimed to oppose all forms of totalitarianism and to have
been frequently at odds with both Fascists and Nazis. He saw
Fascism as an agricultural response to things urban and in *Italia
barbara* (1925) celebrated the bucolic, down-at-heel, atavistic
parts of Italian life—a far cry from his spoof, *Sodoma e Gomorra*
(1931), in which Voltaire tries to discover what malpractice the
people of Gomorrah really committed. His best writings have
grown quite naturally from his spectacular and, it seems, ingeniously improvised career. *Fughe in prigione* (1936) describes
his incarceration on Lipari, and his later writings, better known
and less obviously influenced by Futurism, compose an extravagant, grisly album of our times. Out of his Second World War
experiences as a correspondent, he wrote *Kaputt* (1944), in which
the fatuities and horrors of modern war are made into legends,
fantasies and derisive, paradoxical nightmares. It is an anguished
yet gloating book, full of shudder-provoking pageantry and corrosive loathing. It is as if D'Annunzio had swallowed a Silone-
type conscience; and beneath the assembled grotesquerie of faint
humans and resolute animals there is a kind of sustained, structural hysteria similar to that we find in Céline. *La pelle* (1950),
again in the form of imaginative memoirs, concentrates on the
period from 1943 to 1945 and a group of American officers in
Naples.

None of this is without merit, but Malaparte's fondness for the
gruesome and the showy, the clever-clever and the farcical, gives
almost all his work an inhuman flavour. There is always an un-
stable-sounding cacchination to split the surface of the compassionate passages; always a suggestion that humans, to
Malaparte, are just another species of circus animals. But his
visions—long-distance for suffering, close-up for idiocy—define
in bravura language the kind of muddle which gives cartoonists a
good start and propagandists no hope at all. Where Silone elicits
something fundamental and positive from modern man's misadventures, Malaparte fantasticates the human equation he cannot factorize. He gives, in fact, a futurist's version of despair—

rather German in its blithe excesses and, for its intensely personal rearrangement of familiar events, a danger-signal to the neo-realists because it makes eloquently plain the subjectivity of objective reporting.

Vasco Pratolini (1913–), on the other hand, austerely, impersonally shows how so-called history-in-the-making affects the lives of the humble, and especially of the urban poor. At eight Pratolini sold caramels in the theatres, at twelve was apprenticed to a printer, at twenty became a vendor of iced drinks and then spent two years in a sanatorium, where he began to write. He knows the mean streets as well as does any Italian novelist writing now, and his account of how war and Fascism affected those who lived in '*Il quartiere*' (1945) is often brutal and sometimes monotonously shocking. Pratolini's compassion operates through calculated repetition; he pushes his point without commentary, without indignation, and his own feelings are compressed into the resolve to document bluntly. Out of thousands of touches—smells, sounds, quarrels, gossip, encounters, the texture of the air, the slant of the light, the susurrus of insect and vehicular life—Pratolini assembles a chastening fresco of life in the Sanfrediano and Santa Croce areas of Florence. Like Bacchelli, he is concerned with people in their numerousness, but his multitudes quiver with living individuals in whom one can believe and about whom one can become indignant. From 1941 onwards Pratolini has been most prolific, adding one exposé to another. *Cronache di povere amanti* (1947) shows how Fascism (in spite of the Duce's occasional bursts of bucolic fervour) was essentially an urban movement. Life in the *Via del corno*, an obscure little street, becomes an image of Italy between 1925 and 1926. There is no main character; instead, the beautifully integrated depth-study of Maciste, the smith whose end is tragic, the two Fascists Carlino and Osvaldo, the vicious Signora and the two lovers, occupies the mind almost as if we have been eavesdropping. The prose is accurate and cool although a little over-adjectival during lulls. There is no doubt of Pratolini's gifts and achievement, but one cannot help wondering if in such novels as *Mestiere da vagabondo* (1947), *Un eroe del nostro tempo* (1949) and *Le ragazze di Sanfrediano* (1953) Pratolini has not over-duplicated. With *Metello: una storia italiana* (1955–), a vast fresco-novel, he finds himself at the point where Verga faded out. It remains to be seen whether or not he can tackle the community at all levels without favouritism and without losing, in modifying, the technique which he has made such a specialized success.

Giuseppe Berto (1914–) saw military service in Ethiopia and North Africa, and then spent thirty months in a Texas P.O.W. camp. He began to write after seeing how some American writers (especially Hemingway) 'boldly and without too great a concern with fine writing' confronted life in the raw. In America he wrote a volume of stories, and the novel *Il cielo e rosso* (1947), a poignant exploration of the impact of war on four adolescents. Berto carefully disentangles the pity from the political and military commotion, but without quite discovering the deeper wells of personality—the things which, trivial as they may seem, ultimately justify men and even adolescents to themselves. There is something external in the treatment, something which prefers the vivid outline to the interior chiaroscuro, as *Il brigante* (1950), set in post-war Calabria, makes plain. Compared with the novels of Pier Paolo Pasolini (1922–), Berto lacks knowledge of the human spirit's hinterland. Pasolini, attempting in such novels as *Ragazzi di vita* (1955) and *Una vita violento* (1959) to present the tough boys of the Roman slums, manages to pursue motive and fantasy without over-developing the boys' sensibilities and, also, to interweave the starkness of treatment with deftly compressed ideology. Part of Pasolini's success in this can be attributed to his accurate and thorough knowledge of several related things: Italian popular verse, Roman dialect and the psychology of the young. As a result, one day with the Roman *ragazzi* becomes more illuminating (and disturbing) than a war studied through Berto's adolescents. Pasolini has now turned to the art of the film, and his *Accatone* is much less melodramatic and superficial than Visconti's version of Berto's *Il brigante*.

Pasolini is one of those who have profited from the example of Verga, and *Ragazzi di vita* loses nothing in being compared to *Mastro-Don Gesualdo*. All the same, their respective accounts of slum-boyhood expose one of the main temptations of the Italian novelist: that is, to resort to poverty as a literary motif simply for the opportunities it confers of being basic. For the most part, Pasolini, like Verga, curbs the subject's sensational potentialities with cool, matter-of-fact prose. But where Verga overdoes things philosophically, Pasolini sometimes overdoes them through excessive recourse to slang; and any kind of heightening takes the novel into the swamplands of D'Annunzian hyperbole. The neo-realists know this and write with great restraint about poverty or choose a different social class. Carlo Cassola, for instance, in *La casa di Via Valadier* (1956), studies anti-Fascism in a middle-class ethos, taking pains to prevent one character from sounding like another—from appearing to be just one of half-a-dozen variations on one theme. The problem is to be passionately factual without being melodramatic or simplistic, and this is what mars the reso-lute work of such young writers as Antonio Guerra (*Dopo i leoni*), Italo Calvino (*L'entrata in guerra*), Elémire Zolla (*Minuetto all' inferno*) and Nello Saito (*Gli avventurieri siciliani*). The difficulty emerges most clearly in the work of Carlo Levi, whose *Paura della libertà* (1946), purporting to discuss the major themes of our time ('Sacrifice', 'Slavery', 'Blood' and so forth), develops into a subtle, argumentative prose elegy, while *L'orologio* (1950), set in post-Liberation Rome, loses itself in kaleidoscopic confusion. To care deeply—as Levi evidently does—is to become rhetorical; yet to be rhetorical is to leave realism behind. And most Italian novelists from Verga on have been haunted by the chimaera of a complete realism: so complete as to evict the author from his own work. So the choice has become one between documentary, in which there is no need to maintain fictional conventions, and highly imagina-tive writing which its exponents try to protect from rhetorical excesses. Italians are still opposing a sane, compassionate factu-ality to their recollections of Fascism.

Mario Soldati's *Il vero Silvestri* (1959), with magnificent economy of means, shows how difficult it is to define the essence of anyone: after all, what *is* real? How many people's accounts do we need? Soldati makes his Pirandello-like case through juxta-positions of varying accounts, and such subtle, almost Jamesian analysts as Giorgio Bassani pursues intimate truths even more deeply. Among other writers, Dino Buzzati has turned to the moral fable, Giose Rimanelli to primitive intensity (especially in *Il peccato originale*), Ugo Pirro to lurid, Goya-like vignettes, Brunello Vandano (*Il quando e il come*) and Ercole Patti (*Il punto debole*) to a cinematic terseness or elliptical method, Raffaele le

Capria (*Ferito a morte*) to almost evasive technical experimentation, and Furio Monicelli in *I giardini segreti* to the ironic swirl of effects we find in Bely the Russian. The best women novelists —Elsa Morante, Giana Manzini and Anna Banti—go in for scrupulous, flowing analyses which recall Dorothy Richardson and re-prove Virginia Woolf's assertions about reality. Where indeed is fancy bred? One answer could be, 'In the head of the neo-realist.' We have only to study two parallel developments— the new vogue for the old-school novel (*Il gattopardo* and Alberto Denti di Pirajno's *Ippolita*) and the cult of documentary—whether about priests or Sicilian squalor. The one restores to the novel a certain sophisticated irony and a more complex attitude than either Verga's attempted objectivity or the committedness of social realism. The other shows the novelist what he does not need to do. The two together make it likely that the Italian novel will soon, without becoming wildly experimental, yield to the film its own (as to the documentary), and start to regain the Manzoni heritage. In other words, make room again for amusedness, sophisticated probing of motives, expression of a narratorial point of view, a wider range of subject-matter and, above all, a sense that the social panorama is not always sordid. But, of course, individual temperaments lead themselves, and all one has to rely on is the assumption that the majority of novelists are bound to find a limited social realism just as confining and un-representative as the *chosisme* of the French. Giuseppe Borgese, the novelist (*Rubé*, 1921) who went to America and there embraced sociology (*Goliath*, *The City of Man*, *Common Cause*), corresponds to Carlo Levi, but goes further, arguing for combined aesthetic and historical views of works of art. In Italy, now, it is just as important to argue that the virtues of *ermetismo* have been obscured by its faults, and that the personal, private alchemy which makes an *art* of fiction now needs to catch up with an overdeveloped, over-zealous attention to social conditions; the humanist with the humanitarian, which is what De Sanctis always insisted on and what the most enterprising younger novelists, Natalia Ginzburg (*Tutti i nostri ieri*, 1953) and Guglielmo Petroni (*La casa si muove*, 1950; *Noi dobbiamo parlare*, 1953), have made the basis of their gifted audacity.

3

Soviet Russia

I

SO FAR we have noticed how the English novel is handicapped by excessive concern with class-distinctions, from worm's-eye to bird's-eye views; how the Americans try to create a *Summa* of their society by documenting massively or resorting to myth; how some French novelists try to eliminate psychology by cataloguing the external world; how the Italians fight a tradition of *ermetismo* by an almost over-compensatory *verismo* whereas the West Germans counter painful recollections by turning to Parnassianism and fantasy.

I want now to examine the Soviet novel, source of the East German novel's debility and antithetical to the romantic or subjective type of fiction. Ilya Ehrenburg, laboriously stating in his memoirs that he can pay tribute to Hemingway without 'degrading' himself, ignores Hemingway the romantic who has much in common with the Pasternak of *Dr Zhivago*. It is easy to overestimate the class-feeling expressed in *To Have and To Have Not*, but a Western reader approaches that feeling with the notion of 'commitment' at the front of his mind. In the West, being '*engagé*' or 'committed' is a condition the writer squares his shoulders for: he assumes the label selfconsciously and (as Camus, Sartre, Silone, Malraux and Dos Passos remind us) not always without pomposity. In Russia, however, being *engagé* is an obligation taken for granted as an old national habit. Belinsky's idea that 'art without ideas is like a man without a soul' finds an echo in Virginia Woolf's essay 'The Russian Point of View', in which she says: 'In reading Tchekov we find ourselves repeating the word "soul" again and again. It sprinkles his pages. Old drunkards use it freely. . . . Indeed, it is the soul that is the chief character in Russian fiction.' She goes on to explain 'why it needs so great an effort on the part of an English reader to read *The Brothers Karamazov* or *The Possessed* a second time. The "soul" is alien to him.' And she is right. But when she uses the word 'soul' she thinks of Dostoevsky's 'seething whirlpools, gyrating sandstorms, water-spouts': high somatic drama in the inward amphitheatre. But Belinsky's idea of the soul is much more philosophical and social-political, rather like Virginia Woolf's idea of the English novelist: 'inclined . . . to scrutiny of society rather than understanding of individuals themselves'. A change has come about. If we want old-fashioned soul we have to go to Faulkner and Mauriac; the new kind of soul—that is, the new kind pursued with something of the old fervour—is what we find in Ehrenburg but not in Dostoevsky, in Dudintsev but not in Pasternak. Soviet Russia has exploited that part of the Russian character which made Virginia Woolf brood hard on Pozdnyshev's question in *The Kreutzer Sonata*: 'Why live?' But it no longer puts that question. Whereas the great Russian novelists advanced on two fronts—the social and that of the soul—the Ehrenburgs and Dudintsevs advance on the former only; the question has turned into an imperative 'Live!' and the life-devouring is according to the state's menu.

We have to distinguish between compassion for man in general (which both Virginia Woolf and Pasternak, both Hemingway and Silone have in common) and concern for man expressed through rigid doctrines. 'Commitment' is used to refer to both, and it is only recently that Russian writers have felt free to compare the second unfavourably with the first by protesting lengthily against the Stalin cult. Yet, in noticing this, we have to remember that even the anti-Stalinists do not, cannot, separate compassion for man in general from communism; the for merentails the latter. Those who suffered worst under Stalin were those who had been the most fervent supporters of the Bolshevik Party, and those who fared best—Alexey Tolstoy and Ehrenburg—were those who repudiated the October Revolution. And now, with Stalin gone, there is a natural enough attempt to see communism plain, to cleanse 'commitment' of its personalist associations: not to recur to any pre-revolutionary past (as in Hungary and Poland) but to make writing live up to the heroic commitment epitomized by the

October Revolution. It is not to Andreyev, of the last pre-revolutionary decade, that the moderns look, but to the golden first decade of the achieved revolution when 'commitment' was defined generously and debated openly; it is the decade of Blok, Mayakovsky, Yesenin, Pilnyak and Babel, between which and the early sixties there is precious little.

To look back to Maxim Gorky (1868–1936, 'Alexey Peshkov') and Leonid Andreyev is saddening. Gorky, who in his youth had as many kinds of jobs as John O'Hara and Saul Bellow, could always convey the sharp desirability of the world at hand without losing sight of something better. In him soul and realism never parted company. As well as making his Satan exclaim, 'Man— that sounds proud!' in *Na dne* ('The Lower Depths', 1902), he could expose the corruptness and crudeness of his fellow-men with all the undistracted mordancy of an Aldous Huxley, the Huxley who himself recently echoed that Satan (see p. 63). His hobo stories, *Meshchane* ('The Smug Citizen', 1902), *Foma Gordeyev* (1899) and *Troye* ('Three of Them', 1901), extol the life of the floater and send us forward to Thomas Wolfe and Kerouac. He could always, even in his early ingenuously individualistic work, answer the question, Why live? The autobiographical *Detstvo* ('My Childhood', 1913) tells us why: all tenacious euphoria and ebullient faith, he sweeps confidently through the self-imposed elenchus of his mature period (*Mat'*, 'Mother', 1907–8; *Ispoved'*, 'The Confession', 1908) to idealize the collectivity, espouse the Bolshevik experiment and finally, in 1928, to quit Italy and risk his lungs by returning to Russia. His four-volume panorama *Zhizn' Klima Samgina: sorok let* (1927–37, composed of *Bystander*, *The Magnet*, *Other Fires* and *The Spectre*) creates plethoric streams of life and thought and, although amorphous, remains enthralling even now. What Gorky derived from Chekhov and developed into forceful realism, he gave back in the form of his publishing firm, Znaniye, which nourished V. V. Veresayev (anti-tsar in *Na voyne*, 'In the War', 1908; Christian and submissive in *Bez dorogi*, 'Without Road', 1895; anti-Bolshevik in *V tupike*, 'In a Blind Alley', 1923; but eventually reconciled to the Soviets), Alexander Serafimovich (*Gorod v Stepi*, 'The City in the Steppe', 1910; *Zhelezny potok*, 'The Iron Flood', 1924, a master of popular panache), as well as A. I. Kuprin, I. A. Bunin and Andreyev.

Kuprin (1870–1938), after holding a Gorky-like variety of jobs, first of all wrote some stories about factories and army life, then made his name with the novel *Poyedinok* ('The Duel', 1905), an articulate, Chekhovian onslaught on the military mentality. His principal excellence is his power of vivid characterization, occasionally lapsing into the lurid—as in *Yama* (1912), about prostitution in Odessa—and lambent romanticism (*Koleso vremeni*, 'The Wheel of Time', 1930; *Zhaneta*, 'Jeanette', 1932–3). These last two reflect his own experience as an *émigré* in France (where he went after the Revolution) and recall both Turgenev and the shorter Tolstoy. Bunin (1870–1953) too owes more to the old masters than to Gorky, advancing after a rather sentimental apprenticeship to the corrosive realism of his novel about peasant life, *Derevnya* ('The Village', 1910). Although given to protracted bouts of commentary, Bunin (who won the Nobel award in 1933) rarely fails to overpower the reader with sheer portraiture: *Sukhodol* ('Dry Valley', 1911–12), presenting the fall of a landowning family, the Khrushchovs, through the mind of a woman servant, is a powerful and majestically compressed novel, while *Gospodin iz San Frantsisko* ('The Gentleman from San Francisco', 1916) points the sudden death of an American millionaire on Capri with brilliant, ingenious brevity. Another anti-Bolshevik, Bunin went to France in 1919, where he wrote *Mitina lyubov'* ('Mitya's Love', 1924–5), a Moravia-like exploration of young, misty sensuality; *Zhizn' Arseneva*; *istoki dney* ('The Well of Days', 1930), autobiographical, dark in mood, and analytical; and the even more sombre *Tyomnyye allei* ('Dark Alleys', 1943). Bunin is a most impressive writer—for his unflaggingly poetic response to the mystery of life, his acid social realism, his lavish pictorial sense and his skill with atmosphere. He has a keen eye and a romantic's respect for the exotic and the spiritual. A patient, methodical writer, he sometimes sacrifices plot to local texture and even character to physiognomy, but he never makes the mistake of most novelists who deal in emblems and symbols: he never fails to convince us of the colour, texture and validity of the thing in hand before showing what lies beyond it, as in his stories of peasant brutality (some told in vernacular), and such exotic themes as a Colombo rickshaw man and oriental erosion of the will.

Andreyev (1871–1919) took some of his inspiration from the

later Tolstoy and from Gorky, but he was always drawn to morbid or carnal themes, and as he grew older became increasingly hysterical and lurid in style. He speaks for the *fin-de-siècle* intellectual, more interested in analysis and discussion than in direction-finding, and emerges as a voluptuary of the unanswerable. His early stories are much concerned with death and human vulnerability, and *Krasny smekh* ('The Red Laugh', 1904), ostensibly about the Russo-Japanese war, develops into an onslaught—both anguished and gaudy—on war in general. *Tak bylo* ('Thus It Was', 1906), made similar points, or, rather, released similar cries, about the French Revolution and revolution itself. Andreyev's nihilism is often suicidal; he suffers from too much Schopenhauer mixed with more than an average share of personal melancholia. Groping in his own wild way for the noble image of the selfless leader, he is a demented Silone. *Rasskaz o semi poveshennykh* ('The Seven Who Were Hanged', 1908) is a fierce and shocking work, savage from its opening, 'As the minister was a very stout man, inclined to apoplexy', to its last poignant words, 'And on the snow lay Sergey's black rubber-shoe, wet, trampled underfoot. Thus men greeted the rising sun.' The hanged bodies are transported back along the road they recently travelled alive, and Andreyev's description spares us nothing: 'With stretched necks, with bulging eyes, with blue, swollen tongues, looking like some unknown, terrible flowers between the lips, which were covered with bloody foam.' Compassion and morbidity combined to derange him, and he three times attempted suicide: he was one of those who asked, Why live? He spent most of his life in the sort of spiritual darkness which Tolstoy experienced just before composing *Smert' Ivana Ilyicha* ('The Death of Ivan Ilyich'), but he lacked mental resourcefulness. He could not invent answers but he could empathize to a phenomenal extent.

Rasskaz o semi poveshennykh is his best novel, largely because it expresses a luminous adjustment to horror, whereas *Krasny smekh* upsets us and feeds on bitterness, and *Gubernator* ('The Governor', 1906) makes its point resignedly and almost apathetically. Andreyev's lucid intervals became fewer, especially as his anti-Bolshevik hatreds became a substitute for his dwindling creative power. In one of his most powerful plays, *Tsar' Golod* ('King Hunger', 1907), he reviles all classes of society, and his last

novel, *Dnevnik Satany* ('Satan's Diary', 1921), no more than a
draft, compresses a suffocating pessimism that leaves as little to
heaven as to the imagination. In his play, *Anatema* (1909), he
sketched a Christlike hero who reappeared as Duke Lorenzo in
the tragedy *Chyornyye maski* ('The Black Maskers', 1908). In some
ways Andreyev is close to Dostoevsky and, had he lived, might
have developed further the heroic, almost hopeful Samson of his
last play, *Samson v okovakh* ('Samson in Chains', written in 1914),
who, because he trusts vaguely in some larger hope, destroys himself in order to destroy the forces which angered Andreyev himself.
One cannot help feeling, however, that he took a child's as well as
a visionary's delight in the images of horror he devised. Rather
too irresponsible to be an utterly convincing novelist, he is best at
theatre and effects; but *Rasskaz o semi poveshennykh* shows what
brilliance of detail and dignity of idea he could occasionally
achieve and, in sending us forward to Camus, makes us wish
Andreyev had done more in that vein. Yet he is not half so
theatrical as M. P. Artsybashev (1878–1927), his apparent rival
in gloom, whose *Sanin* (1907) electrified a bored, disenchanted
public with a creed of lurid carnality. A sweatily erotic novel, it
created an appetite for which Artsybashev wrote another sexual
novel, *Milliony* ('The Millionaire', 1910), but which led eventually, for him at any rate, into the Andreyev region of suicide as the
only way to freedom. *U posledney cherty* ('Breaking-Point', 1912)
gives us Naumov who regards all faith in life as vacuous super-
stition. But the point is better proved, if proved it has to be, by the
suicide of Mayakovsky and Yesenin and by the fact that by 1938
other leading poets had killed themselves or, like Ivanov, left
Russia (1924, when Trotsky was cast out), or, like Pilnyak, been
purged (1937). The question, Why live? becomes as much a social
as a cosmic one although the negative answer to it remains one
and the same. There is room here only to mention and commend
the aesthetes who countered the civic-minded optimists (Gorky)
and the Andreyev pessimists. Panache and refinement, as well as
a willingness to play zestfully with ideas, characterize the work of
D. S. Merezhkovsky (1865–1941: *Tolstoy and Dostoevsky*, 1901),
his wife Zinaida Hippius (1869–1945), N. M. Minsky (1855–1937),
A. Volynsky (A. L. Flekser, 1863–1926), V. V. Rozanov (1856–
1919), author of a brilliant commentary on Dostoevsky's 'Grand

Inquisitor' which also includes a superb chapter on Gogol, and Leo Shestov (1869–1938), all of whom ranged far and wide in their critical works, tried to evolve original religions (not without many debts to Dostoevsky) and helped to create a climate for such symbolists as Ivanov, Bryusov, Balmont and Annenski. It is perhaps significant that the Russians, not the French, elaborated a whole philosophy of symbolism, feeling the need to theorize against the menacing articulations of the civic-minded. Upper-middle-class attitudes, far from crippling the new school of poetry, gave it a cosmopolitan, gracious flavour, as well as fostering a civilized acknowledgment of the play-element in literature.

Fyodor Sologub (1863–1927), perhaps the most interesting member of this set, came from poor circumstances but took no part in the events of 1917. He must be noted here for his bizarre novels, of which *Melki bes* ('The Little Demon,' 1907), *Tvorimaya legenda* ('The Created Legend', 1908–12 serially) and *Zaklinatel'nitsa z'mey* '(The Snake-Charmer', 1921) are the best and the most characteristic of his weird fusion of realism with vivid, Manichean fantasy. The hero of *Melki bes*, Peredonov, is a carefully calculated and brilliantly imagined goblin of squalor—as arresting a character as anything in Dostoevsky and a foretaste of the thick citizen, Vladimir Globov, in *The Trial Begins* by 'Abram Tertz'. One of the most neglected and, because he wrote rather like James Joyce, baffling writers in the group is Andrei Bely (B. N. Bugayev, 1880–1934). His first effort, *Dramaticheskaya simfoniya* (1902), showed which way, as both poet and novelist, he was going, *via* the anthroposophy of Rudolf Steiner's Dornach colony, 'the Society for the Study of Poetic Rhythm', and the Revolution. Bely invented the symphonic novel which can evoke a real world underlying drifting phenomena; to him life was a decrepit dome of many-coloured glass, not to be too much respected. An over-riding concern with prose rhythm (*Ritm, kak dialektika*, 'Rhythm as Dialectics,' 1929) accompanies his almost riotous comic sense (evident in the sympathy of *Masterstvo Gogolya*, 'Gogol's Mastery', 1932). Of his novels, at least two may be regarded as outstanding achievements, especially *Peterburg* (1912), which is more recklessly inspired than *Serebryany golub* ('The Silver Dove', 1910). Always close to caricature, Bely's wildest pages go back to Gogol and Dostoevsky as well as forward to Joyce and Beckett.

Peterburg dazzles with its array of suspenseful flashbacks, symphonic anaphora, dreams, levels, hallucinations, crowded bravura, echoes, symbols and asides. But it is just as gripping as giddily clever. The action occupies a couple of days in the geometrically planned city of the title, seething with the revolutionary energies of 1905. Senator Apollon Ableukhov, who, deserted by his wife, has developed a colossal pattern-complex, senses desperateness and misrule on the orderly air. And well he might: his son has pledged himself to the revolutionaries, who equip him with a bomb in a sardine-tin. The target, his father; the method and occasion unspecified; the time twenty-four hours, for the muddled young man has managed to start the thing ticking. It ticks throughout the second half of the novel and its final ineffectual explosion is symbolic. The self-important senator shrinks when he is sacked; his perfidious wife glides back in rage; another world—that of proletarian squalor on Vasilyevsky Island (woodlice, peelings, cockroaches and all)—looms and swells. Lippanchenko, the *agent provocateur* 'with lips that resemble slices of salmon', gets grotesquely murdered. An army officer, whom young Ableukhov has cuckolded (or seemed to), shaves off his beard and tries to hang himself. But the ceiling falls in, and he survives for new indignities. The whole novel provokes one to snatch at (or fend off) meanings; and the reading is strenuous but it brings swarmingly alive a population with a doom complex. Bely refuses to simplify his people and his crowds or to complicate his prose, which is sharp, brassy, nervous and vivid. Atmospheric details, much gusty talk and the precise use of characterizing images build up a total effect of appalling originality; appalling because the structural tricks look a bit wilful beside the heartrendingly funny, gravely compassionate conception of the whole.

Bely's later novels, such as *Moskva* (1927) and *Maski* ('Masks', 1933), are less pyrotechnical and, which is much more serious, less spell-binding. One looks away more often. But certainly they ensured that he would be a strong influence on almost all other Russian novelists of any mental dexterity and spiritual originality. Of course no one in Soviet Russia speaks much of him, largely because there are few who for sheer imagination can touch him, and therefore—whatever his subject-matter—he would now not be approved of. But his 'formalism' is an exciting experience for readers not afraid of textural surprises. A writer with similar methods is Alexey Remizov (1877–1957) whose fantasies of evil, folk-nightmares and urban monstrosities owe something to the *skaz* (peasant narrative), to the virtuoso of *skaz*, Leskov, and to Gogol and Dostoevsky. Such lurid novels as *Prud* ('The Pond', 1907), about city life—which Remizov sees with creative loathing, *Chasy* ('The Clock', 1904), *Neugomonny buben* ('The Unhushable Tambourine', 1909), *Pyataya yazva* ('The Fifth Pestilence', 1912) and *Slovo o pogibeli zemli russkoy* ('Lament for the Ruin of Russia', 1917) present his uncontrollable aversion to townscapes and westernization. His style is baroque and bloated, like the English of Thomas Nashe or Carlyle, and he creates gargoyle characters with extraordinary facility and much originality. His later style is tamer and so reveals the great deal he has in common with Boris Pilnyak (1894–).

II

Futurism coincided with the First World War, the February and the Bolshevik Revolutions; between 1917 and 1920 Russian writers necessarily marked time. After this there could be no place for aestheticism, for genteel stylists, for satire or Parnassianism. Mayakovsky trumpeted a poetry of catchwords and Yesenin combined a barbaric yawp of his own with tame, bucolic lyrics. Writers were obliged to clarify their politics, and many left the country. The notion of class literature was advanced but failed to catch on immediately; there were too many moderates for that. And those whom Trotsky called fellow-travellers were able to write their own kind of literature while yet accepting the fact of the Revolution. This was the last respite before the watershed, and it produced some stirring novels about Revolutionary experiences. Boris Pilnyak's *Goly god* ('The Naked Year', 1922) is typical of these: it celebrates the violence rather than the desired reform and its panorama of the Russia of 1921—all rapine, hunger and blood—assaulted the popular imagination in much the same way as Dimitri Shostakovich's Fifth Symphony (first performed in 1937): bumptiousness and tenderness violently juxtaposed, both strident and mellifluous, confidently orchestrated and yet rather formless as a whole. Self-concern had to shrink: that appears to be the theme of Shostakovich's orchestral dialogue and it is the structural basis of Pilnyak's novel. Pilnyak followed with a torrent of work, ranging from *Ivan-da-Marya* (1923), on the Cheka inquisition, *Tret'ya stolitsa* ('The Third Capital', 1923), a quiet anthem to pastoral Russia, and *Mashiny i volki* ('Machines and Wolves', 1925), to *Makhogany* ('Mahogany', Berlin, 1927), which Pilnyak eventually incorporated into *Volga vpadayet v Kaspiyskoye more* ('The Volga Falls to the Caspian Sea', 1930), his famous epic about the construction of a dam to change the Volga's course. Pilnyak celebrates the industrial initiative of it all but also rebukes the wastage of the Revolution, and sustains his criticism in *Rozhdeniye cheloveka* ('The Birth of a Man', 1935) in which a hard-headed female comrade suddenly softens into ecstatic motherhood. But in *Sozrevaniye plodov* ('The Ripening of the Fruit', 1936) the villagers who used to paint ikons now paint other objects, and we have to guess what Pilnyak thinks.

Of 'construction' novels, F. V. Gladkov's *Energiya* ('Energy', 1933) is the most tedious and Valentin Katayev's *Vremya vperyod!* ('Time, Forward!', 1932), about teams who compete in the pouring of cement, is cinematically and technically the best. Those readers who can take such a theme seriously will take it, and others will have to abandon it as jejune. Certainly Mikhail Sholokhov (1905–), recording the Cossack epic, has a more fruitful theme as well as the imaginative power to make it live within the ideological frame he has had to acknowledge. His *coups d'essai* at the Cossacks, his own people, can be found in two books of stories, *Donskie rasskazy* ('Tales of the Don', 1925) and *Lazorevaya step'* ('The Azure Steppe', 1926), both of which, tackling the Cossack class structure, have something of the exuberant density we find in Alexey Tolstoy's *novella, Kazaki* ('The Cossacks'), and bustling panoramic trilogy, perhaps too little known outside Russia, *Khozhdeniye po mukam* ('The Road to Pain', 1921–41). But Sholokhov consistently provides a grim ending, and the titles themselves indicate the mood: 'Dry Rot', 'Alien Blood', 'Deadly Enemy'. The aloof patriarchs will eventually be immersed in the society they control and made intimately responsible and responsive. This theme swells into the major work called *Tikhy Don* ('The Quiet Don'), and to some extent obliterates the idiosyncrasies and deeper reaches of character. 1,300 pages should be enough to include everything, especially about a nation of atavists and even about complicated people of high etiquette (which Sholokhov's Cossacks are not). The old way yields to the new; there is pain and awkwardness but none of the tragic resolution of the stories. Sholokhov sounds tromboning notes of hope, faith and life-affirmation. Gregor Melekhov, torn between ancient-and-honoured and new-and-national, progressively loses all—like Hemingway's Harry Morgan and Santiago. He cannot successfully contend with history and he cannot take a stand on the present for the present is never still. *Tikhy Don* (1928–40) is as much propaganda for human nature as for any political dogma, and the same is true of *Podnyataya tselina* ('Virgin Soil Upturned', 1932–3) in which commissars try to establish collective farming among the same highly individualistic Cossacks. Publication, however, was held up while Sholokhov briefly defied the authorities; he then made the required revisions, and *Podnyataya tselina* is now set reading for Russian schoolchildren.

Revisions or no revisions, the author who once described Soviet literature as a 'grey flood of colourless, mediocre' matter won the Lenin and Stalin prizes and spent two years modifying the original version of the second volume of *Podnyataya tselina* (1960), known as 'Harvest on the Don' in English. For a hero who, it is said, committed suicide after being jailed on false charges, Sholokhov substituted death inflicted by White counter-revolutionists. Semyon Davydov, a solemn, gat-toothed man from Lenin-grad, is one of 25,000 workers sent to get collective farming on its feet in the Don region. He soon finds everything going wrong: his assistants are manic, one staying up all night learning English, the other slaughtering cats to protect his pet pigeons; the farm manager is a crook who is concealing Whites and peculating; the Cossacks dilly-dally, misunderstand and object; rival collectives raid the hay; the wanton Lukeria distracts him, and the Cheka police are monsters who eventually get murdered. The characters are convincing and the writing is carefully pared. There are even cracks at the régime; but there are also long voluntaries on the bravery of party officials, the devotion to duty of the G.P.U. and heart-to-heart talks between earnest party officials (none of whom, it seems, is happily married). *Harvest* is much less theoretical than

Virgin Soil, and Davydov is no exemplar: he blunders, cannot keep order during an enrolment meeting, and fornicates; he is often impolite, too, and likes to delegate work. There is some sentimentality, especially in the portrayal of Shaly the blacksmith and Shchukar the windbag, and the landscape is in places too animated: 'Not one grave was tended, and the wind blowing from the east gloomily stirred the last year's scrub on the clayey mounds, and tenderly, as though sorting it over with fine feminine fingers, rustled the twigs of the faded, darkened wormwood', which surely would have read just as informatively: 'Not one grave was tended, and the wind from the east, stirring the last year's scrub on the mounds as though sorting it with feminine fingers, rustled the wormwood'. Sholokhov, racy and wide-ranging as he is, gets sentimental when he has to be sociological (as in *Virgin Soil* and *Harvest*) and superficial when, as in *Tikhy Don,* he tries to mythologize his own people. When we think that every supervisor of a collective farm was required, by government order, to read *Virgin Soil,* we cannot help wondering to what extent Sholokhov thought he was writing a textbook for the Russian people: after all, during the early days of the collectives, the Associations of Proletarian Writers sent journalists into the field to collect and process the raw material for a class literature to be used as a doctrinal instrument.

From earnest insistences to satire it is not always as far as Soviet Russians think; the propagandist often topples into self-parody and his arguments immediately reverse themselves. Of the deliberate satirists, Y. I. Zamyatin (1884–1937) made a habit of making a nuisance of himself. The manner of both Gogol and Remizov reappears in *Uyezdnoye* ('District Tales', 1911), and the journal which printed his *Na kulichkakh* ('At the World's End', 1922) was confiscated. His best-known novel is *My* ('We', 1922), sometimes likened to *Brave New World* and *1984,* but it was not permitted to appear in the Soviet Union. In 1931 Zamyatin left for Paris where he worked on a study of Attila whom he saw recrudescent in his own times. His other works, *Vzroslym detyam skazki* ('Fables for Grown-up Children', 1922), *Peshchera* ('The Cave', 1922), *Mamay* (1922) and *Blokha* ('The Flea', 1925), are written in his usual showy prose and present a peculiarly festive type of distortion. He removes all excrescences from a ridiculous situation and then develops the idiocy in depth. Small wonder that

Zamyatin is attracting the attention of young Russian writers who disdain 'flat' Tolstoy and laconic, grey Chekhov in favour of Gogol and Leskov: in other words, in favour of some spunky, inelegant knockabout touched with grotesquerie. And 'touched also in the sense of moderate derangement.

Ilya Ehrenburg (1891–) is a prolific writer who once thought of joining the Benedictine order. He was a fellow-traveller, he worked with Durov the animal trainer and Pavlov the physiologist, and has always made literary capital out of his rootlessness. Ehrenburg the satirist vacillates between slick cynicism and ruthless derision, but is often steadied by his passion for vivid, cinematic reporting. *Lik voyny* ('The Face of War', 1920) is both honest and persuasive, and his picaresque panoramic spoof on the nations, *Neobychaynyye pokhozhdeniya Khulio Khurenito i yego uchenikov* ('Julio Jurenito and his Disciples', 1921), presents the jocoser side of what are euphemistically called 'national differences'. *Lyubov' Zhanny Ney* ('The Love of Jeanne Ney', 1924) is a love story with spies, much more playful than the novels that followed: *V Protochnom Pere-ulke* ('In Protok Lane', 1927), about the slums, the dialectical steel-plant novel, *Vtoroy den'* ('The Second Day', 1933), *Padenie Parizha* ('The Fall of Paris', 1942) and *Voyna* ('War', 1943). It was a different Ehrenburg who in 1954 published *Ottepel'* ('The Thaw'), a cautious attack on Zhdanovism. After Ehrenburg's came such other nonconformist works as the *Literary Moscow Almanac*, since condemned three times over, and Dudintsev's *Ne khlebom yedinym* ('Not by Bread Alone'), both published in 1956. Pukhov, the painter in *Ottepel'*, destroys his personal and artistic integrity by constantly accommodating himself to bureaucratic formulas; one suspects a *persona* here just as, in such utterances as the following, Ehrenburg's daring commonplaceness mocks his former ironies: 'It is not enough for a Soviet man to control Nature; he has to control his own feelings.' That gives us a start but hardly prepares us for direct onslaughts on factory-managers and the astounding, rehabilitatory groping of this: 'so often people do one thing in their private life but say something quite different'.

Similar points are more ingeniously made through the contrast of Pukhov the opportunist with Saburov the diffident, dedicated artist. But we have to study *Vesna* ('The Spring', 1956), the sequel to *Ottepel'*, before we can understand what is going on. The engineering plant is apparently going to become a reality; the head designer is forgiven by the Party Bureau for getting cross; Lena settles down with the worthy Dmitry; Pukhov vows to discipline his envy of Saburov and—well, everything else comes right too, just as it goes wrong in Moravia and Verga. The thaw leads to a false spring; the characters, lapsing only so far, snap back into poses of frozen rectitude. In fact this is some of the feeblest, thinnest Ehrenburg ever, and even if we read *Vesna* as complete irony we are nowhere near the region of Gide or William Golding. Instead, we discover the fatuous unanimity of Russians on all matters. After Bulgakov's *Dyaboliada* ('Deviliad', 1925), with its far from genial mockery of the Soviet way, and Katayev's *Rastratchiki* ('The Embezzlers', 1927,) which applies a sharp knife to officialdom, we might have expected better. But, then, the period 1955–6 is marred by 'revisionism' and Russian writers are back to the private and public dishonesty which saps all moral intelligence, separates thinking man from thinking man and defeats even the ironist. Who can say what the Ilya Ilf (1897–1937) of today is doing, or the Evgeny Petrov (1903–1942)?

Ilf and Petrov collaborated to write *Dvenadtsat' stul'yev* ('Diamonds to Sit On', 1928), a spoof about capitalists who hunt diamonds in chairs only to find the stones have been sold to build a club for workers. Ilf's *Zolotoy telyonok* ('The Little Golden Calf', 1933) is another picaresque financial thriller in which Ostap Bender the arch-criminal reappears but again to no purpose: the money he acquires is of no use to him in a virtuous socialist republic. No indeed, and neither is spiritual capital. Anyone in Russia can poke fun at petty officials and small-time bigwigs: there is an honoured tradition of doing that; but, to say what is fundamentally wrong, the Soviet Russian has to allegorize: for petty official, read leader—and so on. Where does it end? For instance, Pavel Nilin's *Zhestokost'* ('Cruelty'), set in the early 1920s, tells of a serious young member of the N.K.V.D., tracking bandits through thick Siberian forests. Although sympathizing with the bandits, he brings them in, but shortly afterwards shoots himself in a fit of despair brought on by remorse and a mixed-up love-affair. The duty-versus-heart theme is solid, the snowscapes are deliciously exotic, and the author has a keen eye for people's characteristic gestures. But these things are no match for vast wastes of earnest *Komsomol* debate, the general woodenness of the characters and the narrator's relentless eulogizing of his heroic friend. Is it an allegory, with the dull debates thrown in for camouflage? We cannot tell, and neither can the novelist. Compared with the profound psychopathology of Sergei Sergeyev-Tsenski whose *Preobrazheniye* ('Transfiguration', 1923) explores the mind of a brooding, cuckolded architect against a vivid Crimean tapestry, Nilin's account of the new society and its man seems vapid and unreal. Again, Panteleymon Romanov (1884–1936) created in *Rozhdeniye geroya* ('The Birth of a Hero,' 1930) and *Sobstvennost'* ('Property', 1933) catalogues of everyday life in the U.S.S.R. which did not need to be allegorical because they were accurate about ethical and social problems.

III

It is obvious that an official aesthetic can stunt a national literature beyond repair, forcing upon it slavish socialist realism of a drab variety or the philosophical fable in the form of a monstrously obvious or monstrously esoteric code. There remains one other answer, however: Zamyatin's *My*, Ehrenburg's *Khulio Khurenito*, Pilnyak's *Makhogany* and, recently, Pasternak's *Dr Zhivago* and Abram Tertz's *The Trial Begins* were published abroad. How it must feel to write with no thought of a censorship to come, we can only guess. Isaac Deutscher sneeringly referred to Pasternak as 'a voice from the grave'; that is, a freak survival from the pre-revolutionary intelligentsia, and it is indeed odd to recall the Boris Pasternak (1890–1960) who wrote cryptic poems, sometimes called 'futurist' largely because of their involved syntax, who took little active interest in politics, counselled slow thinking in an accelerating society and published a collection of verse called *Poverkh bar'yerov* ('Above Barriers', 1931). Pasternak, like Bely, was strongly drawn to music and thought at one time of trying to become a composer. *Dr Zhivago* (1958) is as 'symphonic' as Bely's *Peterburg* but without that novel's tricksiness; it is certainly no duty-novel but the resolute defence of certain values by a man not entirely comfortably in the novel-form. Pasternak's unfrocked priest puts the main point clearly. Christ, he says, put the individual, his conscience, his power to love, at the centre of life. There is no room in such a doctrine for stereotypes. It is true that a life-force—whether or not through illegitimacy, the marriage of incompatibles, whether against or according to human wishes— perpetuates the species. Whatever the human person's entry into life, he can achieve what might be called the resoluteness of kindness. Political revolutionaries cannot countenance this fact. We are, says Pasternak, the partly self-controlling products of the mechanical life-force: while we live, we exercise conscience; when we die, we live on in our offspring who, in turn, will have the chance to rise above mere Nature.

The narrative which illustrates these principles is really a very up-to-date version of the progress of the wandering pilgrim. Yury Zhivago, a doctor and poet, is appalled at the social chaos brought by the Revolution. So he and his family leave Moscow for a village in the Urals, where they manage to make ends meet by tilling the land. While here, Yury encounters an old sweetheart called Lara, who revives in him his love of life. She is the one who makes Yury's tribulations worthwhile; she is the spiritual mainstay of the book —as Pasternak himself has said. When he finds her, she is married to a non-party revolutionary called Strelnikov. During the civil war, Yury is kidnapped by the Reds, and has to stay with them for some years. His family returns to Moscow. Yury eventually finds Lara again and realizes to the full his love and its futility; for Lara has to escape to Eastern Siberia; and Yury goes back to Moscow. He dies of a heart-attack in a street-car, and Lara returns to Russia only to vanish into a concentration-camp. The story is not an attack on any particular political creed; it serves to show how all mass movements whether in ideas, in politics, in history, in industry, in agriculture, disrupt the life of the individual. This is Sholokhov's point too. Yury is tossed about on the tide of history; strive as he does, he can achieve very little. He ends up a broken man, haunted by the memory of a brief, perfect love, the many wasted years, his exiled family and the prospect of his own redundancy. Between the mere causality of history and the idiocy of revolutionary and post-revolutionary politics, man has little chance. For what we glibly call history-in-the-making is a force of Nature too.

Compared with Pasternak, 'Abram Tertz' seems to be writing in acid, resolved to do damage with each sentence. *The Trial Begins* (London, 1960) amounts to an illustration of his critique *What is Socialist Realism?* (Paris, 1959). This *novella* satirizes the last year of Stalin's reign. We find the regimented mind recoiling to lechery, beauty-parlours, jazz, secret societies, dirty post-cards and, of course, thought-crime, of which the novel's optional symbolism is an interesting sample. The public prosecutor, pre-paring to arraign an abortionist, finds that his own unfaithful wife has sought the services of that trade already. So: what trial? Of what? Certainly not the reader's patience. Desperate and ironic, with a bite to its every sentence. *The Trial Begins* resumes for a brief spell the foaming social art of the Russian novel's (as the narrator says) 'prehistoric' phase. The style is not in isolated phrases but dispersed in a thousand slight twists of familiar utter-ances on stock occasions:

The music flowed. It oozed like oily, rainbow-patterned puddles. It rose. It roared and stormed off the stage into the body of the hall. Seryozha thought about the cloudburst in the streets outside and wriggled with pleasure. The music was like his private image of the revolution. The flood drowned the bour-geoisie in a most convincing way.

A general's wife in evening dress floundered, tried to scramble up a pillar and was washed away. The old general swam with a vigorous breast-stroke, but soon sank. Even the musicians were, by now, up to their necks in water. Eyes bulging, lips spitting foam, they fiddled frenziedly, randomly, below the surface of the waves.

A lone usher, riding on a chair, is swept past. This is Bely, verging on Andreyev. Tertz's own account of such writing can be found in his study of socialist realism:

I place my hopes in a phantasmagorical art: an art which would have hypotheses instead of goals, an art in which the grotesque would replace the realistic in the description of every-day life. This is what would best respond to the spirit of our

age. May the unearthly imaginations of Hoffmann and Dostoevsky, of Goya and Chagall, of Mayakovsky . . . may these
teach us how to express truth through the fantastic and the
absurd!

Tertz, with little to be thankful for, should at least be grateful he
is not trying to write such surrealism in England, about the
English; for in England by an odd coincidence 'socialist realism'
has taken over the younger novelists, and any kind of phantasmagoria is out. Vary the daily actuality only slightly, and English
critics become as pompously censorious as the 'line' critics of
Zhdanov. Tertz's comment that Soviet literature has become the
false bible of communism, in which 'whores are as modest as
virgins and hangmen tender as mothers', puts paid to Ehrenburg's
Vesna and also explains an important characteristic of his own
novella.

If Soviet society is so hypocritical and unanimously good, then
the only way of writing the novel of manners about it is to
travesty; and that method, starting with Bely, say, leads eventually to the wildness of a D'Annunzio and the chaos of *Finnegans
Wake*. Obviously there is a point beyond which social comment
becomes self-indulgence, and there is a chance of the Tertzes' getting back to Futurism or, on the other hand, to Dostoevskian
phantasmagoria, to the best in Sologub as to the worst in Remizov.
Aestheticism may well take over for a while: the novelist will have
to go Gothic to make the duty-versus-love theme (as with the
father in *The Trial Begins*) viable without a surrounding mesh of
manners. After all, what sort of books would Henry James have
written if he had spent his life working in a steel-mill? Or down a
mine? Or on the staff of a workers' club? It is not so much the
perniciousness of Russian society that cramps the novelist: on the
contrary, that would be his theme if only he could publish books
about it. What really nullifies him is the drab pageant of tamed
social units, the pack of other-directed spiritual eunuchs afraid to
demur. When Alexander Werth writes in the *New Statesman* (29
October 1960), in the blandly reminiscing tones of Sir Harold
Nicolson, 'I remember a conversation in Moscow, a few months
ago, with my old friend Boris Polevoi, one of the masters of the
socialist-realist novel . . .', we are tempted to laugh: Werth's

phrasing is the sort of deliberate irony we find in Tertz; and the
two idioms—the encrusted mannered, treasured by connoisseurs,
and the right-minded panegyric of the official line—consort oddly
together. You cannot adore eccentricity or practise it if you are
obliged to genuflect before (in Werth's next few words) Boris
Polevoy's *Povest' o nastoyashchem cheloveke* ('Story of a Real
Man', 1946), 'a story of Russian wartime heroism which has sold
no fewer than six million copies'. Reading such sentences we must
surely see why Tertz is tempted into hoots of enraged dismay.
And the terrible predicament of the Soviet writer is made plain:
he is out of touch, and begins to wonder if he really is justified in
laughing privately when, apparently, so many do not, and there
is only the world outside Russia to test things against. Tertz's
Karlinsky, arguing, lost his temper but

> Checking himself in the nick of time, he switched back to
> more current forms of speech:
>   'Objectively speaking ... the logic of the struggle ... the wheel
> of history . . . He who is not with us . . . Encirclement . . .
> Socialism in one country . . . In essence . . . Speaking object-
> ively . . .'

We have foresuffered all, on this same platform or, in nightmare,
before being sentenced. This kind of absurdity is all Tertz has to
work with; no wonder his novel has something of the 'cubist'
angularity and thinness of Zamyatin's satires. Tertz is obliged to
make the most of his material when his main point is the presence
of a dividing line: dividing mindless assent from mockery, hebe-
tude from sensitivity.

There is another point. When Camus writes of the absurd, he
is making an old-fashioned Russian point: Why live? When Tertz
looks at cosmic absurdity he has to add to it a social absurdity
which pains him just as deeply: no wonder he elects to write
superficially about society rather than apocalyptically about the
'human predicament'; the one travesties the other. In his work
the Russian appetite for soul is restored, but by implication only:
he writes about the predicament of the old appetite and the old
tradition in which society was at least on its own side *versus* the
universe. Tertz states a malicious negative, Pasternak a lyrical

positive, but they coincide in their regard for the intactness of souls. Tertz's narrator starts out receiving instruction from the Master (Stalin, surely) on how to write the story and ends up, with two of his own characters, in a concentration-camp, having been denied the chance to rectify parts of the story which fail to square with socialist realism. So there is the hapless narrator who is Tertz's guinea-pig, and Tertz, savagely manipulating. In his essay *Socialist Realism* there are also two personae: one which compares communism to medieval Christianity, and one which argues the nobility of the Cause. Another, third voice, packs the interstices with irony. A fourth, Tertz, concludes the essay.

The argument is ingenious, but we have to track it through a clutter of polyphonic duplicity, defining as we go the boundaries of the irony and deciding which double negatives cancel each other out. It is the idiom and method of the deadpan comedian. First of all, we learn, 'the highest idea which is accessible to us, if not through our understanding, then through our wish that there should be such a purpose,' is the idea of divine purpose. After the 'inaccessible' Purpose of Medieval Catholicism there came 'the era of individualism which proclaimed the freedom of the individual as the Purpose and set about worshipping [it] with the aid of the Renaissance, humanism, superman, democracy, Robespierre, banquets and other forms of prayer'. Third came communism: but if Purpose is merely the product of the wish for purpose, has not communism repeated the old self-deceptions? Well, then, if the goal is unknowable, the emphasis falls on the means and the means has lapsed into the refutation of the goal:

> To abolish prisons for ever we have built new ones, to bring down the frontiers between states we have ringed ourselves round with a Great Wall of China, to make our work in the future restful and pleasant we have introduced forced labour, to avoid spilling a single drop of blood we have killed and killed endlessly.... In the name of our Target we have had to sacrifice all we inherited and to use the same methods as our enemies: proclaim the omnipotence of Russia, write lies in *Pravda*, put a new Czar on the empty throne, bring officers' epaulets into fashion again and with them torture. .... Sometimes it seems as if all that was needed for the final triumph of Communism was

one last sacrifice: the renunciation of Communism. . . . Lord,
Lord, forgive us our sins! After all, this world was created in the
image and likeness of God. Communism has not yet become
Him, but it is near enough. And we arise, staggering with weari-
ness, gaze round the whole universe with our blood-filled eyes,
and see nothing of all we hoped to find.

Communism is just a diabolical prank; and even the phrase
'socialist realism' is foolish. For 'socialist' implies the dream, the
wished-at goal, whereas 'realism' means the life we have on our
hands already, and you cannot write prophetically about what
already is. The author of *The Trial Begins* has nothing to live by,
neither goal nor recent history, and the present is hopelessly corrupt.

Tertz's is the right footnote to add to the officially approved
historical novels of Alexey Tolstoy (1882–1945) and Sergeyev-
Tsenski, Alexey Chapygin (1870–1937) and Alexey Novikov-
Priboy (1877–1944). To the unnerving impermanency of the surface
of communist society—all emergencies, purges, redefinition and
revisionism—these novelists opposed the universality of past heroisms: all, of course, in the light of present virtue. Alexey Tolstoy
compares modern Russia to that of Peter the Great, who is made
to appear as a precursor of Lenin and Stalin, but *Pyotr Pervy*
('Peter the Great', 1929–34) is superficial compared with Sergeyev-
Tsenski's voluminous study of the Crimean War in *Brusilovsky
proryv* ('Brusilov's Breakthrough', 1944). Chapygin's *Razin
Stepan* (1926–7) presents the seventeenth-century Robin Hood as
a Bolshevik before his time and Novikov-Priboy's *Tsushima* (1933–
4) describes the sinking of the Russian fleet in the Russo-Japanese
War. Tertz, who seems to revere Mayakovsky the prophet
(rather than Mayakovsky the poet of bread-prices and economic
policy), has something in common with Yuri Tynyanov (1894–
1943), the author of *Kyukhlya* (1925), a tribute to the Decembrist
poet Küchelbecker, and *Smertt' vazir-Mukhtara* ('Death and
Diplomacy in Persia', 1929), about the playwright Griboyedov,
and the quietly glorifying but tedious *Pushkin* (1936). Literary
homage to literary figures is all very well, but it merely reintro-
duces Tertz into the region of Purpose, which is a delusion anyway. History, however, is even less comforting. Why, asks
Seryozha in *The Trial Begins*, was the Russian conquest of the

Caucasus an enlightened humanitarian gesture and the British conquest of India vicious imperialism? 'Seryozha felt sorry for Shamil. After all, how could Shamil know the Revolution would take place in Russia? All he wanted was to free his own people; it was only afterwards that it turned out to be wrong and even anti-socialist as well.' Why deny hindsight to exponents (Globov is one) of the 'Glorious Aim'? Seryozha deeply admires Rakhmetov, the main figure in Chernyshevsky's tract *Chto delat'?* ('What's To Be Done?', 1864); but talking about the noble means to the Glorious End gets him nowhere. Tertz's portrait of a morally dislocated society is really a collection of impatiently juxtaposed and acerbly accurate vignettes; a technique very different from Pasternak's rhapsodic, meandering stream.

But the two come together in several ways. When Seryozha visits his grandmother she tells him about the manuscript she is typing: 'It tells you all about a model farm . . . It explains all about it so that other farms can follow the example'; we remember Sholokhov. Then she says 'there's too much about love', which is obviously what is wrong with *Zhivago*. Again, Rabinovich the abortionist discovers a dagger in the prison camp, its handle shaped like a crucifix. He interprets thus: 'God was the end and they turned Him into the means—a handle. And the dagger was the means and became the end.' A little farther on he has an outburst: 'In the name of God! With the help of God! In place of God! Against God!' He is pointing the dagger towards the sky at arm's length: 'And now there is no God, only dialectics.' One last quotation will indicate how Pasternak erred through providing the thing whose absence Tertz anonymously describes:

> The universe was empty, and its emptiness was so enormous that it was unimaginable, and so purposeless in its infinity that Yury felt almost as unwell as that other time, in bed.

What Camus called 'the wine of absurdity' abounds in Pasternak and comes to us sour from Tertz; but it does come, and it flickers at us even in the second volume of *Podnyataya tselina* when Sholokhov confides to us that the hero cannot remove his undershirt because he has (a survival from his Imperial Navy days) an obscene tattoo on his stomach, imprinted one night by his shipmates while he lay in a drunken stupor. The unutterable in modern Russia does indeed appear in a hundred different ways and prompts us to think of Mao's 'hundred flowers' in a new light.

It must be remembered that even Pasternak and Tertz turn back to the original puritan vitality of the Bolshevik Revolution: they are not willing to jettison everything. Pasternak exonerates the system and blames the premisses of Marxism-Leninism: in other words his point is a religious, not a social, one. It is the natural standpoint of a martyr, and his arguments in favour of Russian vitality are natural too. So are those of Tertz, safe from martyrdom only by virtue of pseudonym. Zhivago implies all the possibilities of being reborn, of living on: a writer through his book, a spirit after its body, one man in his life several times, and so on. And one may even wonder about the possible relevance of Abram, son of Terah, whom God proved by asking him to sacrifice his son.

In a similar way Lopatkin, the tough-spirited inventor hero of Vladimir Dudintsev's *Ne khlebom yedinym* (1956), eventually triumphs when his revolutionary pipe-casting machine is vindicated. By that time he has been obstructed by bureaucrats and rivals, tried, exiled to Siberia and then reprieved; but those who opposed him seem to be doing well for themselves at the end of the novel. It is unfortunate that Dudintsev should have worked out his theme so mechanically and left his characters, in the main, so wooden, especially the hero himself and the appealing Nadia. There is much in the novel which cries out for further exploration; indeed, there was enough grit in it to incur official displeasure although enough of the innocuous to make Khrushchev eventually forgive the impenitent author. It was therefore intriguing to see *Novogodnyaya skazka* ('A New Year's Tale'), published in *Novy Mir*, complete with such supposedly Aesopian items as a mysterious gang of bandits, an unspecified 'dark continent' upon which the two scientists will bestow artificial sunlight, and an owl which augurs death. Having already made a case for the lonely individualist who helps the Cause in his own weird way—as long as officials do not pester him—Dudintsev might have expected to reinforce the theme. Instead he splits it into two men who, although haunted by death in the form of the owl, press on to the greater triumph of immortality. (That is, the immortality of being national heroes.) The younger scientist is somewhat petty, the older one a reformed bandit anxious to complete his work before death, in the shape of his former associates in crime, catches up with him: they regard him as a traitor and finally knife him to death, in the back. In other words, they do what Karlinsky does to Seryozha in *The Trial Begins* (he denounces him to the police for Trotskyism). It is difficult to establish what this fable 'means', but the burden surely cannot be harmful to Russia; after all, even if there is mention of the disreputable and corrupt (in the two scientists as in their enemies, and of the backward) surely these fit into the policy which regards a bit of public self-criticism as the subtlest form of propaganda. The censor can, in every sense, help himself to Dudintsevs who cast the themes of Pasternak in an inscrutable idiom. It is a matter of sly pawnbroking, and for every subversive meaning the Western reader can extort there is a harmless one which the official censor can comfortably nod at. It is a different matter when we read the poems of Yesenin-Volpin, son of the great Yesenin:

> O Prophet, plainly no mere bird!
> Is there no foreign country
> Where to argue freely about art portends no peril sore?
> Shall I ever reach that region, if such be, and not get
> shot? . . .
> Croaked the Raven: Nevermore!

This parody of Poe, published in *The Leaf of Spring* (New York, 1961), returns us to the reality of Lubyanka, Karaganda and Chernovtsy prison in which Yesenin-Volpin has spent many years and which he uses as titles for his pathetic poems. Released on the death of Stalin, he was jailed again in 1959, but resigned in his view of himself as a hidden corm which has put out its crocus of defiance and derision. It is an oddly Zhivago-like notion, and one which we have to respect.

In the harsh light shed by his example, a great deal of the blithe nationalist literature looks blank and sham. There is no need to list all the tractor novels; it is enough to mention Ostrovsky's *Kak zakalyalas' stal'* ('How the Steel was Tempered', 1936) and Pavlenko's *Na vostoke* ('In the East', 1937), both of them packed with chauvinistic clichés and hectic righteousness. There is a place, however, for such vivid novels as Konstantin Simonov's *Dni i nochi* ('Days and Nights', 1943-4) about the defence of Leningrad, his *Tovarishchi po oruzhiyam* ('Comrades in Arms', 1952) set in Mongolia, Galina Nikolayeva's *Bitva v puti* ('Battle on the Road', 1957) and V. A. Kaverin's *Skandalist* ('The Brawler', 1928), the satirical realism of which anticipates the pious social precisions found in *Ispolnenie zhelaniy* ('The Fulfilment of Desires', 1935-6) and *Dva kapitana* ('Two Captains', 1940). One young writer, Vladimir Tendryakov, has attempted Chekhovian subtleties in such stories as 'Miraculous Ikon', 'Bad Roads' and 'Three-Seven-Ace' and has been rebuked for misrepresenting Soviet realities (as when, in the last-named, he makes Siberian lumberjacks succumb to a confidence trickster as well as indulge in fornication, gambling, boozing and brutality). What chance, then, has a Yesenin-Volpin? How can such an interesting novelist as Leonid Leonov (1899–), being a stylist and in his *Vor* ('The Thief', 1925) one of the finest writers in the Dostoevskian tradition, avoid the eventual decline into such a tract as *Sot* ('Soviet River', 1930)? And it is worth noting that in *Skutarevsky* (1933) he arrives at that favourite cliché of the post-thaw writers, the pioneer victimized by local bureaucrats but really at one with the masses. Skutarevsky the scientist sheds his aloofness and loneliness by mixing in, and his ultimate triumph is to read a treatise to the workers. Anyone who can write his own language can concoct such stuff, and modern Russia has many utterly undistinguished journeymen who have climbed on to the socialist-realist bandwagon. After all, to acquire the privileged, lucrative status of writer, they have only to make the right salutes and noises. No one is concerned with quality, especially with the quality of style. The sad thing is that, in this respect, there are people in the West who have no more feeling or respect for style than have the Russian literary whips. When nothing vital to a novel is lost in the translation, then the novel will have become a dramatized pamphlet. The Russians are already condemned to shuffling cards which read either: Good Party Man or Correctly Orientated Innovator. It is all as simplified as a John Buchan spy story; a bit of fun creeps in when, as was suggested in *The Times Literary Supplement*'s 'A Sense of Direction',[1] such a novel as *Ne khlebom yedinym* 'offers to masses of

1. 16 August 1957, iii.

readers *relief from awe*'. But that is not enough; what Russia needs is what set off most of its nineteenth-century intellectual movements: European influence—a care for style; for playing with (as distinct from *using*) ideas; a disdain for all absolutes and all tamperings with the truth. *Zhivago* is not too far in spirit from Yesenin-Volpin's *Tractatus*; both argue against Russian ideological nympholepsy and particularly that form of it which has lost Marxism only to create Stalinism and other personality-cults. When the young Russian writers discover the magnificent heritage of the twenties, for instance, and begin to assimilate Western literature (through reading the original, for foreign-language teaching in Russia is intensive), the post-Stalinist awakening will have reached its logical conclusion: getting up and moving round. The Russian experience in this century has been colossal and intense, and when it is allowed to pour out in all its variety and conflict, with all the depth and grandeur of its great tradition behind it, a great deal now being written in the West will look rather trivial. But, curiously enough, Russian writers are unlikely to achieve anything of major complexity and absorbing subtlety until they have rediscovered not so much the Gorky-Andreyev school as the brilliance of the nineties writers who opposed that school and created the idea of literature as, first but not necessarily foremost, expression of oneself.

Such recent developments as official denunciation of novelist Viktor Nekrasov and poet Evgeny Evtushenko confuse a picture which also includes Fedor Abramov's disabusing story, published in the Leningrad *Neva*, about *kolkhoz* life, and Alexander Solzhenitsyn's *Ivan Denisovich* (*Novy Mir*, 1962). The latter work describes a Siberian labour camp (Solzhenitsyn having himself spent eight years in one) and how Shukhov the hero sees how many camp rules he can get away with breaking in one day. The laconic, plain style has a debility all of its own, and the report (in every sense) is all exposure. But, surely, little has changed at headquarters: a glad hand to another anti-Stalin piece means nothing. *Dr Zhivago* remains unread in Russia and seems likely to stay so. The centipede, it is well known, may die or stumble, but he never falls down.

4

Spain

I

THE characteristic novel of nineteenth-century Spain was that of the *costumbrista* or specialist in local life. The best work of José María de Pereda (1833–1906), for instance, deals with village life in northern Spain; his later novels show a good deal of earth atavism (*Peñas arriba*, 1894) and unashamed pantheism yet fail to transcend the provincial. We see man close to the earth: as close as the *pueblo* ever can be, and yet miss that sense of interpretation and universality we find in the work of such similar writers as Hardy, Giono and Sherwood Anderson. The irony is that the Spanish novel, with a few notable exceptions, has developed from regional to esoteric without much in between. In fact the craftlessness and awkwardness which typify Pereda's undeliberate approach to the novel reappear in the Spanish novel of the twentieth century as items in a specific technique.

If Pereda is too diffuse, too little the polished literary artist, his contemporary Juan Valera (1824–1905) overdoes the sense of man in outline. His personages are more mythological than social, more like demonstrations than like people. Something effete in his best novel, *Pepita Jiménez* (1874), deters the reader who thinks the poem and the novel should at least start from different positions. The psychological insight is impressive and the irony reminds us of Forster at his best. But the principal character, a young novice whose sense of vocation fades away under the impact of sexual love, is too Gidean: an illustration of a theme. He seems contrived, and one would never believe he was substantial enough to feel even metaphysical yearning very deeply.

The most considerable figure is the Spanish Balzac, Benito

Pérez Galdós (1843–1920), who amassed a cycle of novels based on Madrid. But where Balzac is always theorizing, Galdós lets an ethos speak for itself: his method is that of exposure, with himself well out of sight. *La de Bringas* (1884) depicts the Spanish court in all its impecunious hypocrisy, and exploits, for extra irony, every aspect of a world in which face-saving is the principal concern. Galdós probes behind the gracious, brittle front, typifying high-born decadence in such characters as the pretentious Señora Bringas and her ally, the extravagant-minded sham the Marquesa de Tellería. Señora Bringas pays for her own weakmindedness: an expanse of spirit in a waste of posturing. Galdós does well to reconcile his serious moral concern with his gift for unlaborious comedy. He writes with a light touch that belies the exploratory part of his mind. That part, fascinated and appalled by the spectacle of human turpitude and back-sliding, gets to work in *Fortunata y Jacinta* (1886–7) on a young, indecisive man vacillating between Fortunata, his tumultuous and plebeian mistress by whom he has had a son, and Jacinta his childless bourgeois wife. Two worlds are rammed side by side: that of the wife's family, prosperous through the manufacture of silk, and that of Fortunata—squalid, unpretentious and animally vital. It is a novel of the city; stone and asphalt challenge the characters as they go about their daily business and their regular illicit errands. It is also a novel of nerves, and this is where the Dostoevskian element shows. Fortunata has an abject, crazed admirer called Maxi Rubén in whose twisted mind Galdós shows more than sociological interest. Throughout the Madrid cycle one can see Galdós the religious psychologist trespassing on Galdós the Balzacian. He tends to let the *comédie de mœurs* slip away a little while he probes into the souls of the near-demented, of monomaniacs and cranks. It is as if he suspects that truth is no longer to be found on the social surface but in man's suppressed lusts, dreams and sensitivity. The later novels concentrate on odd men out: Torquemada the miser, Nazarín the oddly Dostoevskian cleric, and all manner of layabouts. From Galdós's concentration on such types we get something like the upsetting reversions that Forster achieves when he unleashes Pan or Hindu awareness among the quiet, dull conformists of his middle class. But, notice, the direction is inwards, away from the conscious, sophisticated art of social comedy. It is the direction of the Spanish novel as a whole; *mores* have not inspired many modern Spanish novelists. But (to borrow two of Galdós's titles) *Realidad* (1889) and *Misericordia* (1897) have.

One novelist to whom the younger Spanish novelists of today owe a great deal is Pío Baroja (1872–1956). Baroja, doctor, baker and perpetual wanderer, described himself as a Rousseau-type nihilist. He would just sit down and write, believing that any attempt at design perverted genuine impulses. Not for him the slow gestation according to plan; he improvised both his life and his works. *La dama errante* (1908), for instance, appears to be about the flight of a terrorist from Madrid to London, but quickly degenerates into a phantasmagoric picaresque fable. As with the stream of consciousness, we never know what is coming next; and when it comes it may have no bearing on the matter preceding. From such an unsystematic approach to the novel it is easy and just to deduce some kind of philosophy. When man repudiates his organizing ability—and especially that side of it which shapes a work of art—he is re-creating original chaos: not suggesting its presence by trying to control it, but surrendering hope. Many of Baroja's works show this apathetic drift, both structurally and in theme. This is the aesthetics of the agnostic: he does not know the plot or pattern of the universe, and therefore mimicks his ignorance in aesthetic terms.

Individualism and pessimism contend in all his work. He praises those who defy convention and yet, in singling out adventurers, picaros, hobos and drifters, seems unable to endow them with any sense of purpose. He idealizes 'the life of action' but in his novels makes it lead nowhere. He extols the rebel but deprives him of a cause; no cause outside oneself is worth while. And his unpolished panorama of Spanish life is a disorderly exemplification of life-savouring. In his eighty or so novels he expounded no programme or credo beyond his oddly defeatist anarchism. Even some of his so-called trilogies are just three novels grouped together, as with *El passado, La raza, La vida fantastica, Tierra vasca* and *Las ciudades*. But the three parts of *La lucha por la vida* (1904)—*La busca, Mala hierba* and *Aurora roja*—interpenetrate to form a colourful record of Madrid low-life. A muddled but overwhelming and memorable pageant results.

Baroja did better when he had an idea to offer, or at least, as in *El árbol de la ciencia* (1911), attempted to philosophize. The best in him responded to discipline; so that when he really got a grip on himself he overcompensated: his acute sense of life's jumble is beautifully controlled in *Aventuras, inventos y mystificaciones de Silvestre Paradox* (1901) and *Paradox, rey* (1906), both of them feats of hilarious imagination. *César o nada* (1910) is a clear-cut account of the rise and fall of a supreme individualist: like *Zalacaín el aventurero* (1909) it is coherent and deft, vastly superior to the series of twenty-two historical novels he enthusiastically and romantically called *Memorias de un hombre de acción*. It is a high-spirited nihilism which animates even the best of this series, such as *El aprendiz de conspirador* (1913), almost as if Baroja, himself convinced of the futility of striving, took a malicious delight in studying men of action: contemplating the life of action from his quiet vantage as writer, he plays the game of action—of commitment—no less futilely than they. It is odd how Baroja the sitter compares the heroic favourably with the unheroic while Hemingway the man of action never underesteems the man whose heroism is not blatant. Hemingway's pessimism is stoical and tragic; Baroja's is just stoical, an ideal example in fact for a generation who have to mute their opinions into mere depiction and can suggest discontent or rebellion only by disorganizing the world of their fiction. It is in the novels of Baroja at their most sprawling and most incoherent that the blur-muddle begins which is to characterize the writing of the younger Spanish novelists. It is to him and his authoritative creedlessness that a cautious, censor-conscious generation looks.

His own favourite authors—Dickens, Poe, Balzac, Stendhal and Dostoevsky—can all be found in his novels in the form, respectively, of hyperbole, luridity, voluminousness, self-scrutiny and heavy melodrama. The acrid, compressed prose style mocks (because it is so blatantly disciplined) the laxities of conception: the combed, starched idiom floats about on the meandering flood of narrative. And this is not the only paradox in Baroja: idealizing the divine in man, and especially in 'the obscure and despised masses', he indulges himself, is always ready to let a conception flop to the ground or to overexploit a peripheral episode. He is

lax in the way Céline is lax but is deficient of the fury which keeps
Céline driving forward. Baroja does not insist; he just repeats;
does not present a point so much as allow it to work to the surface. And this is all he has in common with such a writer as
Ramón Pérez de Ayala, whose 'poematic' novels recall the
Generation of 1898 and (especially such later works as *Luna de
miel, luna de hiel*, 1923, and *Tigre Juan*, 1926) offer characters
whose main force is that of symbols, transcending and transfiguring every context.

The poet Gómez de la Serna once explained his gnomic,
aphoristic prose-poems (*greguerías*) as 'attempts to define the in-
definable, to capture the fugitive', and their counterpart in the
Spanish novel is surely provided by Ramón del Valle-Inclán
(1866–1936) who derives equally from D'Annunzio and Villiers
de l'Isle-Adam. His *Sonatas* (1902–5), four long stories about the
love-life of the passive Marqués de Bradomín (*'feo, católico y
sentimental'*, ugly, pious and sentimental), present affairs which
attune themselves to the seasons of the year. Valle-Inclán special-
izes in talk and keeps analysis and portrayal to a minimum. He
is readable now only because his dialogue is jerky and harsh
enough to keep us from surrendering completely to the anodyne
of his mannered, cadenced prose. *Flor de Santidad* (1904), about
Galician beggars and peasants, is just as abrupt and laconic, but
on a larger scale. He cannot stay with a theme: he deals in cuts,
explosions of emotional energy, lunges at irrelevant notions and
acerb reversals of tone. No wonder he turned eventually to the
theatre: his *Comedias bárbaras* are really histrionic novels on the
occasion of epic subjects, and his last novels—*Tirano Banderas*
(1926), which satirizes a Mexican dictator, *La corte de los milagros*
(1927) and *Viva mi dueño* (1928), both exposing the corruptness
of aristocratic life before the revolution of 1868—typify what he
called the *'esperpento'* method: that is, reducing all to the absurd
and grotesque. For him, only the deformed is eloquent and he
himself seems like some cavorting Goya of prose. Swaggering,
reckless, impulsive, self-obsessed, ever suspicious of formal
literary purpose, he is essentially the stylist, the effects-man,
looking forwards to the anti-novel, giving a technicolour version
of the unsystematic Baroja, and looking back to the generation
of '98. In him, something contorted and wilful, which is truly

Spanish, assumes dandified form and evokes the techniques of cinema without going quite so close to them as Blasco Ibáñez, his equally spectacular, less 'precious' contemporary.

Vicente Blasco Ibáñez (1867–1928), commonly referred to as the Spanish Zola, was an altogether more impulsive person than the Frenchman, from whom he carefully distinguished himself: 'Zola was a reflective man . . . and I am an impulsive one. He attained his final result slowly, through perforation, while I proceed through explosion, violently and loudly.' Blasco Ibáñez, master of the naturalistic novel, was also an agitator, dueller, free-thinker and an editor, and in his mid-thirties founded two colonies in South America. He seems just the sort of man envied and revered by Baroja. In addition he was a dashing, impressionistic and sometimes meretricious writer with something of Hemingway's sensuous romanticism, as is evident and rather cloyingly so from the famous war-novel *Los cuatro jinetes del Apocalipsis* (1916). His Valencian novels are essentially less dramatic, and, with more time to spend on description, he achieves subtler effects. In *Arroz y tartana* (1894), *La barraca* (1898) and *Cañas e barro* (1902) he is a more patient writer, more so than in his Second World War novel, *Mare Nostrum* (1918). He needs either melodrama or lush scenery, sense-impressions rather than ideas. Thus, Julio Desnoyers in *Los cuatro jinetes*, trying to avoid the war, brings more out of his creator than, say, the social themes of *La catedral* (1903) and *La bodega* (1905). The Argentinian landscape, the brilliant sea and the pastel walls of the Balearics (*Los muertos mandan*, 1909), like the gaudy rituals of the bull-fight (*Sangre y arena*, 1908), stimulate him into the kind of lurid set-pieces we have noticed in Andreyev and Durrell. The execution-scene in *Los cuatro jinetes*, for instance, is just a little too stylish: 'Two uprights flashed up above their heads—the arm of the priest making the sign of the cross, and the sabre of the squad-commander glistening at the same instant.' Or again: 'Some collapsed like half-emptied sacks; others rebounded from the ground like balls; some leaped like gymnasts. . . .' It is almost as gratuitous as the gauntlet execution of the local Fascists in *For Whom the Bell Tolls*, except that Pilar is doing duty for Hemingway and in Hemingway's own style when she describes it, whereas Blasco Ibáñez is acting in his own right as ringmaster.

After such livid vignettes, the archaeological *Sónnica la corte-sana* (1901), the patriotic novels *El papa del mar* (1925) and *A los pies de Venus: Los Borgia* (1926) seem tame and flaccid. He has no flair for the *entr'acte* and, in such historical grandiosities as *En busca del Gran Kan: Cristóbal Colón* (1929) and *El caballero de la Virgen* (1929), he lacks Baroja's ability to let things slide, to make vivid capital out of musings. Action or the picturesque: that is Blasco Ibáñez, a not very sophisticated D'Annunzio who sends us forward to Juan Goytisolo and also exemplifies the hazards of being gaudy in an inflexible prose.

Ramón José Sender (1902–) is a severer figure. His first novel, *Imán* (1930), is a brilliant and searing record of war; his interpretation of suffering is not only philosophical but also leftist—as his essay, 'El novelista y las masas', explains. He always seems immersed in the twentieth century, and his best work—*Imán* and *O.P.* (*Orden público*), 1931, based on his experiences as a political prisoner—is comparable with the best of Malraux. *El verbo se hizo sexo* (1931) is a fictional life of St Teresa but constitutes only a brief respite from the violent century which eventually put Sender's first wife to death for being a republican sympathizer. *Siete domingos rojos* (1932) describes a futile workers' revolution in Madrid while *Viaje a la aldea del crimen* (1933) deals with the brutal suppression of a peasant uprising in an Andalusian village: the first event is fictional, the second real. After this, Sender composed an acerb, furious fantasy called *La noche de las cien cabezas—novela del tiempo en delirio* (1934), which resembles Malaparte's *Kaputt* and Céline's *Mort à crédit* and recalls both Goya and Quevedo. *Míster Witt en el Cantón* (1935) looks back to a popularist effort at Cartagena in 1873—yet another unsuccessful attempt to crack the surface of oppression. Sender has made a speciality of such events, almost turning them into metaphors of the human condition. The Civil War forced *Contraataque* (1938) out of him, this time an almost prosaic account of the defence of Madrid. *Proverbio de la muerte* (1939), crammed with Heath-Robinson philosophizing and foggy scientific theorizing, shows Sender groping for adjustment or faith and finally hitting on something like Baroja's cult of the individual. *El lugar del hombre* (1939) takes this cult into a pastoral setting where man's wolfishness to man seems even more pernicious. The search for 'man's place' goes on, hampered by forces that Ortega summed up as 'The Other' and, in *Epitalamio del prieto Trinidad* (1942), set in a Mexican penal colony, develops into an almost hysterical exclamation against non-human forces which deprive man of dignity and peace.

His progress, obviously, has been from the social protest to the metaphysical quest. His method has become increasingly surrealistic but at the same time more abstract and theoretical. Since 1938, when he settled in the United States, he has written nostalgically about his youth and childhood in the *roman-fleuve* which begins with *Crónica del alba* (1942): Pepe Garcés drifts gradually from place to place, hemmed in at first by an excitable father, a jeering older sister and a weeping younger one; then escapes to a steadfast sweetheart called Valentina, with whom he hunts grasshoppers, sacrifices a pigeon and eventually practises free love. The second section of the trilogy deals with schooldays in the monastery at Reus, where the fiery boy and a humble lay brother achieve a profound friendship that Sender has the sense to present without philosophizing, but studs with little items from the boyhood caper—communal yawns during the Good Friday sermon, jaundice induced by taking saffron, and gulling the devout young Catalonians. Such a return to the source, a movement backwards and then forwards into our own times again, is a natural enough action: Sender, in exile, is retracing his steps, becoming more and more mystical as he goes. The struggle upwards (of man in general) and the individual effort to attain self-definition (sometimes through a Cause, a revolt or a passionate defence) are Sender's themes. Arturo Barea's estimation of him as 'the only important novelist of the young pre-Civil War generation' is just. But Sender, like Malraux, reaches a vision of plenitude and peace only through increased inattention to the immediate contemporary scene. The compassionate, deep, brave, active man of the world is still there, but he has to be inferred from beneath the veils of mystagogy. Previously, we had to take care to credit the man of action (Malraux too) with his mystical inwardness, which it was easy to overlook.

Another expatriate, Arturo Barea (1897–1957), better known as a critic and essayist, published his first book, translated as *The Struggle for the Spanish Soul* (1941), in Spain in 1938. Obliged in

1938 to go to France, Barea finally found his way to England and pursued his writing career by writing in Spanish and then publishing in England, with an edition in Spanish following later. In this way he produced his autobiographical trilogy, *The Forging of a Rebel*, composed of *The Forge*, *The Track* and *The Clash*—frank, vivid, never pretentious and rarely as intellectual as the similar works of Salvador da Madariaga and Sender. One of the saddest, as well as one of the most stimulating, spectacles of our time has been the expatriate nostalgia of such writers as these, who lose awareness of the contemporary world the more they try to approach it with a characteristically Spanish eye. An inevitable consequence is the scattering of the mind and the almost voluptuous picking-up of the pieces in Mexico or Paris, in Buenos Aires or London. A Pasternak arrives through Italian; a Nabokov reappears in English; a Beckett elects to write in French; a Koestler belongs everywhere and yet nowhere. It is small wonder that those novelists who can freely represent the society they live in lapse into near-possessive caricature. It is almost time we had a study of the special strains and virtues and defects of expatriate writing, whether the writer left of his own volition or was compelled out. This is the basis of the vogue for picaresque, the explanation of much fragmentary writing and the occasion for distinguishing between the turbulence of 'safe' societies and the upheavals of those which resemble prisons. When the novel becomes oblique and cryptic, when it has to close its eyes and affect opinionlessness, it has willy-nilly been forced into the region of poetry. In other words, the novel's evasions themselves have become metaphorical; and between the significantly disjointed or dark and the merely sloppy, it is not always easy to distinguish.

Miguel de Unamuno (1864–1936) is at the opposite pole. To him the novel was a way of avoiding the systematizations of philosophy. Not that he went as far as Baroja in rejecting the organizing mind; he just felt that the novel's illustration gave vitality to ideas. Consequently his own novels are somewhat functional; nothing spills over except the exhibitionism inseparable from his personality. He is always making a point about the creation of faith out of inner conflict (*Niebla*, 1914). He is always pitting man against God, and a man's sense of himself against temptations to hypocrisy. His 'tragic sense of life' too readily develops into the portentous in much the same way as it does in the novels of Sartre. Unamuno deals in acerbity and violence, does not bother much with psychology and usually creates a parable of man's cosmic plight. All he needs (and all he gives) is one strong-willed character whom he can, in a manner almost diagrammatic, push to destruction. Raquel in *Dos madres* (1920) and Caroline in *El Marqués de Lumbria* (1920) are typical; they are maniacs of the maternal instinct. Alejandro Gómez in the powerful *Nada menos que todo un hombre* (1920) is the embodiment of sheer will—almost, in fact, a reduction to absurdity of Unamuno's preferences. Alejandro wants to assert the Self against everything; against what Ortega called 'The Other'. Confronted with these, all other characters melt away. As studies of pathological egoism these three novels, together composing the book called *Tres novelas ejemplares* (1920), set the reader philosophizing almost at once. He sees what Unamuno called 'the brusque affirmation of a thing because I wish it to be so, because I need it to be so' steamrolling over other lives. Unamuno does not bother to condemn; after all, these are *exempla* and self-evident. If you are the kind of reader he wants, you interpret for yourself. Domestic life emerges as unmitigated hell; all that matters is advantage and expediency. Life is to be interpreted in terms of selfishness, drive and greed. A family swallows its pride; a father exploits for his own ends his daughter's beauty; brother, in *Abel Sánchez* (1917), turns against brother. It is not enough to point out that Unamuno is mordant about the self-seekers, the upstarts, the sumptuously vulgar amorists and the honour-mad antagonists: like it or not, he says, they exist because we all need to assert ourselves. He is not concerned with personal motives but with general significances: the wives evoke barren Rachel; Joaquín in *Abel Sánchez* evokes Cain; and Abel evokes his namesake. Such, says Unamuno, is the mythology of human nature. We are destructive: in *Nada menos que todo un hombre* Alejandro and Julia destroy each other. Will, therefore, is not enough; it has to be informed with something else, and the will that batters on has to realize that its failure might stir the heart of someone else. All failure, he says, is relative; to win would be to cheat God's inscrutable design. The trouble is that Unamuno pares so much away; half the time, social context is omitted and the drama seems remote and irrelevant (*La tía Tula*, 1921). But the short-comings of what he agreed to call his '*nivola*', and its 'agonic' dialogues, are those of the fabulists: the Ernst Jüngers, the Camus's and the Gides. The author exposes himself as a specimen. In *Abel Sánchez*, for example, Unamuno divides himself up into Abel (calm and obliging) and Joaquín (restless and assertive); Abel is the artist, Joaquín the interrogative spirit. One is a Stephen Dedalus, the other a Faust. Abel is a success and Joaquín is envious. Yet it is obvious that Unamuno is of Cain's party, and knows it: in the second edition of the novel, Unamuno wrote: 'In re-reading my *Abel Sánchez*, I have felt the greatness of my Joaquín's passion, and his moral superiority to all the Abels. The evil is not in Cain; it is in all the petty little Cains, and in all the petty little Abels.' The novel ends with Joaquín repudiating hatred and extolling love. It sounds facile, but the novel reasons its way towards such an abstract conclusion; and the reasoning, as we might expect from Unamuno, is tortuous, paradoxical and sometimes savage. He is a neglected author now, and his appetite for spiritual heroics survives in the young novelists as nothing more than a preoccupation with extravagant effects. But at least the religious *costumbrista* in him, exemplified in his last novel, *San Manuel Bueno, mártir* (1931), augurs the rural playing-safe of his successors. In fact, the peasant stoicism which he admired as a kind of anaesthesia has, nowadays, become an essential part of the novelist's armour. To go on writing in adversity the Spanish novelist of today has to develop his own stoicism: in other words an eclectic blindness implying proscribed truths. And it could be argued that the *costumbrista* genre is as much a deliberate terminology of mute protest as it is homage to peasants' tenacity and the national tradition they embody. Through the image of peasant life, the novelist can show something crude, but uncorrupted, in the Spain of today.

II

If we add Unamuno's concern for the Nietzschean, the violent, even the demonic, to Baroja's rejection of systematic assembly, we have something close to the essence of Camilo José Cela

(1916–). Cela prefers the weird, the apparently meaningless and the amorphous. The world of his novels has been likened to that of Hieronimus Bosch and Brueghel; he sees man as a prisoner in a forbidding universe where chaos and imperfection always defeat the idealist. His first novel, *La familia de Pascal Duarte* (1942), exemplifies his objective technique: Pascal Duarte, epitome of the unlucky and the lowly, tells his story from the prison cell to which he has been condemned. One thing follows another; there is no distinction made according to quality. In fact the evaluating mind is quite absent—a technique that we find in the rather more outlandish novels of Robbe-Grillet. Pascal is a kind of camera: no intentions, no prophecies, no hopes. He takes things as they come in much the same way as the traditional picaro of the Spanish novel always did. Just as the main characters of *La Vida de Lazarillo de Tormes* and *Gil Blas* allowed the current of life to take them where it would, so does the typical Cela character embody the qualities of the anti-hero, the man who just cannot be bothered to persist in the chase after any chimerical Good.

Gil Blas is not a moralizing book; perhaps the earliest picaresque tales might have been so described, for they showed a slow progress of the soul from the follies of the world to a sane, mature and contrite wisdom. Gil Blas ends up in luxury and unrepentant. The picaro attaches himself to, and in literature is a rebuke upon, a society that has lost faith in its own moral code. Between *Gil Blas* and Pascal Duarte he has become more a piece of flotsam than an enterprising scoundrel. He has become submissive and apathetic, a symbol of disaffection. And, of course, in the Spanish novel he necessarily represents the writer who cares still but finds his version of the truth suppressed by censors.

Cela's second novel, *La colmena*, was published in Buenos Aires in 1952. Again the account of life, this time of proliferating Madrid, is amorphous, nihilistic and distorted. The dialogues are squalid exchanges between persons of whom the novelist has no expressed opinion. The novel reads like the fragmentation and recombination of several Zola documents: the scenes follow one another in meaningless succession. It is bitter honey that he crams into the combs. There is nothing here of Galdós's symmetrical, coherent, patiently expository image: instead the method is cinematic: it flickers, falters and bewilders. The whole kaleidoscope is based on one day in Madrid in 1943. There are plots but they are so intricately interwoven as to remind one of Dos Passos. There is no hero; rather, the intricacy and 'swarm-ingness' of life are shown to preclude heroism of any kind. But if there is no hero, there are at least objects of respect: the white-collar and manual classes, slaving away to no purpose beyond surviving to slave again tomorrow. This is a vision of disintegration, chastening to read and obviously indebted to the example of Baroja.

Cela's own view appears in the prologue to *Viaje a la Alcarria* (1948). He explains that he will deny himself the role of 'being meddlesome and so risking a setback for drawing conclusions philosophical, political or moral'. But his opinion of modern life is eloquent in every capricious transition. He not only takes considerable trouble with his style; he weights it heavily with popular idiom. Cela is the 'tramp' who wanders about, record-ing with a hard and experienced eye the landscape and other travellers in Alcarria, only about forty miles from Madrid. The absence of meditation and discussion is occasionally frustrating; it is just as tedious to read a brilliant catalogue as to wade through lengthy disquisitions that hold up the action. The main thing in this novel, however, is the traveller's frame of mind: not daring an opinion; noting the external world like a man who needs to cling to it in order to preserve a sense of his own reality. Cela is a prolific novelist. With over a score of books to his name he still pursues the bizarre and the sordid grotesque, almost as if he thinks that a heightening of the everyday will amount to an opinion expressed. It does, provided we can attune ourselves to his stylish garbling of an already garbled society. Cela is the Goya of Franco's Spain.

From Cela to the style of writing called *Nadalismo* is a logical transition. In 1944 the Barcelona publishing house 'Destino' founded a literary prize in memory of Eugenio Nadal. The first Nadal Prize went to a novel called (oddly enough) *Nada* by Carmen Laforet, a young writer in her twenties. Plotless, event-less, shapeless, *Nada* recounted some episodes in the life of Andrea, a young student in humble lodgings in Barcelona. The award canonized the new mode, the apathetic picaresque. Not only that: as the prize is given to an unpublished manuscript, the temptation for an unknown author to conform to the Nadal manner is considerable. The main thing is not to seem to know how to write a novel at all: in fumbling there is sincerity—or so one might rationalize. We are back to the novel which pretends it is not a novel at all. Subtract plot, narrator and reflective intelligence and, certainly, what is left cannot be accused of looking like a novel. On the credit side, however, the cult of unsystematic observation has sharpened the senses of some of the younger Spanish novelists. Instead of dismissing a stone as grey, they look intently and record purples, reds, blues as if in mescalin-inspired vision. The trouble is that the reader too gets myopia from this and eventually longs for anything a bit vague. Once again, Robbe-Grillet comes to mind.

In 1955 the Premio Nadal was given to Rafael Sánchez Ferlosio for *El Járama*, a conversation-piece dealing with young people on a Sunday afternoon by the Járama river, near Madrid. Everyone is bored. The river goes by, no doubt bored itself. The boys and girls talk and talk—the last resort of their unsatisfied minds. But their prattle is at least idiomatic and pert; they are working-class and indifferent about it. Ferlosio records and then analyses, but almost as if he were a sociologist-cum-philologist taking a busman's holiday. He creates a flashing, rhythmic and eventually tragic tapestry of vernacular motifs, but parts of the novel have no more drive than a tapestry, and the inertia of the young passes into the quasi-structure. Ferlosio is a long way from the swarming microcosm presented so garishly by Cela.

Yet in 1951 Ferlosio published at his own expense a little fable called *Industrias y andanzas de Alfanhui*. This strange fantasy, evocative of many of the frail stories that appeared in *The Yellow Book*, has nevertheless a substantial Moravia-like theme: it explores the dawn of adolescence, the slippery problem of self-definition perched on the edge of mature sexuality. This is a subtler piece of work than Moravia's *Agostino*, for it traces not only the growth of self-awareness but also the sudden sense of release into the fertile springs of a previously unknown cosmos. Obviously the opportunities for bathos were many, the chances of finishing without sententious whimsy small. But, slight as the piece is, it is miraculously judged: not too delicate, not too pretentious, not too physical. It would not be too much to compare this short evocation to Gide's *Les Nourritures terrestres*: there is the same slightly bewildered, increasingly rapturous exploration of a world that was waiting all the time. *Alfanhuí*, then, is a novel of awareness and a standing rebuke to the young cataloguers, not because lists are bad in themselves, but because compiling them mindlessly is. And that applies to Ferlosio himself, going from *Alfanhuí* to record the Sunday colloquies of young mooners.

When the exponent of high literary art decides to mingle among ordinary folk, it often seems to him enough to record them as exotics and have done. If your material is colourful enough, you do not have to animate it yourself: that is the principle, felt even if often unformulated. Cela himself is too familiar with all sorts and conditions to confuse the exotic with the spectacular. But another novelist, Miguel Delibes, presents in *Diario de un cazador* (1955) an almost curtly economical account of an ordinary life: the facts are all there but Delibes writes as if adding them up would wreck the fictional illusion. Jesús Fernandez Santos does much the same thing in his *En la hoguera* (1957) on the subject of a student who, physically ill, wanders around a strange village. The same writer's *Los bravos* (1954) is considerably better. A doctor goes to live among the peasants and eventually manages to identify himself with them. When he stops a lynching he finds the whole village turned against him; but he resolves to stick it out, feeling that it is a man's duty to invade the islands of others' pretended self-sufficiency. He wants the villagers to realize that he is taking notice of them, and to be repaid in kind. Ritual surrounds such a theme, as well as implications about the nature of bureaucracy. But one cannot help wondering how much pioneering the reader will stand without asking for other aspects of life. These novels have an oddly American—Huck Finn, Thoreau, Steinbeck—flavour. Meant as homage and written in the simplest prose, they have dignity and worthiness of a narrow kind. Certainly the incoherence of Cela gives one more of the feel of life and also reminds one that all that is primal is not rural.

One young Spanish novelist who has become quite well known in translation is Juan Goytisolo, a specialist in the urbane urban sordid. Goytisolo takes naturally to the gaudy and creates a prose style to match. Fundamentally, such a novel as his *Juegos de manos* (1954) portrays the moral debility of the fairly well-to-do; but Goytisolo also takes considerable pleasure in creating the rather stagy characters who enact his homily. *Juegos de manos* gives an exciting account of how a bunch of Madrid students plan, as an *acte gratuit*, the murder of a politician. Uribe, a dipsomaniac des Esseintes ('I want to steal the frost from the rooftops and make a gift of it to the blind doves'), inadvertently causes the role of executioner to fall on David, the ditherer, the good boy anxious to prove himself. The last seventy pages or so, in which climax and anti-climax force maturity, self-denial and conscience into the hermetic world of these well-heeled delinquents, are hypnotic and profound. The characterization is steady throughout and the prose is harsh and agile. Goytisolo catches the eye and dazes the mind. His beatniks have all the colour of those close to the inferno. The Spanish title, 'Juggling', suggests his interpretation: the young men will do anything to pass the time—anything, that is, likely to give them kicks. It is a novel worth dwelling on, for it supplies an intriguing antithesis to the much less violent work of John Wain and Kingsley Amis. The reader may also catch the flavour of Hitchcock, for Goytisolo's technique is essentially cinematic and flamboyant.

Goytisolo's subsequent books are in much the same vein. *Campos de Nijar* (1960) is a colourful, stylishly written travel book, as vivid in its way as *Juegos de manos*. *Duelo en el Paraíso* (1955) shows that Goytisolo can manage a light though apocalyptic touch. In *El circo* (1957) he returns to harsh contrasts. A little girl, Pira, is murdered by a sex-maniac; a sailor called Gorilla pursues his crass, bestial way until his twelve-year-old companion, Pipo, drinks too much and informs on him to the police. The novel is lush and vivid, but Goytisolo is too fond of the diabolical-Hogarthian grotesque, and the general statement he seems to be attempting disappears in a blaze of spectacular effects. Self-indulgence defeats the urge to imitate. *La resaca*, published in Paris in 1958, is a panorama of the Barcelona suburbs. Once again, the squalid is the mainstay: not squalid personages, for the characters are very sketchy, but squalid circumstances created by a squalid regime. As a novel, *La resaca* is hardly satisfactory; but it is a first-class social document and, despite its blunt realism, a long way from the self-indulgent lavishness of the other novels. *La isla* (1961) has the same documentary aim, exposing the boredom of the fashionable set at Torremolinos. The odd thing is that Goytisolo seems himself bored with the technicolour boredom of his characters. But his motives and, in some ways, his method bring him close to the Moravia of *Gli indifferenti* and *La noia*. Goytisolo has the makings of a great novelist; but he will always, one suspects, have to damp down his natural inclination to the phoney melodramatic. Some of his writing is every bit as much an *acte gratuit* as anything done by his own 'jugglers'.

A maturer novelist, a Catalan and the 1946 winner of the Nadal Prize, is José María Gironella whose first novel, *Un hombre* (1946), has been translated into several languages. His main project is a trilogy about the Civil War. The first volume, *Los cipreses creen en Dios* (1952) sets the eve-of-war scene in a small provincial town. The compendious second volume, *Un millón de muertos* (1961), mightily detonates the uneasy calm. This may well become a classic; Gironella writes with mature spareness (he is already in his forties) and indulges in none of the pyrotechnics we find in Goytisolo. Such a theme calls for courage and objectivity; and this novelist has both in abundance, reminding one in some ways of Camus. A younger novelist, Ana María Matute, has grappled with the same subject in *Los hijos muertos* (1958), a study of muddle and mixed loyalties every bit as moving as Malraux's Civil War novel, *L'Espoir*. Well known for her novels and short stories, Ana María Matute moves easily from specific to abstract, and her book of modern fables, *Los niños tontos* (1956), displays an intellectual grasp and power of generalization not often found in women writers. She won the Nadal in 1959 for an autobiography about the Civil War's impact on several young people. Again, this book, *Primera memoria* (1959), shows an unostentatious compassion and a decisive approach to a complicated theme. She is a writer of immense promise, but so far is at her best in miniatures and in the collection together of episodes. When she has achieved, say, Galdós's or Gironella's inclusive sureness of grasp, she will be a formidable writer indeed.

The qualities that characterize the modern Spanish novel, then, are confusion, morbidity and formlessness. The reasons are not far to seek. Here is a society still tormented by its allegiances in a civil war and held arrested in a totalitarian aftermath. The war drove many of the best novelists into exile: Arturo Barea, Ramón Sender and Salvador de Madariaga were among them. Those who write in modern Spain have to reckon with the censor: Cela, for instance, had trouble getting *La familia de Pascal Duarte* accepted by the authorities, and *La colmena* was forbidden. Again, when Sartre added his name to the international protest against the imprisonment of Luis Goytisolo (Juan's brother), the government proscribed both the importing and sale of all Sartre's books. Some of the best contemporary work has achieved publication only in Paris and Buenos Aires. A good many translations have been made, especially into English and French, but the Spanish case is somehow not as spectacular as the Russian. When, for instance, a Pasternak and an 'Abram Tertz' rebel and publish abroad—in Italy and Paris—the world watches avidly. The Spanish dissident, however, lacks news-value—for what that is worth.

The Spanish writer is not only isolated; isolation itself has fostered lack of interest in what is outside. Timidity, cowardice, hypocrisy and conformism have already taken their toll of the Spanish novel. The choice is simple: between saying what you are allowed to say and saying nothing at all—in print at any rate. No wonder, then, that the novel has become 'objective' and 'photographic': not that a wealth of implication cannot be put into such writing. It can, and Cela does this most skilfully. But some sights cannot be photographed at all—by order; and some emotions and states of mind simply have to be analysed and discussed. The result is that those Spanish novelists who are exiles have to grapple with nostalgia and also with a new ethos; those who stay at home have to avoid many worthwhile themes. C. P. Snow's study of bureaucratic man, for instance, would be impossible in Spain. True, a novelist interested in such a theme might tackle it obliquely through, say, the image of a village or through a phase of distant history. But the novel is essentially of the here and now; made too oblique and indirect, it becomes tame and debilitated.

There is another consideration. Cela himself has expressed it unequivocally: 'Spain is a country', he says, 'where people read little. . . . In Spain the writer is a man who every morning, as well as writing, has to apologize for doing so. . . . In Spain the writer is always a suspicious character, a presumptive heretic.' It is not surprising that the writer, needing to identify himself with some social group, has gone rural, seeking a *planche de salut* from which to operate as best he can within the ideological prison. Paradox and conflict have always been a part of Spanish culture: Spain, as well as sharing in the Western heritage, has participated in other experiences. During the middle ages she experienced eight centuries of lively contact with the Arab and Jewish worlds; she is, so far, the only European country to have won and entirely lost a considerable empire. She championed the Counter-Reformation and so was isolated even as early as 1600. Torn between the Faith and the claims of the European intellectual tradition, she has, from the Age of Reason on, preserved her identity only through refusing to participate and leaving modernity to a few outward-looking marginal groups. Unamuno embodies the conflict; he wished to do so, and it was used against him on the seventh centenary of the University of Salamanca when the diocesan bishop banned a tribute to him.

Suffocation and ambivalence have worked on the peculiar twentieth-century predicament of Spain. The novel as a commentary on society has become exiguous, incoherent and non-committal. A safe piety has replaced satire: 'safe' themes, especially those bound up with the fecklessness and inertia of the young (which the Church will corroborate), have ousted themes more deeply felt. Some novelists have got their frustration into their style; their energy goes into the grotesque or into the development of a neutral, plain mode of expression. Inevitably things look stunted; but at least they do exemplify and supply metaphors for the society that makes them. The novel has become symptomatic rather than discursive. And, a few brave efforts apart, the scene is one in which the *roman-fleuve*, the stream, satire and comedy play little part. The novel survives only through untendentious reporting and thus supplies, for special reasons, another instance of art's disowning its own nature. After all, if the Spanish novelist needs to find a form of writing in which he cannot be impeached for doctrine or onslaught, then surely the meta-novel is it. The sad thing is that only the writers with the strongest consciences will be driven into such aestheticism. The reader can only make allowances for that fact, and lament it. If he looks at the non-representational daubs of such modern Spanish painters as Antoni Tàpies, Manolo Millares and Modest Cuixart, he may well see the way the novel is going: towards an exercise in surfaces which throws the burden of interpretation on the baffled spectator. We can only look on, and hope to infer correctly the truth, the home-truths, intended.

Conclusion

> 'The modern novel! The *grumus merdae* left
> behind by criminals upon the scene of their
> misdeeds.'
>
> (Pursewarden, *Justine*)

TRYING to sum up brings me back to the snags of portrayal: to distortions both deliberate and inevitable. We have seen how, realism being imperfect, some modern novelists have insisted too dogmatically on one way of conveying the mysteries of streaming consciousness and how, in consequence, the anti-hero has emerged, spawned partly by a literary technique and partly by modern man's sense of being powerless. And this anti-hero, exposed variously by Joyce, Beckett, Kerouac, Mann, Moravia, Tertz and Sánchez Ferlosio, and many others, has attracted the scorn of the more old-fashioned novelists.

It is easy to see why. The anti-hero, essentially a symbol of undynamic man, fosters uneventful, passive novels in which everything seems accidental and the old skills of manipulation and architectonic count for little. Further, the anti-hero, varying in kind according to the national circumstances he is supposed to develop from, is a way of expressing defeat by society: in fact he brings about, once again, after the cult of flux, a reflux which works private and abstract views of man against a view that is primarily social. In other words, the anti-hero and the anti-novel sum up modern man's literary and social sense of powerlessness. And the picaresque, itself essentially disorganized, is really a limp protest against 'anti-literature': it makes much of society without going deeply and depicts the restless without creating purposes for them.

The novel, as blurred and dissolved by such as Durrell, Robbe-Grillet, Faulkner, Jünger, Malaparte, Bely and Baroja, has become a document of metaphysical defiance distinct from the novel of social analysis attempted by such as Snow, Romains, O'Hara, Doderer, Pratolini, Ehrenburg and Gironella. Neither mode of novel is likely to 'oust' the other: the one, acutely modifying the facts of life, suffers from too extreme a response to the limitedness of realism compared with 'reality', while the other, written by men acutely conscious of the novel's role as a social document and of the timidity implicit in aestheticism, makes an unfailing appeal—witness the success of *The Leopard*. In Britain the private and abstract views become extreme because English society and English social novelists tend naturally towards idiosyncratic comedy, and Snow, avoiding comedy at all costs, is an exception. What Moore and Bennett took from the French Naturalists, and Moore from Dujardin, not to mention parallels between Proust and Dorothy Richardson, should prepare us for further borrowings and other parallels. In France, Russia and Spain, protest against the nature of their respective societies leads the most thoughtful novelists into cipher, obliquity, experimentation and plotless blur. In Italy the tradition of social reporting is strong: no wonder, either, after the silence imposed by Mussolini. And the West German novelists are gradually beginning to look squarely at the new society, even if that means adding new vice to old guilt; but the tradition of fable and fantasy persists as an essential escape-hatch. Of East Germany it is enough to say, as of Russia, that where honest portrayal is forbidden the novel is pushed towards the poem's modifying and distorting habits and, even then, not allowed into print. A *Zhivago* makes its poignant, awful point to a guessing outside world and an 'Abram Tertz' keeps getting the occasional manuscript through to Paris and London.

One's final view is not heartening: of a world divided between totalitarian and gentler societies, the one run by childishly closed-minded overseers, the other by demagogic manufacturers intent on keeping the majority of adults childishly fixated on advertised paraphernalia. For those who are allowed to write about it, and dare to, the bewildering and violent century is there; but one cannot be surprised if the best talents produce increasingly evasive parable-novels in which mid-century man prefers his cosmic and private doom to the doom of attrition by society. After the absurd universe the absurd society; and after that the absurdity of writing at all, save for oneself. The temptations are there; the techniques of self-isolation are to hand; and whether the novel will become as private as the poems written by patients in mental homes depends, surely, much on individual whim—the impulse to have a go—as on the conduct of international statesmen. If we hate our society we either write about it to tear it to bits, or we fantasticate it. Setting things down, coldly, for what they are, denies to the novelist the personal fulfilment which, within the limits of art, is what he has always wanted. But when things get so bad that the medium of words cannot convey them or when words make them more palatable than they are, then the novelist might well say: 'Enough. Let each man meet actuality for himself at first-hand; away with my kind of informative portrayal. I will amuse myself with fantasies, tricks and little noises.' My own belief is that we shall eschew fiction only when human society is too bad to know about or when it is too satisfactory to need art's rearrangements. Against infinity we have only human affinity, whether that is expressed in words or communal charity; and it is on such affinity that the novelist who communicates has to rest his case. He is unlikely, I think, to regard himself as an end in himself as long as most people are communicating in the known languages.

Suggested reading

General

Block, H. M. and Salinger, H., *The Creative Vision: Modern European Writers on their Art* (1960) (Gide, Proust, Thomas Mann, Pirandello, Giraudoux, Malraux, Sartre, Dürrenmatt)

Brown, E. K., *Rhythm in the Novel* (1950)

Burgum, E. B., *The Novel and the World's Dilemma* (1947)

Daiches, David, *The Novel and the Modern World*, rev. (1960)

Gregor, Ian, and Nicholas, Brian, *The Moral and the Story* (1962)

Lewis, R. W. B., *The Picaresque Saint* (1959)

Lubbock, Percy, *The Craft of Fiction* (1921)

Lukács, George, *Studies in European Realism* (1950)

ed. Scholes, Robert, *Approaches to the Novel* (1961)

ed. Smith, Horatio, *Columbia Dictionary of Modern European Literature* (1947)

Stallknecht, N. P. and Frenz, Horst, *Comparative Literature: Method and Perspective* (1961)

Trilling, *The Liberal Imagination* (1950)

Zabel, M. D., *Craft and Character in Modern Fiction* (1957)

England

Allen, Walter, *The Novel Today*, rev. (1960); *The English Novel* (1954)

Church, Richard, *The Growth of the English Novel* (1951)

Gindin, James, *Postwar British Fiction* (1963)

Karl, Frederick R., *A Reader's Guide to the Contemporary English Novel* (1962)

Kettle, Arnold, *The English Novel*, 2nd vol. (1953)

Lawrence, D. H., *Phoenix* (1936)

Leavis, F. R., *The Common Pursuit* (1952); *The Great Tradition* (1948)

Leavis, Q. D., *Fiction and the Reading Public* (1939)

Murdoch, Iris, 'The Sublime and the Beautiful Revisited', *Yale Review* (Winter 1960)

Newby, P. H., *The Novel 1945-50* (1951)

Reed, Henry, *The Novel since 1939* (1946)

ed. Schorer, Mark, *Modern British Fiction* (1961)

Simon, Irène, *Formes du roman anglais de Dickens à Joyce* (1949)

Stevenson, Lionel, *The English Novel* (1961)

Van Ghent, Dorothy, *The English Novel: Form and Function* (1953)

Wain, John, 'The Conflict of Forms in Contemporary English Literature', *Critical Quarterly* (Summer 1962), pp. 101–19

France

Boisdeffre, P. de, *Métamorphose de la littérature*, 2 vols., 3rd ed. (1953)

Brée, Germaine and Guiton, M., *An Age of Fiction* (*Gide to Camus*), (1958)

'Le Nouveau Roman', *Esprit* (juillet-août 1958)

Magny, C.-E., *Histoire du roman français depuis 1918*, vol. I (1950)

Mauriac, Claude, *L'Allitérature contemporaine* (1958)

Peyre, Henri, *The Contemporary French Novel* (1955); 'Trends in the Contemporary French Novel', *New French Writing* (1961), pp. 73–87

Pingaud, Bernard, 'Roman réflexif et roman descriptif', *Le Français dans le monde* (octobre–novembre, 1962)

Poulet, Robert, *La Lanterne Magique* (1956)

Robbe-Grillet, Alain, 'Une voie pour le roman futur', *La Nouvelle Revue Française* (juillet 1956); 'Nature, Humanisme et Tragédie', *La Nouvelle Revue Française*; (octobre 1958)

United States

Aldridge, John W., *After the Lost Generation* (1951)

Chase, Richard, *The American Novel and its Tradition* (1957)

Elliott, George P., 'A Defense of Fiction', *Hudson Review* (Spring 1963)

Frohock, W. M., *The Novel of Violence in America*, 2nd ed. (1957)

ed. Gardiner, H. C., *Fifty Years of the American Novel* (1952)

Geismar, Maxwell, *The Last of the Provincials: The American Novel 1915–1925* (1947); *Writers in Crisis: The American Novel 1925–1940* (1947)

Gloster, Hugh M., *Negro Voices in American Fiction* (1948)

Hassan, Ihab, *Radical Innocence: The Contemporary American Novel* (1961)

ed. Hicks, Granville, *The Living Novel* (1957)

Hoffmann, Frederick C., *The Modern Novel in America, 1900–1950* (1951)

Kazin, Alfred, *On Native Grounds* (1942)

Magny, C.-E., *L'Age du roman américain* (1948)

West, P., 'The Fear of Possibility: American Myth and French Mimesis', *Chicago Review* (Summer 1960), pp. 1–42

West, Ray B., *The Rise of Short Fiction in America, 1900–1950* (1952)

Germany

Bithell, Jethro, *Modern German Literature, 1880–1938* (1945)
Boucher, M., *Le roman allemand et la crise de l'esprit, 1914–1933* (1961)
Lange, Victor, *Modern German Literature, 1870–1940* (1945)
Waidson, H. M., *The Modern German Novel* (1959)

Italy

Arrighi, P., *Le vérisme dans la prose narrative italienne* (1937)
Bertacchini, R., *Figure e problemi di narrativa contemporanea* (1960)
Fernandez, Dominique, *Le roman italien et la crise de la conscience moderne* (1958)
Lombardi, Olga, *Scrittori neorealisti* (1957)
Pacifici, Sergio, *A Guide to Contemporary Italian Literature* (1962)
Pasolini, P. P., *Passione e ideologia* (1960)
Pullini, Giorgio, *Il romanzo italiano del dopoguerra* (1961)
Riccio, P. M., *On the Threshold of Fascism* (1929)
Sticco, Maria, *Il romanzo italiano contemporaneo* (1953)
Whitfield, J. H., *A Short History of Italian Literature*, chs. 13–15 (1960)
Wilkins, E. H., *A History of Italian Literature*, ch. 52 (1954)

Russia

Mirsky, D. S., *Contemporary Russian Literature* (1926)
Lavrin, Janko, *An Introduction to the Russian Novel* (1942)
Simmons, E. J., *Russian Fiction and Soviet Ideology* (1958)
Steiner, F. G., *Tolstoy or Dostoevsky?* (1960)
Struve, Gleb, *25 Years of Soviet Russian Literature* (1944)

Spain

Barja, C., *Literatura española: libros y autores contemporáneos* (1935)
Bell, A. F. G., *Contemporary Spanish Literature*, rev. (1933)
Brenan, Gerald, *The Literature of the Spanish People*, 2nd ed., ch. XVI (1953)
Eoff, Sherman H., *The Modern Spanish Novel* (1961)
Goytisolo, Juan, *Problemas de la novela* (1959)
Salinas, P., *Literatura española siglo XX* (1941)
Vézinet, F., *Les Maîtres du roman espagnol contemporain* (1907)

Index to both volumes

*Bracketed references are to works or characters
whose author is not cited on the page in question*